All about the
Yorkshire Terrier

'Beautiful to look at; Active as a Kitten, Vivacious as the "Most Perky Pom", the perfect Yorkshire Terrier is the acme of Toy Dog Virtue and Perfection, looked on from every Standpoint.'

THEO MARPLES
Show Dogs
Their Points and Characteristics

'Nation has, before now been congratulated upon the non-possession of a history and we are not at all sure in our own minds that the Yorkshire Terrier is not fortunate in finding itself in the same lucky category. So many breeds have been the subject of acrimonious and narrow-minded disputes and petty quarrels, that a variety which has, comparatively speaking, been let alone, is certainly not to be commiserated with when it finds itself permitted to stand or fall on its own merits. Whatever the varieties of dogs may have been which were called upon by breeders to combine and form the present beautiful Yorkshire Terrier it is proved by results that the judgment of their earliest supporters was sound and the trouble spent amply repaid by the Successful Termination of their Labours.'

VERO SHAW
writing a century ago about the Yorkshire Terriers lack of background in his
Illustrated Book of the Dog 1879–81

All about the
Yorkshire Terrier

MONA HUXHAM

PELHAM BOOKS

For Serroll, Hamilton and Purdey and All My Family
also
Emmrill Paddie Wack . . . the First of the Many
Emmrill Christmas Fuzz of Blue Peter Fame, Paddie's son.
Emmrill Jig Saw . . . Imported by the Author from Beryl Hesketh of the
famed Heskathane Yorkshire Terriers of America.
Little Evie, her son Emmrill Adams Apple whose sire Chantmarles Much
Ado was the Litter brother to Mrs Mary Hayes delightful little Champion
Chantmarles Snuff Box whose beautiful picture on the Cover of the first
three Editions of this book did so much to popularise it.
and
To all the little Yorkshire Emmrill Champions all around the world that
make such good little ambassadors for the Breed.

First published in Great Britain by
Pelham Books Ltd
44 Bedford Square
London WC1B 3DU
1981

Huxham, Mona
  All about the Yorkshire Terrier. – 2nd ed.
  1. Yorkshire terriers
  I. Title
  636.7′6   SF429.Y6

ISBN 0 7207 1318 8

Typeset, printed and bound in Singapore

Contents

Illustrations

Figures

Photo credits

BIPS photos 19, 24; Martin Booth photos 56, 59; Cassidy & Leigh photos 16, 25; C.M. Cooke & Son photo 33; Thos. Fall photos 9, 10, 12, 15, 38, 40, 44, 51; J.K. & E.A. McFarlane photos 53, 54, 55; Sally Anne Thompson photo 42; Diane Pearce page 9 (right),

Champion Blairsville Royal Seal

On the cover of this book and on the page opposite I am delighted to be able to show photographs of the most remarkable little dog in all the long show history of the Yorkshire Terrier breed. I am indebted to Mr and Mrs Lister for supplying the photo opposite and to Mr Harold Holborn of the *Sunday People* for taking it. My thanks also to Mr Franz-Otto Reiners who lives in FRG Krefeld who took the excellent cover picture.

Ch. Blairsville Royal Seal, (Tosha to his friends) was born on 2 May 1974 by Ch. Beechrise Surprise (photo left) out of Champion Blairsville Most Royal (photo right) who was by Ch. Whisperdale's Temujin out of Ch. Blairsville Shirene, who, in turn was by Ch. Blairsville Boy Wonder, so the 'royal' part of the title is well deserved.

Ch. Blairsville Most Royal was Best in Show in Belfast and Reserve Best in Show at Crufts in 1974. Rita and Brian Lister were waiting for a taxi outside Crufts and I stopped to congratulate them. They said they were in danger of missing their bus home to Yorkshire so I took them to my car and taking all the short cuts and cutting all the corners I got them to Victoria just in time.

Royal Seal was the Top Dog for the whole country by 1976 when he won the *Our Dogs* Dog of the Year Award and the one for *Dog World*. He won *Our Dogs* the next year also. By the end of 1976 he had won 201 points whereas his nearest rival only gained 69. By the end of 1976 he had won the record number in the breed of 30 CCs and by the end of his showing career he had won 50 under different judges.

In 1977 he was beaten at Crufts in the breed although he was presented with the 'Yorkshire Terrier of the Year' Award at that show. Had he won Crufts then his owners had intended to retire him but instead they decided to keep him in the ring for another year and that is when he broke all records and when his owners did retire him he had won, besides the 50 CCs, 24 Best in Shows, 16 Reserve Best in Shows, including Crufts 1978, 12 Supreme Best in Shows at All-Breed Shows and 33 Toy Groups.

Acknowledgements

To the Kennel Club my thanks for permission to reproduce the standard of the Yorkshire Terrier.

To Elizabeth Osman for her help with many of the photographs. Caroline Haffner for her illustrated standard and all the line drawings.

A very special thank you to all the very kind people who trusted me with copies of photographs they value very highly and to Clifford Hubbard for all his help and assistance.

Preface

To anyone who has evinced the slightest interest in the Yorkshire Terrier, it will readily be seen that the Show Specimen is a true connoisseur's piece, prized above rubies, handled with the care bestowed on the rarest porcelain, tended with the unfailing attention that her slaves gave to Cleopatra, nurtured from birth, anointed with the finest oils, valeted with silver appointments and bedecked and displayed upon the finest silks and velvets.

From the last paragraph, one might justifiably imagine that the owning of a Yorkshire Terrier would be a cult practised only by the richest in the land. Nothing is further from the truth, for the fact is that a large majority of the owners of some of the most glamorous of the present day show Yorkies come from working-class areas, and the little dogs are kept as members of the family — and very important, demanding members at that — in small houses and even flats, with little or no exercising ground at all. Tending the Yorkie and tying his coat in curling papers is as much part of the daily pattern as washing the children to go to school.

Contrariwise, the Yorkies that are found in more suburban and country areas, where they have the privileges of regular romping and playing in garden and park, and the chance to scamper over the fields and open spaces, are the ones whose coats leave much to be desired and who usually look strangely reminiscent of the familiar 'feather duster'. Make no mistake about it, these 'house pet Yorkies' probably get a good daily groom from their fond owners but, without the dedication and scientific approach applied to the exhibition model.

Without specialised knowledge, alas, the Yorkie coat in amateur hands is a thing possessed, and possessed with all the worst intentions. Brush it with all the loving care in the world and five minutes later it reverts back to looking as if its owner had just been dragged through the nearest hedge, and backwards at that. Neglect it for a day or so through illness or absence from home, and you will find it has tied itself into tight little tiny knots in all the most awkward places. Coping with them becomes an agony both to the poor little victim and to you, for the discomfort you have caused your pet and the actual pain he or she must undergo before the knots are all teased out, especially in the groin and under-arm areas. No doubt about it, a knowledge of some of the arts of the exhibitor/owner would be of great help to the harassed pet owner in these circumstances. While in no way suggesting that the 'pet only' Yorkie should be subjected to the apparent indignity of having his coat tied up in curlers, it is apparent that there is much to be learned from the experts in this particular field. Even if his coat is never intended to be his 'glory' it need not, necessarily, be his 'cross'.

On the other side of the coin, there is the thought that, with his coat all tied up and his freedom curtailed in case he gets wet or dirty, the owner of the show Yorkie never really sees his dog as the game, fearless, sporting and naughty little terrier that he actually is. Will the coiffeuring, beribboning and general 'tarting-up' that he must continually undergo completely submerge the imp, or is he always there just waiting to break loose? Conversely, how is it possible that the mischief-loving, cat-baiting, ball-chasing carefree little tear-a-way with the look of a street-urchin who comes when he thinks he will, and is quite impervious to rhetoric, bullying or chastisement when caught in any nefarious act — can be full litter brother to an immaculately groomed, top-knotted, doll-like creature that allows itself to be posed on a velvet-draped dais with tresses cascading down on either side of him, like a tiny graven image, as still as can be for seemingly hours on end?

Nature being what it is, can it be possible that one mother can whelp two such opposing off-spring in one litter? Do they both start off equal and is it the eventual environment of each that decides its ultimate career? It needs a very wide stretch of the imagination to be able to suppose that, being both tarred with the same brush, as it were, it would make no difference which of these two was chosen to perform two such opposing roles in two such separate worlds. It seems apparent right away that there can never be a dual purpose Yorkie. The Show dog must never be a madcap, and the exuberant little reprobate that most pet Yorkies become, could never calm down enough to acquire the mantle of patience expected of the show exhibit in the ring.

How does the experienced Show breeder pick out his Yorkie pup? Does he pick out the best-coated one and hope for the best character-wise? If, on the other hand, he chooses the mildest temperament he is taking an awful gamble coat-wise as no less than 50 points in the breed standard refer in some way or other to 'coat'. Some old-timers say that it doesn't matter how they start out, they can always make what they want out of a promising puppy. In this case they must be able to practise mesmerism and be very adept at it, as I can think of no accepted means of puppy training that will turn the mischievous little rips my Yorkie puppies are, into the virtuous little models many little six months' old puppies appear in the show-ring. How they do it is a mystery to most people. It can only be performed by those with very special gifts of patience and absolute dedication. It is no question of five minutes now and again when the mood is on one, but of regular, steady training given with kindness and understanding so that it is never allowed to tire the little trainee.

Consider that Yorkies are completely free of fear and, therefore, cannot easily be frightened into submission. Also, as they are not usually particularly greedy little dogs, it isn't the answer to obtain their obedience through their stomachs. There is nothing of the sycophant about the Yorkie and his desire to please his owner is nothing like so strong as that of the Poodle, for instance, who will go to any length he knows and perform any trick, in order to win the approbation of his loved ones. The methods used to achieve the high standard that can be seen in any show-ring in this country today are discussed in further detail later in this book.

It is true that any Yorkshire Terrier born with the correct texture of coat can, in the process of time, in the hands of any of the Breed's experts, grow all the length of coat that is needed for exhibition purposes. It is, however, problematical, that, if he has been allowed to become just an unruly pet beforehand, he will ever be subjugated to the more passive role of the show dog.

When asking what makes the Yorkshire Terrier the 'Top Dog' in Exports and also one of the most sought-after pets not only in this country but in many overseas ones as well, I found the answers I received as completely opposed as 'for his glorious coat', and 'we only like him if he has a brittle coat'. How these two opposing facets of the same little dog can be reconciled, is a question which has fascinated me ever since I started preparing this book. I do not know the answer now, completely, because the more I found out about this delightful breed the more confused the issue became. Even so, I hope that by the time you have reached the end of this book you will have learned enough about whichever side appeals to you most and, at least, enough to show that the Yorkshire Terrier is a very desirable little dog to own.

1 The Origin of the Yorkshire Terrier

It is agreed by everybody who has studied the origin of the Yorkshire Terrier that it was first of all shown as 'The Broken-Haired Scotch Terrier' and at one show in Birmingham in 1860 all the winners in the Broken-Haired Scotch were actually Skye Terriers, so they were at least entitled to the description of 'Scotch'. The next year, in 1861, however at the Kennel Club Show at Leeds all the specimens were of the breed later to be known as 'Yorkshires'. How this came about one can only surmise but the breed had been developed by the people who lived in Lancashire and Yorkshire for that is where all the best ones were to be found when Dog Shows started in 1859. However else it was derived all are agreed that the Skye, Clydesdale or Paisley Terrier had some responsibility for its long coat, the Maltese for toy size, coat and shape, while many people lean to the Black and Tan colour of the finished Yorkshire. It was said at the time that the canny Yorkshireman kept his methods close to his chest and never divulged the source of his breeding policy. However it was done there is a lot of truth in the account of how the woollen textile workers in Clydesdale and Paisley had a smallish terrier with a long coat that they took to work with them in order to rid the woollen mills of the rats and mice that were a constant worry to them. With the coming of the Industrial Revolution Lancashire and Yorkshire became very important centres of the textile industry and with the introduction of the new machinery had an upsurge of trade and many of the mill workers in the Clydesdale area decided to try and improve their working conditions by moving south to the more important centres of Yorkshire and round about. The terriers they had were the pure-bred Clydesdale or Paisley Terrier that were a bit like a Skye Terrier but smaller and with a harsher coat and grey in colour. The Skye Terrier went back to the days when Dr Caius of Queen Elizabeth's time wrote his list of the dogs to be found in England called *Of Englishe Dogges*. The Skye takes its name from that north-western island that bears its name. He is the only terrier belonging to the north-western isles that is not common all over Scotland and he is said to be without rival in his own domain wherever there are rocks, dens, burrows, cairns or covers to explore or waters to take to and his services are required.

Many people are under the impression that the Skye came first and the Clydesdale or Paisley Terrier derived from it. However the late Brian Vesey-Fitzgerald, who I often met while judging abroad as well as in this country, told me and I have no reason to doubt what he said, that the Clydesdale or Paisley Terrier came before the Skye. He said it was absolute nonsense to suggest that the Clydesdale came from the crossing of the Skye with the Yorkshire Terrier as the Yorkshire was a comparatively new breed only evolving in the latter half of the nineteenth century while the Clydesdale went way back before that and were almost extinct in 1856 so that it was in its hey-day at the beginning of the nineteenth century. I show a picture of the Clydesdale taken circa 1878. They have had several rebirths as following its danger of extinction in 1856 a powerful movement sprung up to put it on its feet again. Later on it was in trouble again but in 1887 the Clydesdale Terrier Club was formed and in 1888 it was classified in the KC Stud Book. The Club, unfortunately, did not last long and was followed by the Paisley Terrier Club. This breed was never a 'toy'. It was rather like the Skye Terrier to look at but lighter in weight — between 16 and 20 lb, shorter in the back and was originally a hard, tough little terrier used for ratting and killing other vermin and regarded as a magnificent fighter, afraid of nothing. To start with the coat was long but hard, so much so that pups with silky coats were rejected at once. Gradually with popularity the silky coat came to be the more desirable and that was the beginning of the end for it started to decline. In 1924, 25, 26 and 27 the Clydesdale Terrier was listed in the Kennel Club Entries but 'No Entry' was put against it and so the breed ceased to be recorded over here although it went on in a very isolated way in the U.S.A. Clifford Hubbard in his *Observer's Book of Dogs* says that a revival took place in 1936 but it petered out (perhaps because of the war). He says the height should be 13 to 14 in, weight 16 lb. Colour a fine clear blue (dark preferred) ears erect and coat to be silky and about 5 to 6 in long. So Mr Hubbard evidently took the later preference for a silky coat over the original.

I myself would disallow the admixture of the Dandie Dinmont as an unnecessary admixture except for the fact that the roached back is so often seen in Yorkies even of the present day and none of the other breeds claimed for the foundation of the breed have this ugly failing which even today spoils

Clydesdale Terrier champion Ballochmyle Wee Wattie owned by Sir Claud Alexander. Wee Wattie was said to have a perfect colouring — dark blue body coat and golden tan on his face, paws and legs.

Left Mr G. Shaw's Clydesdale Terrier, Mozart by Hayden out of San Toy.

the outline of so many of the present day show dogs.

The early Yorkies were not tiny being about 14 lb on average, some smaller and a few even larger. The Victorians had a great desire for the diminutive and set about bantamising the breed very early on so that in the space of some twenty years the breed came down to the 2 ½ to 5 lb level that present day devotees think is the ideal size and which makes the breed the smallest British breed and the most popular dog in the world.

It is claimed by nearly all the writers of the Yorkshire Terrier's history that its colouring and markings came from crossing the long coated terriers with the old Black and Tan, now known as the English Toy Terrier. Miners were among the people who had need of a tiny terrier to take down the mines in their pockets. The mines were full of rats and when the miners and their suppliers had bantamised the keen, fearless character of the Manchester Terrier, with the even more alertedness of the prick-eared toy, there never was a more satisfactory rat-catcher. The tiny size and smooth coat so easily washed when in the house was also most suitable for living in the home. Many working families owned these tiny little 'gladiators' and of course, miners had their rat-pits and such above ground where their little terriers would also give a good account of themselves.

With such an admixture it was no wonder that the first Yorkie to make a name for himself as the foundation sire *par excellance* of the breed for all time was the famous Huddersfield Ben. Ben, who died in 1871, was an excellent rat-catcher and was entered regularly in rat-killing competitions in which he did well. He was the sire of so many prize-winning Yorkshire Terriers up and down the country — in fact his name appeared at the back of every important pedigree. Now he didn't get there by the number of rats he killed or the number of shows he won. I have set out to discover what there was behind Ben's breeding that gave him such an incredible superiority in those early times.

To Mr Peter Eden of Cross Lane, Salford, Manchester must go the credit of really producing the first such terrier of blue silky coat, golden tan on head and legs and showing in the beauty classes with a long silky forelock covering head and eyes. Idstone in *The Dog* published in 1872, before the Yorkshire Terrier got that name, tells us that these little terriers were produced in Manchester and that Mr Peter Eden is famed for manufacturing them. He tells us that he saw the 'stock dog' and comments on the quality he found in the class he was in. This stock dog was 'Albert' 1st K. C. Stud Book No. 3586. Other Albert's there were in this issue, but they came afterwards and Mr Eden's 'Albert' was the first name entered under Class XXXII: Broken Haired Scotch and Yorkshire Terriers in the very first issue of the Kennel Club Stud Book of 1874 which covered all dogs up to that time.

Albert's prize-winning performance is recorded below. There is no age given for him and Idstone tells us that the breed are only at their best after two years old as they don't get thoroughly coated until that age.

Albert No. 3586 Performances:

Birmingham	1st Prize	1863
Birmingham	1st Prize	1864
Islington	2nd Prize	1864
Islington	3rd Prize	1865

1865 was the year Huddersfield Ben was born. Albert, so my research tells me was bred by Peter Eden by a dog called 'Old Soldier' out of 'Young's Kelly' who was by 'Pearson's Teddy' out of 'Pink'.

I have been able to ascertain that Mr Peter Eden, whose home bred Albert was the very first entry in the Kennel Club's first Stud Book, was a regular supporter of all the early dog shows that featured Scotch, Broken-haired and Yorkshire Terriers. His name is among the well known exhibitors reported to have been entered at the third Great International Show held at the Agricultural Hall, Islington from 2 to 6 June 1865 where it was reported he entered three Scotch Terriers over 7 lb and won 1st, 2nd and 3rd prizes.

He was at the seventh Dog Show at the Zoological Gardens in Manchester in December 1867, because Charles Henry Lane includes his name in his list of people who had well-known names of the past.

We find Peter Eden judging a dog show when he officiated at the Curzon Hall, Birmingham on 1 to 4 December 1873 where he judged Smooth Terriers with Mr Charles Collins. They also judged Bulldogs, Dalmations, Bull-Terriers, Black & Tan Terriers and Large Non-Sporting Foreign Dogs where it was reported they had a very good entry amongst a total entry of 944.

The next year Peter Eden also judged at the very same show in December 1874 and his breed on that occasion was Fox Terriers. Mr S. E. Shirley, the founder of the Kennel Club was one of the other judges. Peter Eden and Mr S. E. Shirley, M. P. were judging together again at the second International Exhibition of Sporting and Fancy Dogs at the Pomona Palace, Manchester on 6 to 9 August 1875.

At the Royal Pomona Palace, Manchester on 20, 21, 23 and 24 July in 1877 Peter Eden had a very important part to play as a judge at the same show that seemed to have him judging most years. He had a huge entry of excellent Fox Terriers and most of the important kennels were represented — he judged the smooth and wire classes of terriers with Colonel Cowan and Mr W. Lort and with Mr J. Taylor he judged Bulldogs, Bull-Terriers, Black and Tan, White English and Yorkshire Terriers, Dalmations, Pomeranians, Toy Spaniels and Toy Terriers, Maltese Terriers and Italian Greyhounds, then with Mr W. Lort he judged all the Foreign dogs. The most interesting result as far as this book is concerned is that he awarded Mrs M. A. Foster *All the Prizes in Yorkshire Terriers*.

From the above it will be observed that Peter Eden who claimed to be the originator of the Yorkshire Terrier was no back street breeder struggling to produce an ideal terrier from unknown material but a very important and knowledgeable expert for whose opinion on their dogs all the top names in dogdom entered under him. Amongst these were Vero Shaw, Bulldogs and Bull-Terriers, George Stables, English Terriers and George Raper and in Fox Terriers many names of the highest calibre such as Murchison, Burbridge, M.F.H. of Surrey cricket fame, and S. E. Shirley, M. P. the well-liked founder of the Kennel Club.

It is no fluke that Peter Eden's 'Albert' was the first entry of our breed in the first edition of the Kennel Club Stud Book. He was there by design and merit and for his potency as a sire, which goes without saying if we consider how many times he appears in the pedigree of Huddersfield Ben and in his own right as in Idstone's volume *The Dog* under the blue-tan English Terrier and the blue-tan Peter Eden Breed are listed on page 29, of the 1872 Edition, and the eighth edition. On page 208 Idstone tells us:

Manchester has produced a sort of late years called the Scotch Terrier with a long silky forelock covering the face and eyes. These are invariably blue-grey tan or black tan and they are large or toy size. I imagine they are manufactured from those *for which Mr Peter Eden was famed*. (the italics are mine, author). I have seen, I think at Middleton, the stock-dog from which most of these dogs come, and the best class I ever saw was produced at that exhibition; for these, men in rags refused offers of twenty or thirty guineas from the London dealers, and they were not far wrong, as the breed has become exceedingly fashionable and second-rate specimens — first-rate ones are never in the market — readily fetch twenty or thirty guineas each. A good blue, a rich tan length and silky texture of fore-lock, symmetry and clearness of markings are the great points of excellence, whilst the prevalence of the blue tinge is never passed over, and generally carries the day.

These dogs require constant attention and are carefully brushed, combed and cultivated, as one lump of felt is soon succeeded by another, and a tangled coat is fatal to all chances of success. Great roguery is committed by the dishonest in the dressing and staining of these dogs, but the chicanery has hitherto never escaped detection, as the judging takes place in daylight, and even heightened colour is transparently visible to a practised judge.

Dogs of this breed are generally cropped, but it does not add to their beauty, as the ears are scarcely visible. The coat is profuse on the body, the tail is not very bushy; the feet are short-coated, the eyes rather full; the moustache moderate; the tan is profuse and blended into a black saddle and the general texture is soft and silky; the back should be silvery, with a mixture of slate or blue, and this should prevail on face and legs.

The dog is hard to describe and difficult to judge, requiring a practised eye, acute observation and adroit comparison. The oldest dogs are generally the most taking; none are thoroughly coated until they are over two years old, and much allowance must be made for age. They are also called 'Yorkshire' and 'Lancashire' Terriers, and the best I have seen have come from the latter county with the exception of Mr Foster's.

This mention of 'faking' was one that the new Kennel Club was much concerned with but preferred the Breed Clubs concerned to enforce any regulations in the Rules of such Clubs. The Yorkshire Terrier Club was honoured when the Countess of Warwick became their President but the Club lost her patronage on this question of 'faking' as her Ladyship did not feel that they were strict enough in dealing with this very vexed question.

Before the establishment of the Kennel Club, dog breeding had become so popular that big profits were often made and a minority of dishonest exhibitors took advantage of the lack of regulations; in some cases adult dogs were entered in classes restricted to puppies while sometimes well-known winners had their coats dyed and were entered in classes confined to novices.

In 1880 the Kennel Club extended its rules to include penalties for faking by dying coats or by altering by surgery. It instituted rules whereby nobody could show a dog at any show held under the Kennel Club unless it had already been registered with that body. Machinery was set up to hear objections arising from dog shows and where necessary to publish in the Kennel Gazette any punishments incurred for offences of a discreditable conduct. In 1881 the Scottish Kennel Club was formed in co-operation with the parent Club. The following year the French Société Centrale Canine was founded, followed in 1883 by the American Kennel Club. It was not until 1911 that the Fédération Cynologique was formed by a combination of Austrian, Belgian, Dutch, French and German Canine Societies and has become the recognised authority in Europe which like about thirty Kennel Clubs in the free world have reciprocal agreements with the English Kennel Club.

'Huddersfield Ben's' sire, 'The Boscovitch Dog' was a great-grandson of 'Albert' No. 3586, Huddersfield Ben's dam 'Lady' was a daughter of 'Eastwood's Old Ben' so that would make 'Albert' No. 3586 her great-great-grandfather. So with 'Albert's' blood on both sides of his pedigree 'Huddersfield Ben' had all *his* virtues to pass on to his own progeny from both sides of his pedigree. When Ben was mated to 'Frisk' this brought off a really fantastic result as it produced Mrs Foster's 'Bruce' No. 3595 1st Prize winner at Birmingham, Miss Alderson's of Leeds 'Mozart' No. 3629 Vol. 1 a multiple winner 'Charlie' No. 3612 Vol 1. 'Bright' No. 3985 Vol. 1 a 1st Prize winner at Crystal Palace. The reason for such outstanding breeding will be clear when a close study is made of 'Frisk's' background for she was out of 'Lilly' and by 'Whitey's' 'Baron' who was by Peter Eden's 'Albert' (No. 3586 Vol. 1)

Fig 1 Ch. Huddersfield
Ben.

who was out of Young's 'Kelly' by Pearson's 'Teddy' out of 'Pink'.

To anyone who sets themselves up to be a geneticist as I do it will be seen what a striking improvement was made when another dose of 'Albert's' blood was received.

I myself don't need to go further in deciding what it was that gave 'Huddersfield Ben' such a tremendous advantage over all the other Yorkshire Terriers both as a show dog and as a sire. Ben's breeder Mr W. Eastwood of Huddersfield did not value him so much as a 'show' dog however as he was entered regularly at the rat pits. In such places dogs were set to kill rats by the clock. This was in those days one of the working men's popular entertainment in towns as was cock-fighting in the country whenever men required something to bet on. The more violent of them followed bull-baiting, bear-baiting, dog-fighting as well as the ratting exploits of the dogs. There is no evidence of the pit where Huddersfield Ben's prowess was wagered against the rats he killed but before this time there is a record of a villain named Charlie Eastup who kept a dreadful establishment known as the notorious Westminster Pit in Duck Lane near Westminster Abbey in London and as well as baiting a monkey against any dog of its own weight, 19 lb, he had a famous rat-killing dog called Billy whose rat-killing records could hardly be credited except by those people who had bet against him and lost. In this same record there is a report of the second time Billy was engaged to kill a hundred rats in less time than a champion opponent could kill ninety. This aroused tremendous public interest. Long before the Westminster Pit was opened 'lots of carriages were in the lane and several noblemen and M.P.s were waiting to obtain seats at 3/- (15p) each for the pit and 5/- (25p) each for the boxes.' Hundreds of the waiting crowd were unsuccessful and lamented their disappointment. On this occasion Billy beat his own record by killing one hundred rats in 7 minutes 10 seconds. Numerous reformers tried to ban this very cruel sport but Bill after Bill was rejected by Parliament.

In 1850 a group of titled gentlemen held a dog show organised by William Davenport Bromley to raise funds for charity. Tea was handed round a tea-table by liveried footmen but it was a success and was the very first recorded 'Dog Show'. The following year the Great Exhibition drew many thousands of visitors to London and our villainous friend Charles Eastup held an exhibition of dogs of a very different character in the bar parlour of a public-house in London by advertising 'A Fancy Dog Show' for which the exhibits were provided by his former cronies whom he made members of a club especially for this purpose. This show consisted of fancy pets and were mostly toy breeds such as King Charles and Blenheim Spaniels, Italian Greyhounds, Isle of Skye Terriers, (evidently a new novelty breed), toy terriers and a miscellaneous collection of unspecified breeds. An offer of £250 (about £2,500 by today's value) was made for an exhibit called Prince and refused. Also on show was the stuffed remains of Billy of Westminster Pit fame, to give the customers extra value for their entry fee of sixpence. The report was to be read in the *Illustrated London News* of 8 February 1851 and attracted considerable attention.

Jem Burns the champion prize-fighter and landlord of the Queen's Head Tavern near Windmill Street in London started a rival club and advertised Grand Shows of Toy Spaniels, Tiny Terriers and Small Dogs. He advertised that imported dogs would be on show and stud dogs would be available on the premises. Thereafter these two publicans held rival meetings which were more or less for the purpose of selling dogs. Public interest was maintained by the advertisements which were continually announcing new and unusual breeds and prices were exaggerated by the accounts of each dog's breeding and achievement. As there were no official dog shows at this time it is easy to see how the dog loving British people could be fascinated by these advertisements. It was also apparent that the canny Yorkshireman could be encouraged to try to breed his already attractive little toy terrier into something so small and glamorous with a long luxuriant shiny coat something so appealing that buyers at the London Show Sales would pay much 'brass' to obtain.

The first official dog show at Newcastle-on-Tyne was for Pointers and Setters only and took place in 1859. In 1860 the Birmingham Dog Show catered for far more breeds and included Toy Terriers under 5 lb and so was the first general dog show ever known so is the oldest dog show society in existence. In 1861 Leeds and Manchester started their shows and it was 1862 before the first large show took place in London itself and this was held at the Agricultural Hall in Islington (later the site of Crufts International Show) and drew an entry of about one thousand. In 1864 the show at Islington was held as well as another one at Cremorne Gardens in Chelsea, London.

About this time dog-breeding began to be so profitable that a minority of dishonest exhibitors began to take advantage of the lack of regulations. Some tried to 'paint' their Yorkies, while others used colouring agents, which, as the shows were held in broad daylight were very easy to distinguish. Another practice was for adult dogs to be entered in classes restricted to puppies and well-known winners were disguised by dyeing their coats and entered in 'novice' classes. These irregular practices began to get dog showing into disrepute so when Mr S. E. Shirley and his committee had run three successful shows at the Crystal Palace, London and in April 1873 it was asked to form the Kennel Club. Starting in a three-room flat in Albert Mansions, Victoria Street, London this very first Kennel Club in the world set about producing the first Stud Book going back to 1859 and the first dog show. It contained a Book of Rules for the Guidance of Dog Shows. In 1880 it passed rules punishing faking and dyeing and it decided that no dog could be entered at any show held under Kennel Club Rules unless it had been registered with the Kennel Club. These registrations were entered in the *Kennel Gazette* which all members read in those days. Our early Yorkshire Terrier breeders did not get any of these advantages for so many of the early lines were started with Huddersfield Ben. He was purchased by Mr and Mrs Foster of Bradford and in her hands he was subjected to the grooming, constant care and expertise that turned him from a rough coated little ratter to the resplendant owner of that flowing beauty of coat and finish that is to be seen in the picture of Huddersfield Ben with his daughter Little Kate on page 36.

Mrs Foster took the prefix 'Bradford' and she showed Huddersfield Ben, after she had purchased him, everywhere there were shows, up and down the country and he was very popular and recognised by all those breeders who were aiming to improve their Yorkshire Terrier strain, as an outstanding specimen in his own right and as a stud force of the highest merit and because of his own very excellent breeding he had the power of transmitting all he had received himself to his own offspring. Up to his coming the breed had been in the minority always, but Ben had such a distinct and stimulating effect on the breed and gave breeders themselves much encouragement and confidence in the future after they had seen and used him. He was the winner of hundreds of prizes, mostly in Variety Classes but enough in the Breed to show what an outstandingly fine specimen he was. Without doubt his was the impetus that helped most to secure the breed's future prosperity and success in the world of dogs and his influence on the breed was immense.

His untimely death by accident at the age of six and a half took him off in his prime and robbed the breed of its 'leading light'. Among the offspring he sired were the following well-known prizewinning Yorkshire Terriers:

Dogs	Mr A. Boulton's	Ben II	No. 4679 Vol. 2
	Mrs Foster's	Ben II	No. 4680 Vol. 2
	Mrs Foster's	Bruce ·	No. 3595 Vol. 1
	Miss Alderson's	Doctor Spark	No. 3603 Vol. 1
	Miss Alderson's	Mozart	No. 3629 Vol. 1
	Mrs Foster's	Charlie	No. 3612 Vol. 1
	Miss Alderson's	Royal	No. 4686 Vol. 2
	Mrs Foster's	Bright	No. 3985 Vol. 1 Under Toy Terrier Rough & Broken Coated

	Mrs Foster's	Emperor
	Henshall's	Punch
	Hirst's	Peter
	Inman's	Benson
	Manningham's	Charlie
	Hill's	Sandy
	Bank's	Bismarc
	Crossley's	Wasp
Bitches	Foster's	Little Kate (afterwards Lady Gifford's)
	Lucas'	Empress

All the above were recorded but there must have been many breeders who used him at stud who did not register their litters and altogether Ben can rightly be called the foundation stone of the breed.

Sam Jessop in his book *The Yorkshire Terrier*, published in the early 1900s, stated that 'Ben is the starting point to use since in all essential particulars he possessed the points required in a Yorkshire Terrier down to the present day.

Sam Jessop should know for he was the author of the only breed book ever published about the Yorkshire Terrier in his time. His work shows how knowledgeable he was about all aspects of the breed and it is quoted so often that one would almost think he had invented the breed himself. The only thing I find disappointing about his book is his picture of Huddersfield Ben and that will be readily understood when it is realised that it was taken after his death and when the taxidermist had finished stuffing him. This, of course accounts for the 'stiff' wooden appearance of Ben. Jessop says that it was the only photograph of Ben he knew of and it was sent to him by a Mr John Thorpe of Patricraft who had had it removed from its glass case for the photograph. When she knew I was writing this book Mrs Edith Stirk told me she knew a man who when he was quite young — and he was then rather old, had visited a pub in the North of England where he saw the stuffed remains of Ben in a glass case on the mantelpiece. I wonder where it is now?

Dr Stables in his book *Our Friend the Dog* published in 1884 tells us that he saw Ben and he remembers him weighing about 12 lb. Mr Theo Marples in his famous and authentic work *Show Dogs their Points & Characteristics* says of Mrs Foster's immortal Huddersfield Ben that he was the progenitor of all our best Yorkshire Terriers and will ever remain the greatest pillar of the breed — then he names some of his winning offspring.

Dalziel writing for Stonehenge, Robert Leighton, Edward Ashe, Barton, Rawden Lee, Stables, Marples, Jessop and *Hutchinson's Dog Enclyopaedia* were all agreed about Huddersfield Ben's importance in the breed — all that is except the Hon. Mrs Lytton who in her quite comprehensive work on all the toy breeds dismissed the Yorkshire Terrier thus: 'As for the unfortunate show Yorkshire Terrier with his unnatural existence as a "clothes' peg" the less said the better.'

So much for history. Of course it would be questionable how far Ben would have gone in the breed if it had not been his good fortune to be purchased by that wonderfully enthusiastic lady Mrs Jonas Foster of Bradford. All the hundred or so prizes he was to win came after his purchase and his metamorphosis from the rough to the glamour of the show scene. Mrs Foster carried the breed forward in no small way as she showed the dogs she bred herself, always sold good winning types to her many, many eager customers and also had such a good 'eye' for the breed and its future that she was able to pick out likely specimens that would help her promote her own strain and keep her at the fountain head of the breed.

After Ben she could have been bereft but she found a dog that she saw being shown at Heckmondwike Show in 1887 when he was four years old. He was Ted.

Writers of her day credit Mrs M. A. Foster of Bradford, Yorkshire, for many years the head and centre of all that pertained to the Yorkshire Terrier, and it was undoubtedly she who raised the variety to its highest point of perfection. Her success was due to her enthusiasm, to the admirable condition of her pets and to the care which she bestowed upon their toilet. Her dogs were invariably good in type. She never showed a bad one, and all the dogs she exhibited were of a uniform excellence. So keen was Mrs Foster on showing her dogs and so sucessful with her Yorkshire Terriers that we find her travelling from show to show wherever there were classes put on either for her larger Scotch and Broken Haired Terriers over 9 lb and under 9 lb. where in fact she was apt to win every class in both sections. This often happened for on 27 June 1876 she was showing her Rough or Scotch Terriers at Woodside Park, Darlington and won every class in over 9 lb variety and under 9 lb. This was repeated at Burton-on-Trent. That same year on 24, 25, and 27 October she was showing at the Polo Ground at Brighton and she took all the prizes for Yorkshire Terriers there. Lady Giffard made her first appearance at a dog show at this show. In July 1877 at the Agricultural Hall, Islington Mrs Foster repeated this performance again and won all the prizes for Yorkshire Terriers. Among the prizewinners were such names as 'Morning Star', 'Lord Dundreary', 'Emperor', 'Queen of the Fancy', 'Effie',

Ch. Ted owned by Mrs Foster.

Left Mrs Foster's Bradford Dickens, winner of over one hundred first prizes.

Ch. Sneiton Amethyst.

'Alfred the Great', 'Bradford Harry' (later a champion in America), 'May Queen', 'Young Alice' 'Bradford Hero', 'Prince Arthur', 'Young Cobden', 'Minnie', 'Fearnought', 'Bradford Dickens' (see photo above), 'Champion Ted', 'Bright', 'Sandy' and the very tiny 'Bradford Marie' and 'Bradford Queen of the Toys' (24 ozs).

Robert Leighton tells us that while Mr Peter Eden of Manchester is generally credited with being the actual inventor of the Yorkshire Terrier — and with his celebrated Albert and others who were equally admirable specimens — he was, it was true one of the earliest breeders and owners and had other dogs of like quality that he used to try to convince the public of the charms and attractions of that variety of dog — it was admitted, therefore that Mr Eden gave the breed its first impetus, but it was Mrs M. A. Foster who possessed and exhibited the best lot of Yorkshire Terriers ever held by one family.

Robert Leighton mentions Mrs Vaughan Fowler's 'Longbridge Bat', 'Bob' and 'Daisy' and those bred by Lady Giffard, Mrs Bligh Monk and Miss Alderson and also Mr Abraham Bolton who were prominent breeders and exhibitors in the early days. Others of merit were Mrs Walton's 'Mont Thabor Duchess', Mr Mitchell's 'Westbrook Fred' who has deservedly won many honours and Mr Firmstone's 'Grand Duke' and 'Mynd Duchess' and Mrs Sinclair's 'Marcus Superbus' were all highly thought of by the judges. Many judges of that time agreed that one of the most beautiful bitches ever shown was 'Waveless' owned by Mrs R. Marshall, who also owned the admirable 'Little Picture'. Perhaps the greatest Yorkshire Terrier of his day was 'Ch. Sneinton Amethyst' owned by Mrs W. Shaw by 'Ch. Ashton Duke' out of 'Jackson's Vic'.

Mr Jonas and Mrs M. A. Foster started exhibiting in 1864 and were both still showing their toy breeds of dogs forty-seven years later during which time their winners and champions were legion. They travelled up and down the country wherever classes were on offer for their little charges. Mrs Foster was a member of the toy clubs of several breeds and there was a sensation when she was asked to judge the toy breeds at Manchester Dog Show in 1889

Mr & Mrs J. Foster who, over a forty year period, established the Yorkshire Terrier as it is today.

as apparently it was the very first time a lady officiated in that capacity. No one doubted her capability in this respect, she was considered a real expert, but in thirty years of dog showing no lady had been invited to enter a ring and make the awards. Mrs Foster was the first to have the courage of her convictions to exhibit them before a critical public. After this time many ladies, some of them of rank and title acted as judges of various classes of dogs but Mrs Foster had the unique distinction of being the first.

The most devout lover of this charming breed could not claim for the Yorkshire Terrier any descent from antiquity. 'Bradford' and not 'Babylon' was where he was first conceived and it must be acknowledged that he was a modern manufactured article. First dreamed up by the wool-workers he is as man-made as nylon. The creators of the breed were artisans living in the West Riding of Yorkshire some of whom just wanted to breed a straight-forward type of Terrier for their own individual purpose — some small enough to carry in their pockets to hunt rats. The other sort of breeder of that time required a pint-sized glamour coated drawing-room pet that would attract buyers at the newly started London dog markets that had appeared — before the days of dog shows — as the best place to obtain such a desirable commodity to grace the homes of the rich and important gentry that attended these nefarious sales and where huge prices indeed would be available for anything really tiny with a silky shiny mantel of inordinate length. Once the show-going public got started, there was no end to the struggle. But here we are concerned with those people who, like Queen Victoria, her husband, children and everybody in the Royal circle, would vie with one another in a boastful way for the smallest, the silkiest, the prettiest, the longest coated etc. In fact they vied for anything which might be used by organisers of dog sales to advertise their stock in public notices. Eager buyers were attracted to these auctions, which would often take place in public houses. This was in the 1840s and 1850s and before the first Dog Show proper was held in 1858, and the coming of the Kennel Club.

My own researches show that the originators of the Yorkshire Terrier were actually two completely separate entities and their ideals were as opposite as chalk and the proverbial cheese. Each used the same mixture of strains and breeds for two very different reasons — the first was to produce the best ratting terrier it had ever been possible to breed and to this end Yorkshire had in those days several breeds of rather nondescript terrier who, while keen as mustard and willing to go in to kill at the slightest suggestion, because of their shabby looks and mongrel ancestory could not be expected to be able to reproduce himself as there was no pedigree or pattern in their backgrounds. The other group of breeders were single-minded in their search for a possible glamour-coated silver and gold bantamised toy to sell to the wealthy patrons of the pedigree dog market or their agents, who at that time would travel up and down the country searching for the unusual and the most attractive. All the writers of those times are agreed that the Yorkshire Terrier was a composite article and that his blood contained a mixture of Scotch-type Terriers Cairns, Skyes probably Clydesdales from Paisley, the Black and Tan smoothcoat, the Yorkshire Black and Tan rough-coated terrier, the Maltese and even the Dandie Dinmont, made famous by Sir Walter Scott.

One thing is certain and that is that there was a lot of cross-breeding and a vast mixing up of bloodlines until they were almost untraceable in any case, but when present day historians came to record the actual foundation of the Yorkshire Terrier they discovered that the perpetrators had been so jealous of their methods of breeding Yorkshire Terriers and so determined that nobody else would be able to copy them that none of them ever set down on paper the ingredients and methods they used to breed their famous terrier.

For ratting it is certain that those men would want a keen, stout-hearted dog full of good sense that would kill as thoroughly and as quickly as any larger terrier but small enough to be carried in the overcoat pocket for any possible poaching of game.

In the eighteenth century cock fighting was to the simple man what horse-racing was to the rich one. Cock fighting was a country pastime and the equivalent sport for the townspeople was rat-killing and bull-baiting. Gambling was the name of the game in every instance and a lot of their meagre wages were used in betting on the results of the various contests, which would usually take place at the inns and taverns in every district. Nowhere were these activities more popular than in Yorkshire and the owners of the various little terriers never tired of boasting of the powers of their favourite.

'Huddersfield Ben', who is credited with being the foundation sire and was acclaimed by all that saw him as a show dog of great style and merit, was bred by Mr W. Eastwood of Huddersfield as a rat killing terrier and spent his early life in the rat-pits where, it was said, he always gave a good account of himself, killing his share of rats and earning his master both money and acclaim.

As the first Kennel Club Stud Book in 1872 contained Ben's name and gives him the credit with responsibility for over thirty entries in the broken-coated Toy Terrier and the Scotch and Yorkshire Terrier heading, it is remarkable that in such early days the breed had the good fortune to have someone come along with the interest and specialised knowledge to recognise the rare quality of 'Huddersfield Ben' enough to take him out of the rat pit. His history and achievements appear elsewhere in this work, and his picture taken with his daughter 'Little Kate'. Ben weighed all of twelve pounds but Katie was really tiny and weighed much less. Both have had their ears cut. Although the first recorded dog in the earliest Kennel Club Stud Book of 1859 — 1872 was Peter Eden's 'Albert' and his immediate descendants, including 'Huddersfield Ben' who was closely related to 'Albert' on both sides of his pedigree, he no doubt inherited many of his own good qualities from his double-dose of 'Albert's' blood so that he was able to pass on 'Albert's' many fine qualities to his own offspring and this made him the pre-potent sire that he undoubtedly was. And although I have been able to find quite a lot of the background of even 'Albert' himself and it gives me much added interest, Sam Jessop states that to him 'Ben' is the starting point to use since all the essentials required in the Yorkshire Terrier were transmitted by 'Ben' down to the present day. Mind you if 'Ben' got his long back and ratting instinct from the Skye it may have been worth searching the Isle of Skye to obtain some blood for this particular purpose. The same thing applied to the Dandie Dinmont — there is no way that a cross with this roach-backed terrier is going to improve the looks of a show Yorkie — the pepper and salt colour and texture of coat is nothing I would want to travel far to include in my breeding. If I had a big broken coated terrier and I wanted to breed a long-coated small terrier from it I would put in some Maltese blood but would probably do a lot of harm to coat colour and texture — it is much woollier than a Yorkie should be — and of course spoil the ears completely and it would mean that the ears would not always go up.

Once the wool workers and miners from the Paisley area of Scotland had come down with their Clydesdale Terriers there was absolutley no need for the Yorkshiremen to look any further. From the picture of them on page 15 it will be seen just how easily a straight cross with the Yorkshire broken coated terrier could have achieved just was required in the glamour line. There was plenty of glamour about the Clydesdale and it also had the blue and tan markings which the breeders were so anxious to get. The point about the colour and markings is that they are 'doberman markings' and are recessive in inheritance so that when mated together they always breed true, so the Yorkshire breeders of those times may not have had any knowledge of genetic inheritance as such, but were knowledgeable enough to know that when mated together these particular colours and patterns breed true.

At less than 12 lb the Clydesdale was much nearer the size that the breeders wishing to reduce size would need. It was Scotland's smallest breed of terriers and had been very popular for some time. After the Yorkie breed started in earnest the very attractive Clydesdale lost popularity. Several sincere attempts were made to re-establish the breed but without much success. The Stud Book had them listed for years but 1924 – 5 and 6 had "No Entries" after the title. In 1936 another attempt was made to revive the Clydesdale but before it got going properly again the war started and that didn't survive the war years. It has been a rare breed in America and there are one or two about but never in the show ring nowadays. However attractive the Clydesdale was as a show dog he had to be shown under the category of Scotch Terrier, Rough or Broken-Haired Terrier. At Leeds Show in 1861 all the entries in this section were what was looked on in those days as "Yorkshire Terriers" while at Birmingham the following year all the entry in that class were "Skye Terriers". I wonder if those "Skye" could have been Clydesdales? I think they played a far more important role in the development of the breed than they have been given credit for.

In her book the Yorkshire Terrier Handbook Mrs Annie Swan the expert on the breed tells us that Mr P. Edgecombe's "Silk" was entered for a Show — she does not tell us which one though — and she does not know if with a name like that he was a Yorkshire Terrier or a Clydesdale — she was entered with two puppies. She beat Mr H. Smeeton's "Door Mat" — whatever breed that dog represented. Mrs Swan tells us that the first woman to show a Yorkshire Terrier was a Mrs Carr who showed her Jock at the North of England Exhibition of Sporting & Other Dogs at the Royal Agricultural Society meeting at Leeds from 16 to 18 July 1861.

In the beginning dogs were being bred about 12 to 15 pounds in weight but the type was more or less fixed at 8 to 10 pounds when Mr Peter Eden of Manchester took an interest in the breed. He showed his dogs as early as 1861 and his 'Albert' won great renown for him and admiration for the breed wherever he appeared. The Yorkshire first appeared at Leeds Show but were entered there and in the first Kennel Club Stud Book in 1872 as 'Scottish or Broken Haired Terriers'. They were not to be officially recognised at shows as Yorkshire Terriers until the Yorkshire Terrier Club was formed in 1898. All the canine historians of that time were hard put to it to decide how the breed actually came into being. Classes for Scottish and Broken Haired Terriers could have included, Cairns, Dandie Dinmonts, Skyes, Clydesdales or Paisley Terriers, the first one at Leeds drew only Yorkie type terriers and while they were large and inelegant by our modern standards they were a distinct type and varied only from area to area.

Most walks of life required the services of a small terrier of some kind and the woollen mills of Yorkshire were no exception for the bales of skins attracted rats and mice so much that the millworkers were forced to take their toy terriers to work with them and these as we have seen before were always small enough to be carried in the overcoat pocket for rat killing sessions in the pits where the public were apt to bet their money on likely little sportsmen. In the mills the women fussed them and nursed them, often picking them up to nurse when they had their hands greasy from the lanoline in the skins. This free aid to beauty was wasted on the smooth-coated terriers but where there was an addition of any long haired breed mixed up in the background of the little terrier, and they were in no way a pure blooded race, the action of the lanoline from the women's hands was miraculous. When dog showing got started in earnest it was the mill workers and their families who were the most successful in preparing and presenting the show version when it ultimately forged ahead and became such a very desirable glamorous show specimen with long silky luxuriant coat.

Guesses that the black and tan terrier was mated to a Maltese to put the long coat on would be feasible and both being toy breeds it would follow that those that resembled a Maltese could be culled and only long-coated black and tan terriers retained. Unfortunately the Maltese was a rare and expensive lap dog that would not necessarily be very convenient to find for crossing purposes. So the Skye was used which put a glamorous coat on the victim of the experiment. This might give the correct and desired coat but would increase the size of the Yorkie out of the toy class, which the perpetators did not want. So maybe it was back to the original terrier strain and when size had been stabilised and coat and texture lost, an admixture of the lovely silky Clydesdale or Paisley could have been the next blood to be introduced. Though smaller than the Skye the Clydesdale is up to eighteen pounds and so the Yorkie would still be too large. One way was for them to use naturally reduced sized Yorkies to be mated to a naturally small bred male and the smallest of that mating retained for breeding. It took about twenty years or so and in all that time the prudent and careful breeders continued to mate the smallest of their Yorkie litters together retaining only the smallest for the experimental breeding that they were anxious to practise. The Skyes are still with us and very far from our Yorkie breed in every way but I have managed to find a photo of a Clydesdale or Paisley and this will be found on page 15 and this will be seen to be a reasonable possibility. The all-grey coat — or in more official terms the 'all blue coat' — may have been used so that in future litters all one colour ones were mated to the black and tan toy terrier or the Dandie Dinmont (which cross would spoil the coat texture and markings but drop the ears) would then continue along a very severe retain and rejection policy until at last the breed was fixed in body, coat colour and bantam size. No one has any record to prove this theory right or wrong, but there has been such a lot of culling carried out from time to time that even today when Maltese Whites and such like appear. Again sometimes it is the drop ears of the Dandie Dinmont or its broken coat that crops up in the breeding and needs culling again. Actually in the twenty odd years I have been actively involved in the breed I have found some white chests and toes, a tendency to drop ears in some lines which are best avoided and the inevitable breaking coat which is also to be found and is a bugbear and quite impossible to have in a line where show dogs are desired.

Today the Yorkie despite the awesome task of preparing its coat for exhibition and its treatment to avoid damage, is a delightful little dog with an alert outlook, a love of its owner and its own environment and an enthusiasm for going to shows and showing himself off which is infectious and gives a lot of compensation in a sometimes soul-destroying occupation when it comes to his coat care.

2 Introducing the Yorkshire Terrier

When one considers that the Yorkshire Terrier as a breed is now over 100 years old it is astonishing to find that the average owner knows next to nothing about its origins, which even more surprisingly, are shrouded in mystery.

There must be a great number of people alive today who have an intimate knowledge of some of the early breeders and their breeding methods and remember actual dogs.

My own Grandfather was born in 1862 and I am quite sure that had he been even faintly interested in Yorkies, I would have demanded stories, records and pedigrees and first hand information of as much as he knew. It is certain that there are many people alive now who had such first hand knowledge passed on to them.

Unfortunately for this book, although dog breeding and showing and judging were his hobbies, his interest was in the larger terriers — Airedales and such. Others of course must have had family or friends who could pass on intimate details of the Yorkie cult and its beginnings. Why such useful information should be so difficult to obtain is a mystery and it is made even harder by the contradictory fashion of any information when at last it is found.

Opinion is fairly agreed that the breed evolved during the Industrial Revolution. This particular era didn't happen overnight and neither did the Yorkshire Terrier. One of the natural ancestors of the dog as we know it today was definitely of the Terrier type as the name implies — terra = earth — would describe a dog that goes to earth willingly for its prey. This type of dog would need a strong mouth with scissor-like teeth to facilitate the killing of rats, rabbits and other such rodents.

Such a dog would be indispensable in kitchens, stables, barns, warehouses and such-like for keeping the rat population under control, and in the fields to kill rabbits and such for food and sport.

In time, every district had its own particular type which would be determined by the characteristics and fecundity of the local Canine Lothario. If he had a rough red coat, no doubt a large selection of the local cur population would have a rough red coat also. If the dog himself had any claim to having had any sort of reason for his having been produced, instead of the more usual alley-mixture, it is possible that he would have had some favourable qualities to pass on to his offspring. For instance, if he had been owned by a coachman, farmer or inn-keeper who had purposefully mated his two parents together because they were both excellent ratters, by all the laws of nature, this particular dog would just be an 'Excellent ratter'. If he was allowed to roam at will and mate with any bitch he could, some of the resulting puppies would be found to be good ratters. If by any happy chance he mated a bitch who was an excellent ratter then the offspring of this bitch would be even better ratters than those of the other bitches, and more pups in the litter would have these qualities.

It does not take long in any community for any outstanding achievement to gain renown. It would spread like wildfire if the inn-keeper's dog killed fifty rats in as many minutes, and it wouldn't take long before all the local dog owners would be pitting their champions against the inn-keeper's dog. Crowds would gather to watch, money would be wagered and the nearest gentry would be quick to offer many gold guineas for the purchase of the winner. So can fame be achieved. If our original Romeo now found himself in the possession of the local squire and his activities limited to the stable-yard at the Manor, he would naturally avail himself of all the local talent and when these bitches had puppies would be not averse to mating his own daughters too, with no one to say him yea or nay.

He would continue his 'sinful' ways, no doubt, on the subsequent generations until, before a younger dog appeared to see him off, he would have stamped a quite definite type on all the dogs belonging to that particular household. If the Manor was called 'Greenlands' Manor it could easily follow that any dog bred there could become a 'Greenlands' type and, if at all noteworthy would soon be in demand locally when a good ratting terrier was required. If, as we have said, this particular dog, being a rough red colour, also produced a large proportion of stock of similar colour it would follow that folks who were wanting the good ratting potentialities would connect these with the colour and choose one that looked like the original in the expectation that it would make as good a ratter. This is just a rough picture of how different breeds and varieties got started in the days when there was no Kennel Club to keep all the breeds separate.

People have needed dogs for a great variety of purposes ever since the days when the primitive man had a dog to help him in his hunting for food. According to the nature of the food available he continued to breed dogs that would be most suitable to its pursuit. That means that if the country where he lived abounded in deer he would need a fast moving type of dog to help him run it down in order to kill it for food. Likewise if the greater part of the local fauna lived under the earth like rabbits, badgers, foxes and such-like, his dog would need to be capable of burrowing under the ground after them. If the master was clever the dog would only be required to bolt his prey so that the man could catch it when it appeared at the bolt-hole, so a tiny dog would have been all that was needed. If, however, the man was still very primitive, he would almost surely have a dog that could kill the prey and bring it out to him.

Therefore, a larger dog but still one that would go to earth like a terrier, was needed. We are not concerned here with any of the other requirements man, in his early beginnings needed from his dog, but there is evidence enough to illustrate this point if one considers the hundreds of varieties of the species 'Canidae' which have been perpetuated through the ages from the tiny 'Gentle or Comforter' of the Middle Ages when forsaken wives of the Crusaders turned for affection to little dogs that they could fondle and nurse on their laps, to the enormous hounds bred for wolf-chasing and dogs big enough to drag grown men from the snows on the frozen mountain-sides of the Alps.

In tracing back to the origin of the Yorkshire we need only concern ourselves with the 'Terrier' as all the different strains that went into its production fit into this group.

By describing how the terrier became regional I hope I have illustrated how the group became split up into the various varieties that make up the group. The conditions that characterised the difference in looks of these varieties were geographic and climatic. Where the climate was cold and the terrain stony and craggy the terrier would be found to have acquired a harsh, wiry and very thick coat which would adequately protect and insulate him. Similarly those that would willingly go to water or were forced to live in wet conditions soon developed a wavy or curly coat which is more water repellant than a smooth one.

Long-coated, silky haired dogs have been recorded since Aristotle (384−322 BC) gave such a description to the little ones found on the island of Melita (Malta). This particular toy terrier was popular at the court of Henry VIII and his Court Physician, the learned Dr Johannes Caius wrote a remarkable book *Of Englishe Dogges*, in which he referred to them as 'Melite' Terriers having thin, soft and silky coats, sufficient for their native Mediterranean warmth. The cold and wetness of the English climate may have thickened these coats but to this day they have long, silky coats parting down the middle and hanging to the ground in the same way as those of the Yorkshire Terrier. In 1576, one Abraham Fleming translated Dr Caius' Latin into the English language of that day and in 1605 King James I gave us a careful description of the 'earth Dogges' or terriers of his native Scotland, and adherents of the Cairn Terrier claim he was referring to their breed. Be that as it may, it is fair supposition to say the Cairn was used in the formation of the Yorkshire Terrier. Scotland, with its crags and cairns was the domicile of many shaggy and rough-haired types of terrier right up to the present day. These have varied in colour and coat type according to environment and particular use. Sir Walter Scott in his novel *Guy Mannering*, published in 1814, describes a pack of Mustard and Pepper Terriers, also known as 'Dandie Dinmonts'. Skye Terriers were popularised by Queen Victoria, that most ardent of dog lovers, who bred them for thirty years.

Early in the nineteenth century around the banks of the River Clyde in

Scotland lived several communities of artisans that included some mining groups and wool and cloth workers from the Paisley mills. These people indulged in various sports, and hunting the local terrain with their dogs was one of the prime favourites. They acquired a dog that became known as the Clydesdale and sometimes the Paisley Terrier, which was shown in England up to 1902. Mr H.F. Whitehead, in his book *The Yorkshire Terrier* gives us a very clear description of the Clydesdale as being a soft coated Skye Terrier. Its colour is given as a level, bright steel blue, the head, legs and feet a clear golden tan free from grey, sooty, or dark hairs. 'I wish you to note', says Mr Whitehead. 'The word sooty, and how that word comes into the standard of our Yorkie. The parting of the coat (shedding in Scotland) extends from the head to the tail, evenly down each side. What more tempting to infuse into the Yorkie of that day, nameless then, like the Scottie.'

During the Industrial Revolution many wool workers from Scotland made their way to Yorkshire where their trade was at its zenith. The dogs they took with them were soon matched against those they found in their new territory. The Yorkshiremen, a 'canny' race where dog breeding was concerned, were quick to appreciate the capabilities of the newcomers. Already breeding an established strain of Broken-haired Terriers, the Yorkshireman saw the desirability of crossing his type with the more exotic looking Clydesdale in order to achieve a more commercially acceptable proposition. From the royal family down there was tremendous interest in dogs and the public demanded attractive looks as well as capabilities. The Yorkshireman's desire for 'brass' set him out to evolve a breed that would fulfil his usual duties but look desirable as well. Poaching laws at this time were rigid but never stopped the practice, only caused the reprobates to take care not to be caught. To this end they used a tiny terrier, no bigger than a ferret, that was sent down the rabbit holes to bolt the prey into nets spread for the purpose. The dog and his catch were then popped into large poachers' pockets to remain safely hidden on the return home. The miniature black and tan was a commendable choice but his silky coat was slippery to hold and often when a hasty retreat was necessary he was so difficult to grasp that he had to be abandoned. A longer coat was needed to make it easier to pull him out. This is where the Maltese Terrier could benefit the poacher's purpose. These little dogs were often brought back by sailors from the Mediterranean ports where they could be picked up quite cheaply. Mostly these made most acceptable gifts for female relatives but occasionally they would be bartered for beer in alehouses. As time went on they would be sought by corn-merchants for they were surprisingly keen ratters despite their good looks. All the above-mentioned breeds could have gone into the mixing pot and, when the little blue and gold charmer eventually emerged it was the Yorkshireman's canny instinct that told him he had 'struck oil'. Further breeding of these types together proved that the strain was 'fixed' and, in true Yorkshire fashion he straight away hid his methods so that when the buying public started to want them they had to pay a high price.

Their popularity was assured when the Dog Shows acclaimed them, and classes were put on for them at the Birmingham Dog Shog in 1860 where they were just called 'Toy Terriers'. They were also shown as 'Scotch Terriers' and as 'Broken-Haired Terriers'. It was not until 1886 that the Kennel Club, that had itself only been founded by Mr S.E. Shirley, M.P., in 1873, acknowledged the breed as 'Yorkshire Terriers'.

Although the official standard was not to be drawn up until the year 1898 when the Yorkshire Terrier Club was formed for the purpose chiefly of devising such a standard, most of the essential points had been approved and adhered to at least fifty years before. At that particular point in its history the breed could be summarised as a 'Broken-haired or Toy Terrier with strong Scotch connections weighing anything from 5 lbs to over 15 lbs, the desired colours being steel blue with tan markings. There were, unfortunately, no official records until 1874, when Mr Frank Pearse of Faversham in Kent gratified a long neglected need by producing the first Kennel Club Stud Book and from then on we are able to trace the development of the Breed with some accuracy.

Included in Mr Pearse's first Stud Book is the name of 'Huddersfield Ben', Stud Book No. 3612 owned by Mrs M.A. Foster, 21, Lady-lane, Lister Hills, Bradford; breeder Mr W. Eastwood of Huddersfield; born 1865; died in September 1871. The following is his pedigree, which I have copied out of the first Stud Book exactly as it is set out therein:

3612 HUDDERSFIELD BEN
Pedigree:
By Mr Boxcovitch's dog out of Lady, his sire by Thomas Ramsden's BOUNCE by his BOB out of his OLD DOLLY;
BOB by Haigh's TEDDY (from Lascelles Hall, Huddersfield) out of OLD DOLLY;

Fig 2 Mrs Foster's Huddersfield Ben and his daughter, Lady Gifford's Little Kate (note the cropped ears).

TEDDY by J. Swift's OLD CRAB (from Manchester) out of Kershaw's
OLD KITTY (from Halifax);
LADY by Eastwood's OLD BEN, and granddaughter of OLD SANDY;
BEN by Ramsden's BOUNCE out of YOUNG DOLLY, by OLD
SANDY out of OLD JOLLY by ALBERT (from Manchester), by OLD
SOLDIER;
OLD SANDY by Haigh's TEDDY out of Walshaw's KITTY, by the
Healy House dog out of Walshaw's PINK;

Chief Performances:
Manchester, 2nd prize 1869; 3rd prize 1870
Crystal Palace, 1st prize 1870; 2nd prize 1871
Winner of seventy-four prizes, and sire of Inman's BENSON, Forster's
LITTLE KATE and EMPEROR, MOZART, COBDEN, SANDY and
many other winners.

The entry about Ben is found in Class XXXII — Broken Haired Scotch and
Yorkshire Terriers dogs and bitches. He is pictured in Fig. 1 with his tiny
daughter Lady Gifford's 'Little Kate' whose entry in the same Stud Book is in
Class XL — Toy Terriers (Rough and Brokenhaired) dogs and bitches as
follows:

4001 LITTLE KATE — Mrs M.A. Foster, Bradford; also shown by Mr
A.K. Brigg's; born 1867.
Pedigree: by HUDDERSFIELD BEN

Chief Performances:
Birmingham, 1st prize, 1869;
Birmingham, 1st prize, 1870;
Islington, 1st prize, 1869;
Manchester, 1st prize, 1869;
Crystal Palace, 1st prize 1870;
Crystal Palace, 1st prize 1871;
Crystal Palace, 2nd prize 1873.

Some of 'Huddersfield Ben's' prizes were won in classes confined to dogs
with 'cut ears'. He was awarded a 2nd in a class for 'cut ears' and at
Manchester in 1870 he was beaten into 3rd place by his son, Inman's
'Benson' in a class for Scotch Terriers with cut ears. At Edinburgh in 1870 all
the winners in Scotch Terrier classes are entered in the Stud Book in the
Yorkshire Terrier section.

'Ben's' pedigree warrants careful study and it will show how much close
breeding had to be introduced to maintain the type. Today he is acknowledged as the foundation sire par excellence and he certainly stamped a very
decided size and type. If it is copied out on to an extended pedigree form it can
be seen how many generations had been recorded even before official statis-
tics were kept.

While it will be seen that McDonald's 'Jessie', Hansall's 'Punch' 4012, Coupland's 'Shrimp', Inman's 'Tiny' 4023 and James's 'Willa' owe nothing to 'Huddersfield Ben' for their tiny size as some of them were being shown before he was born, it is universally acknowledged that he has had the greatest influence for good in the breed. We are indebted to the writers on dogs of those times for many good descriptions of him. One of the most famous of these — Hugh Dalziel — wrote the chapter on Yorkshire Terriers for Stonehenge's *Dogs of the British Isles* and illustrates his article with a sketch by Baker of 'Huddersfield Ben' and 'Katie'. Stonehenge was the pseudonym of Mr J.H. Walsh, a famous adjudicator in dog shows of those days and an early editor of *The Field*. One of the contributors to *The Field* was the Rev. W. Pearse who wrote under the name of 'Idstone'. The eighth edition of his book *The Dog* appeared in 1872 and contained the correct points of every known breed with some excellent illustrations by Mr Earl. The Yorkshire Terrier had not received this name when this book was written, but 'Idstone' refers to them under the heading of Broken-haired Terriers.

Also on the staff of *The Field* at this time was Mr Vero K. Shaw and he, being in charge of the kennel side of that periodical, concerned himself primarily with canine matters whereas Mr Walsh covered the whole field of sporting life. Vero Shaw had ambitions to edit the Kennel Club Stud Book, but his offer not being accepted, he contented himself with producing the monumental *Illustrated Book of the Dog*, the first part of which appeared in 1879. His chapter on the Yorkshire is illustrated by a painting of Mrs Foster's 'Toy Smart', and he says:

> 'Whatever the varieties of dogs may have been which were called upon by breeders to combine and form the present beautiful Yorkshire Terrier it is proved by results that the judgment of their earliest supporters was sound and the trouble spent amply repaid by the successful termination of their labours. We have no recollection of coming across an admirer of the variety who claimed that the breed was anything but a manufactured article. It is surprising to contemplate the immense amount of trouble lovers of this remarkably beautiful dog must have been at to produce such good results. Judicious selection of parents can produce anything in the shape of dog flesh, the difficulty being to get these productions to breed true, and obviate the inclination to throw back to some remote ancestor. Yorkshire Terrier breeders have overcome this obstacle for although first rate specimens are difficult to obtain there is an identity of type about the offspring of some of the best strains, which proves the breed is practically established as one of the national breeds.'

All illustrations of these early Yorkshires show they had one feature in common — an overlong back. Henry Webb produced a book called *Dogs* in 1872 which was the first to be illustrated by photographs, so one can be sure they would be nearer to life than an impression in an artist's eye. All the same, 'Toy Smart' owned by Mrs Foster had a length of 22", 'Sandy' 19" and 'Pride' 18½". If they were only 9" to 10" in height they were far from typical of the standard. 'Mozart', born 1869 and a son of 'Huddersfield Ben', was owned by Miss Alderson of Leeds. He won 105 prizes but was described by the judges as having too long a back. He won the variety class at Westmorland Show in 1870 whereupon Angus Sutherland, from *The Field* suggested that as his type was so often called Yorkshires and as many of the very best ones came from that county, they would do well to stick to this name for the breed and so it was adopted there and then and soon came into general use.

By the turn of the century the breed emerges as a 3 to 7 lb specimen with long, silky coat now completely built for the drawing room and show-bench, and showing few signs of the gallant little terrier it started out to be. A large proportion stemmed from Mrs Foster's strain and she had now taken the prefix of 'Bradford' and showed her dogs fearlessly wherever in the country classes were on offer for her dogs. In this respect she had plenty of scope and sometimes showed a whole litter at the same show and had them all in different categories, viz.: Scotch Terriers over 12 lbs, Broken-haired terriers and Toy Terriers under 5 lbs. One of Mrs Foster's most notable achievements was to produce the diminutive 'Bradford Marie' at 1 lb 14 oz the smallest Yorkshire to be recorded at this time. Sold for £100 during Mrs Foster's illness, little 'Marie', although a healthy, hardy and lively little thing did not long survive in her new home. Later Mrs Foster bred 'Bradford Queen of the Toys' who was only 24 oz. While the dog buying public of that time were intrigued with the very tiny ones and offered large sums for them, Mrs Foster's greatest success came with her 'Champion Ted', who was born on 20th July 1885 by 'Young Royal' out of 'Annie'. 'Ted' was a direct descendant of 'Huddersfield Ben', weighed just 4 lb, his height was 9" and his length 17", the length of his coat across his shoulders was 18" and across his loins 17". During his show career 'Ted' won 265 first and special prizes. In his report of the Birmingham Show in November 1889, the judge, the Rev G.F. Lovell said of him:

> ' "Ch. Ted" is, of course, the best that we have seen. Good in head
> with the dark stern and a beautiful coat.'

He was advertised at stud in the Kennel Club Gazette of that time at a fee of 1 gn. The K.C. Gazette of 1894 listed 28 Yorkshire Terrier registrations, and of these 8 were by 'Ch. Ted'.

The importance of a dog in the history of a breed is not so much by his own record of wins but rather for the quality and winning potential of the stock he sired and its effect in improving a certain strain. In this respect 'Ch. Ted' could not be surpassed. In his time he sired many outstanding winners among which the inimitable 'Halifax Marvel', later Aspinall's Teddy', was one of the smallest winners of his day weighing only 3¾ lbs and was noted for the beauty, length and colouring of his coat. He sired 'Monarch', Champions 'Merry Mascot' and 'Ashton Queen' and, probably the most important of all his progeny 'Halifax Ben', full brother to 'Ch. Ashton Duke', 'Ben' was a very dark blue on his back and his tan was of a deep rich colour. Born 6th July 1897 he was bred by J. Crabtree and weighed 3 ½ lb. Altogether he sired more first prize and special prize winners than had any other Yorkshire Terrier sire up till that time, one of the best of which, 'Marvel Wonder', born 19th Oct. 1901, weighed 3 ¼ lb and, as he had 'Ch. Ted' on both sides of his pedigree, can be said (in genetic parlance) to be line-bred to him.

'Halifax Marvel' was a son of 'Ch. Ted' by Bank's 'Young Royal' out of Fleming's 'Annie' — the dam 'Schofield's Fan' (this breeding goes back to 'Old Royal', son of 'Huddersfield Ben' who won 129 prizes beating all the dogs of his day). It also included 'Huddersfield Ben II' out of Townsend's 'Nettle' by Foster's old 'Huddersfield Ben' out of Lumb's 'Rose' and 'Marvel' owned by Mr G. Hollas of Halifax who sired Mr Tom Hooton's 'Merry Mascot'.

Pedigree of HALIFAX MARVEL (late Aspinall's 'Teddy'). (as Advertised). . . . Registered in Kennel Club Gazette, weight 3¾ lb, breeder Mr Schofield, Lindley:

Sire   Mrs M.A. Foster's 'Ch. Ted' by Bank's 'Young Royal' ex Fleming's 'Annie'. 'Young Royal' by Bank's 'Old Royal' ex 'Young Alice'. Fleming's 'Annie' by Hirst's 'Peter' ex Brown's 'Fan'.

Dam   Schofield's 'Fan' by Tindall's 'Marwood' ex Schofield's 'Peggy'. 'Marwood' by Tindall's 'Don' ex Dolman's 'Lady Peggy' by Lumb's 'Huddersfield Ben II' ex Townsend's 'Nettle'.

'Huddersfield Ben II' by Foster's old 'Huddersfield Ben' ex Lumb's 'Rose'.

'Marvel' is one of the smallest, longest coated and best-coloured sons of Foster's 'Ch. Ted' at stud. He is bred on most fashionable lines and his pedigree includes some of the most successful prize winners of the breed including 'Old Royal' winner of 129 prizes beating all dogs in his day, 'Young Alice', winner of 36 prizes in one season and never beaten, and Foster's 'Ch. Ted', winner of 265 first and special prizes.

'Marvel' is a prize winner and sire of numerous prize winners including 'Monarch' and 'Ch. Merry Mascot' and 'Ch. Ashton Queen'.

'Monarch', above, was registered in the *Kennel Gazette* and *Kennel Club Stud Book*. He was born on 18 April 1893. He was bred by Mr R. Richardson of Well Lane, Halifax and he weighed 4 lb.

Sire 'Halifax Ben' as above and out of Richardson's 'Gipsy' by Hustler's 'General' ex Richardson's 'Polly'. 'General' by 'Bradford Hero' ex 'Young Alice'. Richardson's 'Polly' by Aspinall's 'Little Swell' ex Richardson's 'Old Gipsy'. 'Bradford Hero' by Foster's 'Bruce' ex Smith's 'Violet'. 'Young Alice' by 'Crack' ex Hustler's 'Old Alice'. 'Little Swell' by the noted Champion 'Manningham Charlie'.

'Monarch' was a combination of the best blood extant and he was a direct descendant from a long line of well-known prize winners, including 'Manningham Charlie', winner of fifty prizes and cups, 'Old Royal', winner of 129 prizes beating all dogs in his day, 'Young Alice' winner of 36 prizes in one season and never beaten, and Foster's 'Ch. Ted' winner of 265 first and special prizes.

Pedigree of 'Halifax Ben'

Born 6 July 1897 and bred by Mr J. Crabtree, weight 3 ½ lb.

He was by G. Hollas' 'Halifax Marvel' out of Crabtree's 'Lady' by 'Halstead Conqueror' ex Robson's 'Bell'. 'Conqueror' by Mrs M.A. Foster's 'Ch. Ted.' ex Crabtree's 'Floss'. 'Bell' by Hodson's 'Marquis' ex 'Rose'. 'Ch. Ted' by Bank's 'Young Royal' ex Fleming's 'Annie'.

'Halifax Ben' was a combination of the best strains of Yorkshire Terriers up to date. He was by the same sire as 'Ch. Merry Mascot' and 'Ch. Ashton Queen'. Winner of more firsts, specials and Championship prizes than any other Yorkshire Terrier that ever lived. He was own brother to 'Ch. Ashton Duke'. 'Ben' was a very rich tanned dog, dark blue coat, long and straight, and he was the sire of some very noteworthy prize-winning stock. 'Marvel Wonder' was born on 19 October 1901, bred and owned by Mr J. Shuffle-botham and he weighed 3 ¾ lb. He was sired by Mr Hollas's 'Halifax Ben' by 'Halifax Marvel' out of Crabtree's 'Lady' by Halstead's 'Conqueror' ex Robson's 'Bell' by Hodson's 'Marquis' out of 'Rose'. 'Marvel' by Mrs Foster's 'Ch. Ted' ex Fleming's 'Annie'.

'Marvel Wonder's dam was 'Marvel Queen' winner of twenty-seven first and special prizes. 'Marvel Queen' by 'Halifax Marvel' ex Canning's 'Nell'. 'Halifax Marvel' by Mrs Foster's 'Ch. Ted' ex Schofield's 'Fan'. 'Ch. Ted' by Bank's 'Young Royal' ex Fleming's 'Annie'. Canning's 'Nell' by Halstead's 'Little Swell' ex Canning's 'Ruby'. 'Little Swell' by J. Taylor's 'Prince' ex Inman's 'Lady'. Canning's 'Ruby' by E. Beaumont's 'Major' ex Thorpe's 'Tiny'.

It was said of 'Marvel Wonder' that he was one of the smallest and longest-coated and best coloured little dogs before the public.

There is no doubt at all that to anyone who has the slightest knowledge of breeding patterns, that Mrs Foster's 'Ch. Ted' was a *potent sire* to use a present day expression. It is obvious that the stock that had him in their pedigree were of a very high order indeed and when, as quite often occurred in those days, the dangers of too close breeding were not realised, a second dose of his blood seemed to add greatly to the quality.

Ch. Miller's Daughter.

Mrs Foster, with her usual enthusiasm and dedication presented a special cup to be won by the Best Exhibit bred by 'Ch. Ted' at the Pet Dog Show. In May 1893 this prize was claimed by a Mrs Walton for her exhibit entered as 'Chelsea Nellie' and duly awarded. Later the Kennel Club was informed by a Mrs A. Vaughan Fowler that 'Chelsea Nellie' had been given a false pedigree and was not by 'Ch. Ted'. Giving evidence at the consequent enquiry, Mrs Pickles, from whom Mrs Walton had purchased 'Nellie', stated that she went to Halifax and discovered that 'Chelsea Nellie' was by J. Nichols' 'Bright' by 'Crack', and 'Crack' was by Mr T. Walker's 'Teddy'. Her husband had told Mrs Walton that the bitch was by 'Ch. Ted' but they had not registered her.

Mrs Walton claimed that she had been told the bitch was by 'Ch. Ted' when she bought her and had entered her accordingly.

The case was dismissed but the registration form had to be amended in accordance with Mrs Pickles' statement. (*Taken from The Kennel Gazette 1893.*)

I wonder if this Mrs Walton could be the same one that in partnership with Mr and Mrs Beard owned the outstanding 'Ashton Queen'. They lived in Ashton-under-Lyne and 'Ashton Queen' had more prizes than any other Yorkshire Terrier living. About this time too a Mr H. Walton of Woodley bred 'Ch. Boy Blue' owned by a Mr H. Lemon. 'Boy Blue' was by Dobson's 'Harpurhey Hero', credited with being the longest-coated Yorkshire Terrier as his coat measured thirty-six inches from end to end when straightened out.

On the subject of Yorkshire Terrier coats Mrs Troughear's 'Conqueror' also had a very long one as on his body it was 26 inches long on his head 23 ½ inches and below the eye and muzzle 18 ½ inches. He was sold for £250 to a Mrs Emmott the wife of an American actor and it was reported that he weighed 5 lb, which was a lot better than some of the earliest exports to America which, according to the *Complete Dog Book* (the official publication of the American Kennel Club) in 1880 were so varied that it was difficult for the show going writers to discover what kind of a dog was to be the style for show records show that the weight varied from 2¾ to 13 lb. In the beginning the weight was said to be as much as 15 lb and some of the American canine journalists made very caustic comments on the fact 'that its type was not very well fixed' and the author of the work agreed that it was not difficult to imagine their perplexity at the wide divergence in type.

The article goes on to say that modern specimens breed true to type and their characterists are well fixed and the writer says that the diminitive size cannot be credited alone to crosses and it took many years before the Yorkshire Terrier was really small enough to be called a 'toy'. The reduction in size was probably due to selective breeding. Still, it says, it is remarkable that within twenty years of its origin the breed had been dwarfed to such an extent that it was now among the smallest of all varities.

As is generally known the first recorded dog show was held at the Town Hall in Newcastle in 1859 and it is amusing to note that the judge of setters, Mr Brailsford, awarded the prize to Mr Joblings's 'Dandy'. The judge for 'pointers', the aforementioned Mr Jobling returned the compliment by awarding the prize to Mr Brailsford's liver and white dog. One of the intriguing situations that come to light from time to time and make the delving into the past so rewarding. It also illustrates the necessity for the establishment of the Kennel Club to straighten out such anomalies.

3 The Yorkshire Terrier as a Breed

THE Yorkshire Terrier Club was formed in 1898 and its first important task after getting a committee together was to draw up a standard for the breed. The one they drew up and the percentage values of the points to be allotted was so clear and concise that it is, with very little alteration, still the standard and points value in use today, which is as follows:

Formation and terrier appearance	15	Head	10
Colour of hair on the body	15	Mouth	5
Richness of tan on head and legs	15	Legs and feet	5
Quantity and length of coat	10	Ears	5
Quality of texture of coat	10	Eyes	5
		Tail (Carriage of)	5
		Total of points	100

Although, today, we do not judge to these points, as the Kennel Club has decided it is not good policy (all the dogs in a class can have points which when added up come to the same value), we still have to study them carefully in order to see how much value is stressed on coat and colour, and to appreciate the importance of coat and colour in assessing this breed.

The standard which follows can be compared with the points value quoted above and the various features are illustrated in the diagram of a Yorkshire terrier in full coat.

The Development of the Breed

Although the Yorkshire Terrier Club was formed in 1898, and the breed thereafter rejoiced in a name to itself, it was to be many years before enough of these little dogs were to be entered at a show to have classes allotted to them entirely. For many more years they were still to share with other Toy and Broken-haired Terriers. This is why the earlier dogs did not get championship status, presumably.

Gordon Stables, M.D., R.N., gave us several very informative books about this period. His *Our Friend the Dog* gave a whole chapter on the Yorkshire Terrier and his book contains photographs of champions and the standards of the various breeds as laid down by the breed clubs. Another very important work published in 1893–4 was Rawdon B. Lee's *A History and Description of the Modern Dogs of Great Britain and Ireland*. 'Volume III — Terriers' gives classification of breeds, and the Kennel Club later adopted these.

In 1904 Frank Townend Barton brought out his *Toy Dogs* which devoted a whole chapter to Yorkshire Terriers.

There is enough information to show that the breed was being recognised as a household pet and some large prices were obtained for tiny well-made little Yorkies. That the owners prized these little dogs highly will be illustrated by the following account of a case tried at Bow Street Court in April of 1893 when a charge of dog-stealing was preferred against George Blower, a brewers' traveller, and Edward Drew, who was formerly in the same employ.

These men were seated in a dray which had been brought to a standstill near Carlton House Terrace. At the same time, dinner being over, Joseph Saxelby, a stableman in the employ of Mrs Mackay, the wife of the American millionaire, was taking his mistresses' two Yorkshire Terriers out for exercise. One ran on in front and, it was alleged, that Drew seized it and handed it to Blower. When Saxelby asked the latter what his 'little game' was, he threatened to 'hit him on the nose'. He, at the same time, raised his arm and, taking advantage of that movement, the stableman seized the dog and went in quest of a policeman. When charged at the police-station Drew said someone whom he did not know gave the dog to him and he handed it to Blower.

At the police-court the prisoners said they thought the dog was lost and had no intention of stealing it.

The dogs were produced in Court by two servants and, eventually, Mr Vaughan discharged Drew with a caution and bound Blower over in £10 to keep the peace for six months.

At the Crystal Palace Show in 1893 the judge, Mr Frederick Gresham said in his report:

'The Yorkshire Terriers were a magnificent lot. Mr Beard's Ashton Fred, who won in the Novice and Limit Classes, is a splendid little fellow, excellent all round, his only fault being that he is a little dark in colour over the tail, which will improve as he gets older.

Mrs Foster's Bradford Princess, who was 2nd is another good one, not so rich in colour or so full in coat.

Mrs Fowler's Longridge Bob, Mr J. Leach's Sir Belvedere, Mrs Foster's Bradford Maggie and Mr Hodgson's Warrior Halifax are all good ones.

In the Limit Class Mrs Foster was 2nd to Ashton Fred with Bradford Nancy, very rich in colour but not so good in coat, and Mr Walton's Merry Prince II, who is rather on the large side·made a capital 3rd.

Mr Foster had Bradford Ben in the Winners Class and he just managed to score over Ashton Fred in the Open Class by dint of his superior colour of tan, and body.'

We are told that the famous bitch 'Sprig of Blossom' was the winner of 26 championship certificates but no information is given anywhere as to why she was so famous. She was born in Leeds on 3rd June 1908 and her sire 'King' and dam 'Minnie' were both unregistered. Mr Dick Marshall bought her but not from Mr W. Wood, who bred her. Mrs Marshall showed her at the Kensington Canine Society's Show in 1915, so she must have been 7 years old. She beat 'Gala Girl' who was formidable opposition, but was herself beaten by Hardman's 'Lady Charm'. Her proud owners presented the 'Sprig of Blossom' trophy to the Yorkshire Terrier Club for the best in Open and Limit Classes. I found a tiny illustration of her in a composite picture in Mr Edward C. Ash's *Dogs* and she was certainly very beautiful.

Mr H. Walton of Woodley bred 'Ch. Boy Blue' owned and shown by Mr H. Lemon. 'Ch. Boy Blue' was by Dobson's 'Harpurhey Hero', about whom it was claimed that he was the longest-coated Yorkshire Terrier, with a coat measuring thirty-six inches from tip to tip across his shoulders. This remarkable dog was also the sire of Dobson's 'Conran Pride' who sired Mr W. Scolley's 'Ch. Mendham Peggy', who won 25 C.Cs and also 'Invincia Romiley Jinks', noted as being the sire of 'Ch. Invincible of Invincia', 'Suprema' (who went to U.S.A.) by 'Supreme' out of Pearson's 'Beauty' who was from the well-known Pellon strain on both sides. This strain was started by Mr Greenwood of Halifax who started with 'Pellon Conqueror' and went back as far as Mrs Foster's 'Ch. Ted', 'Tom Pinch' and so forth.

One of the few Yorkshire Terrier fanciers to register a Prefix, we are indebted to the 'Pellon' for doing so as it is possible to trace the strain and show its influence on present day Yorkshire Terriers.

Mrs Annie Swan, owner-breeder of the Invincia strain, gives us in her very informative *Yorkshire Terrier Handbook*, some very interesting pedigrees of her early dogs. Her 'Ch. Invincible of Invincia' by 'Invincia Romiley Jinks' who went back to 'Halifax Ben' mated to 'Marvel Queen', and 'Marvel Wonder' mated to 'Inglewood Floss', mated to 'Pillar of Invincia', of the Ardwick Prince II strain. He in turn was the great grandsire of 'Ch. Splendour of Invincia', who was born 16th July 1947, so we see how the old strains were mixed to bring us the present type of Yorkie that we see on the show-bench at the present day. This intermingling was responsible for such dogs as 'Ch. Goldmount', owned by Mr J. Hardman. 'Goldmount' was by a son of 'Harpurhey Hero', 'Fenton Hero' mated to a daughter of 'Ch. Westbrook Fred' who went back to 'Ch. Ashton Duke', a son of 'Halifax Marvel'. Another was 'Ch. Boy Blue', also a son of 'Harpurhey Hero'. He founded the Dewsburian strain by a mixture with Overdon blood, which produced the well-known Overdale Regenta.

'Ch. Mendham Prince' sired one of the most famous Yorkshire Terriers of all time in 'Harringay Remarkable', who lived up to his name in all ways and has been immortalised in many of the breed annals, as he it was who was photographed in his wrappings and used in Hutchinson's *Encyclopaedia of the Dog* to illustrate the correct way to wrap a show coat.

'Ch. Harringay Remarkable' was said to be a wonderful Yorkshire Terrier for at the age of 1 year 8 months he had won a Res. C.C. and Cup at L.K.A., 4 firsts at Crufts and at the Kennel Club Show in 1932 he won 1st Limit, 1st Open, the dog C.C. and Best of Breed, the Grand Challenge Class for Best Toy All Breeds, which won him the Send Gold Challenge Vase and also the Theo Marples Cup for Best Non-Sporting in Show, an award that no Yorkshire Terrier had ever won before. This award earned him a photo in the *Kennel Gazette* of 1932 on page 866.

Other famous champions of the twenties and thirties were 'Ch. Armley Principal Boy' owned by Mrs Wood, Champions 'Mendham's Prince', 'Billy' and 'Gay Girl' all owned by Mr Scolley, 'Ch. Mendham's Beauty', winner of the C.C. at the K.C. Show in 1929 under Mr R. Marshall, 'Ch. Eminent' and 'Ch. Invincible' owned by Mrs Swan, 'Ch. Saucy Lad' and 'Ch. Little Comet' owned by Mrs Marshall, 'Ch. Lady Roma' bred and owned by Miss Olive Saunders, 'Ch. Tinker of Glendinnan', bred and owned by Mrs Wollridge.

Lady Edith Windham (later Windham-Dawson) was one of the foremost breeders and exhibitors of this period and well deserves a chapter to herself. At the middle of the period she was showing 'Ch. Victoria of Soham', described as the best Yorkie of her day, 'Ch. Rose of the World', 'Ch. Thyra of Soham', 'Ch. James of Soham' and his little sister, 'Ch. Rose Crystal', to name the most important.

Left to right Little Pimpo, Ch. James and Ch. Rose Crystal of Soham.

About 'Ch. Rose of the World of Soham', K.C. 933 NN SB, it is said that she won numerous 1sts and specials all over the country. Her sire was 'Ch. Mendham Prince' and her dam was 'Rowena of Soham'. Rose gained her first C.C. at Blackpool under Mr Greenwood, her second at Bournemouth under Mr Shaw and her championship honours at the Kennel Club Show in 1933 under Mr Beynon, who said of her: 'A really lovely little bitch, beautiful blue-black; a wealth of straight coat of ideal texture, rich tan and a born shower. A worthy champion which I understand this award made her.' Best of Breed at this show was again 'Ch. Harringay Remarkable' who is described by Mr Beynon as 'the star turn', standing right out on his own; he is undoubtedly one of the very best of his breed we have and was put down in most perfect condition. He well deserved the C.C. and Best of Breed award.

Lady Edith Windham took over the secretaryship of the Yorkshire Terrier Club from Mr J. Dunman who had held that office for many years. She held office until she went to live in Ireland during the Second World War.

Between the two World Wars the Yorkshire Terrier not only became well-established in this country but in the United States of America as well. Lady Edith Windham did much to popularise the breed and many present day successful breeders owe much of that success to knowledge gained during visits to her kennel in Bishop's Stortford. Miss A.E. Palmer of the Winpal prefix spent some years there and subsequently became one of the foremost breeders and exhibitors with many champions and stud book entries to her credit. She is still exhibiting today and, as she spent some years in Theale in Berkshire within 20 miles of where I live I have constantly met dogs she has bred.

One of the most important exports to America about this time was 'Ch. Delia of Erlcour', bred by Mrs E. Batsford. Always a big winner over here she soon majored in points for her American Championship in the care of Mrs Jean Gordon and her sister Miss Janet Bennett of the famous Wild Weir prefix, and because of the number of champions they have made in the breed with their English imports and their own American bred stock, must be regarded as among the leading breeders in the world. Their 'Ch. Starlight of Clu Mor' is featured by *Popular Dogs of America* for their illustration of the Standard of the breed.

Ch. Delia is particularly interesting as regards her breeding as her sire 'Victory Boy' is by 'Monarch of Harringay', son of 'Ch. Harringay Remarkable', and her dam 'Miretta Marianne' was out of 'Mitzi Marabelle', a grand-daughter of 'Ch. Harringay Remarkable'.

For many years I attended the Speciality Show of the Yorkshire Terrier Club of America which is always held at the Statler Hilton Hotel in New York and of course always meet Mrs Jean Gordon Jr. and her sister Miss Janet Bennett. They knew most of the early history of the breed in America and their 'Am. Ch. Wild Weir Pomp and Circumstance' was on both sides of the pedigree of the little stud dog I brought back with me to help improve size, colour and style in my own Yorkies. 'Emmrill Jig Saw' was out of a 4 lb champion mother so he had a great deal to offer the breed and during the years I had him he helped fix a very definite type that I was very pleased with. Because of the withdrawal of the British Forces from Malta at that time I was unable to find a quarantine kennel near my home to take the three dogs I brought back with me at that time so he was placed in a kennel in Norfolk. Whether it was the colder climate or what I do not know but he came out with a huge coat at the end of six months and could easily have been shown. However at that time I was far too busy myself and had neither staff nor family that had any particular interest in the showing of a Yorkie so I never did get him to the shows. He was bred by Beryl Hesketh, one of my favourite people in Yorkshire Terriers. She sees them in much the same way that I do — we like them small and sound and with the correct texture and colour in the coat. This was something it used to be hard to find when I first started going to the Yorkie Shows in the States as a lot of the dogs are handled by professional handlers and they as a rule liked a slightly bigger, up on the leg Yorkie with plenty of dark, woolly textured coat that they could show under their all-rounder judges and win groups with. When I told them they were wrong they told me that a judge did not bother about details of coat colour and texture when judging groups. They took what was sent up to them by the breed judges and were only concerned with the dogs ability to cover the ground, keep up with all the other Best of Breed Winners, look attractive and have a gay and outgoing personality. The handlers had found (as have a lot of other people) that the woolly coat, although it is wrong and often keeps its black colour without 'breaking', really needs very little care and attention. It never needed to be 'tied' up when the kennel staff were busy doing other things, more profitably, and they liked the darker ones because they could put a 'shine' on the dark coats that would look wonderful under the bright lights of an indoor show or in the sunlight at an outdoor one.

At the time I am telling you about the handlers were very powerful and they could really dictate to a large extent what sort of dogs they wished to handle — right or wrong. Things are different now and the American Kennel Club has done away with the licensing of handlers, which kept them in a very small and powerful circle and anybody can set up as a handler if they have the inclination. The handlers are very important to exhibitors in America where shows are held on circuit all over the different states and it would mean one would be away from home a great deal of the time. Handlers take as many dogs as they can manage, stay in their large motorised homes or put up in motels and spend a whole week showing in a certain controlled area when every dog club in reasonable distance can hold their shows in that one week.

Going back to Mrs Gordon and Miss Bennett again I saw them last when I was in Chicago in October 1980 for the International Dog Show there. They were showing their latest flyer, the five year old dog 'Ch. Wildweir Bumper Sticker' under Mr William Bergum, who made him Best of Breed and then he won the Toy Group under Mrs Sari Brewster Tietjen. With this revised version of this book in mind I was pleased to be able to arrange with the official photographer for the show to send me the photo you can see on page 198 of 'Ch. Wildweir Bumper Sticker'.

Among the older breeders Mr Austin Hollingsworth had had a life interest in the breed, Mr George Tomkins founded his kennel in 1900 and has been active in the breed ever since and owns the Charleview prefix. Mr Dave Batty sold many of his breeding to Mr J. Wood of Armley prefix, Mr J. Jackson of Dewsburian, Mrs R. Green with her Overdon and Mr J. Hardman.

The first champions to be made up after the hostilities of World War II were over were Mr Williamson's 'Bens Blue Pride' — born 8.7.44, by 'Blue Flash' out of 'Jill' and bred by Mr Roper — who attained his championship in 1947, and 'Lady Nada' born 9.9.42 owned by Mrs Hebson and bred by Mrs R. Allen by 'Wee Willie Winkie' out of 'Little Flower'.

One of the reasons why lines are difficult to follow is the fact that many of the owners and breeders with only one or two dogs did not bother to register a prefix. Some probably did not have the means and others who bred but did not show were quite content to sell their progeny for others to register.

1948 saw Mrs Hebson make up another champion bitch, 'Hebsonian Jealousy', by 'Gay Prince' out of 'Hebsonian Harana', this time bred by herself. Also made up that year were 'Weeplustoo of Achmonie', another bitch by 'Sweet Memory of Achmonie' out of 'Isolda of Achmonie', bred and owned by Miss Macdonald. The only dog to achieve his championship that year was 'Starlight' born 15.10.45 by 'Marten Teddy' out of 'Adora', owned by Mrs Hargreaves and bred by Mr Orford.

In 1949 'Wee Don of Atherleigh' by 'Don Progresso' out of 'Beauty of Atherleigh', bred and owned by Mr W.M. Hayes and born 13.9.45, was to achieve great success, and Miss Macdonald made up 'McCay of Achmonie', another dog by 'Nigella of Pagham' (grandson of 'Ch. Harringay Remarkable') out of 'Sophie of Achmonie', born 21.4.46 bred by herself. He in turn sired 'Ch. Someone of Achmonie'.

One of the most important dogs to become champions that year was Mrs A. Swan's 'Ch. Splendour of Invincia' by 'Invincia Masher' out of 'Ollie of Invincia', born 16.7.47. He sired two champions, 'Ch. Stirkean's Chota Sahib' (owned and bred by Mrs E. Stirk) who, in turn sired 4 champions and the bitch 'Ch. Martini', bred by Mrs A. Swan out of 'Cherie of Invincia' and owned by Mrs Beech. 'Splendour' was by a wonderful dog, 'Invincia Masher' who, because he was born during the war years never became a champion but he sired five champions of outstanding merit, namely:

1. 'Ch. Splendour of Invincia' (as above). Dog. 17 C.Cs.
2. 'Ch. Hopwood Camelia', bred by Mrs A. Swan out of 'Invincia Margretta' and owned by Miss Martin. Bitch.
3. 'Ch. Martinwyns Surprise of Atherleigh' out of 'Pat of Atherleigh', bred by Mr Hayes and owned by Mr Coates. Dog.

Ch. Martinwyno
Surprise of Atherleigh.

4. 'Ch. Adora of Invincia' out of 'Ollie of Invincia', bred and owned by Mrs A. Swan. Bitch.
5. 'Sunstar of Invincia' out of 'Margie of Invincia', bred and owned by Mrs A. Swan. Dog.

'Ch. Splendour' made history through his son 'Ch. Stirkean' Chota Sahib', who in turn sired five champions:

1. 'Ch. Stirkean's Kandy Boy' out of 'Trix of Invincia', bred and owned by Mrs Stirk, born 23.12.53. Dog.
2. 'Ch. Deebees Stirkean's Faustina', out of 'Stirkean's Astolat Enchantress', bred by Mrs Stirk and owned by Mrs S.D. Beech.
3. 'Ch. Stirkean's Rhapsody' out of 'Stirkean's Anne Marie' of Winpal, bred and owned by Mrs Stirk. Dog, born 21.2.57.

Ch. Mr Pimm of
Johnstounburn owned
by Mrs Crookshank.

4. 'Ch. Deebees Campari' out of 'Deebees Lillet', bred and owned by
Mrs S.D. Beech. Dog, born 1.5.59.
And out of the same litter:
5. 'Ch. Deebees Isa Le Bella', a bitch also owned and bred by Mrs
Beech.

Another famous little stud dog about this time was 'Parkview Prince' who
sired three champions:

1. 'Vemair Parkview Preview', out of 'Parkview Dinky', bred by Mr
Bain and owned by Mrs Mair. Dog, born 12.5.46.
2. 'Mr Pim of Johnstounburn', out of 'Flea of Johnstounburn', bred
by Mr Sturrock and owned by Mrs Crookshank. Dog, born
29.2.47.
3. 'Vemair Principal Boy' out of 'Frosty of Johnstounburn', bred by
Mr Bain and owned by Mrs Mair. Dog, born 28.6.49.

Of these 'Ch. Vemair Principal Boy' sired 'Ch. Vemair Uncle Sam', but
perhaps the one that is best known to present-day adherents of the breed is
'Ch. Mr Pim of Johnstounburn', who sired seven champions in this country
and many more abroad. He has probably caught the public imagination more
than any other Yorkie as his picture appeared in many magaziners and press

Ch. Pansy of Winpal
bred by Miss A.E.
Palmer.

articles. He is still pictured in reference books as the most typical Yorkie and he certainly appears in hundreds of pedigrees. His champion children are:

1. 'Wee Eve of Yadnum' out of 'Scotford Queen', owned by Mrs E. Munday and bred by Mr Scott. Bitch, born 10.8.51.
2. 'Myrtle of Johnstounburn' out of 'Misty of Johnstounburn', bred and owned by Mrs Crookshank. Bitch, born 8.7.49.
3. 'Pipit of Johnstounburn' out of 'Pixy of Johnstounburn', bred and owned by Mrs Crookshank. Bitch, born 6.9.54.
4. 'Buranthea's Angel Bright' out of 'Buranthea's Paris Jewel', bred and owned by Mrs Marie Burfield. Bitch, born 29.4.54.
5. 'Prim of Johnstounburn' out of 'Lady of the Lake' bred by Mr Brown and owned by Mrs Daphne Rossiter. Bitch, born 25.7.55.
6. 'Pimbron of Johnstounburn', also out of 'Lady of the Lake', bred by Mr Brown and owned by Mrs Crookshank. Dog, born 4.7.54.
7. 'Buranthea's Doutelle' out of 'Buranthea's York Sensation', bred and owned by Mrs M. Burfield. Dog, born 8.5.57.

In the K.C. Stud Book this entry is credited to 'Ch. Mr Pimm of Johnstounburn'. As there is no record of such a dog becoming a champion I am treating it as a misprint. Mrs Crookshank preferred 'Pim' and tried to change but the Kennel Club insisted much to her annoyance.

Mrs Seymour's Ch. Martynwyns Adora bred by Mrs Latliff.

Ch. Heavenly Blue of Wiske bred by Mrs K. Renton and owned by Mr & Mrs L.F. Palframan.

Mrs Crookshank of the Johnstounburn suffix resided in Scotland and was an ardent worker for the Yorkshire Terrier cause in that part of the world but travelled south with her dogs and had many champions to her credit.

Another worthy stud dog of the nineteen-forties was 'Little Blue Boy' who sired four champions:

1. 'Wee Blue Atom' out of 'Our Sue', bred by Mr Latliff and owned by Mrs Overett. Dog, born 20.7.48.
2. 'Jacaranda Beauty' out of 'Bridle Sweetbriar', bred and owned by Mrs Montgomery. Bitch, born 25.1.51. Sire of 'Ch. Blue Belle'.
3. 'Martinwyns Debonaire' out of 'Our Sue', bred by Mr Latliff and owned by Mr Coates. Dog, born 4.10.49. Same breeding as 'Ch. Wee Blue Atom'.
4. 'June's Boy' out of 'Dainty Princess Suzanne', bred by Mrs E.F. Latliff and owned by Mr J. Latliff. Born 19.10.53. Dog, sire of 'Ch. Leyam Mascot'.

'Burghwallis Waggie', owned by Mrs Betton, sired 'Ch. Burghwallis Little Nip', who, on the occasions he was mated to 'Prism of Johnstounburn', produced three champions, and one when mated to 'Little Sheba':

1. 'Pagnell Prima Donna of Wiske' out of 'Prism of Johnstounburn', bred by Mrs S.I. Groom and owned by Mrs K.M. Renton. Bitch, born 1.5.57. Best in Show winner.
2. 'Burghwallis Vikki' out of 'Prism of Johnstounburn', bred by Mrs Groom and owned by Mrs M. Betton. Dog, born 1.5.57. Sire of 'Ch. Sundance of Wiske' out of 'Vanessa of Wiske', owned and bred by Mrs Renton.
3. 'Burghwallis Brideen' out of 'Little Sheba', bred by Mrs A. Brown and owned by Mrs M. Betton. Bitch, born 15.2.58.
4. 'Pagnell Peter Pan' out of 'Prism of Johnstounburn', bred and owned by Mrs S.I. Groom. Dog, born 17.10.61, and himself the sire of some of the most outstanding champions that the breed has known, such as 'Ch. Beechrise Superb' out of 'Beechrise Pixie', born 5.8.63, a dog owned and bred by Mrs H. Griffiths; 'Ch. Heavenly Blue of Wiske' out of 'Ch. Doone of Wiske', born 28.2.63, bred by Mrs K. Renton and owned by Mr and Mrs L.F. Palframan; 'Ch. Pagnell Blue Peter', a dog, born 4.4.64, out of 'Isabel Lady', bred by Mrs D. Smith and owned by Mrs S.I. Groom. Ch. Pagnell Peter Pan Best in Show winner.

Midge's Pal', owned by Mrs Crookshank, was another dog that produced four champions:

1. 'Tufty of Johnstounburn' out of 'Hazy of Johnstounburn', owned

A group of
Johnstounburn
Yorkshire Terriers; *left
to right* Ch. Pimbrou,
Ch. Mr Pimm, Ch.
Myrtle, Ch. Tuffy, Ch.
Medium, Ch. Pipit.

and bred by Mrs Crookshank. Born 3.5.45. Bitch.
2. 'Firhill Fairy' out of 'Miss Monty', bred by Mr Anderson and
owned by Mrs Pannett. Bitch, born 30.9.48.
3. 'Vemair Spider' out of 'Coogee Dinah', bred by Mr Johnstone and
owned by Mrs Mair. Born 30.9.48. Dog.
4. 'Medium of Johnstounburn' out of 'Misty of Johnstounburn',
bred and owned by Mrs Crookshank. Born 23.10.50.

'Pagham Sehow Special' sired three champions, as did 'Marten Teddy',
'Totis Treasure', 'Ear-wi-go of Tzumiao', 'Ch. Pimbron of Johnstounburn',
and 'Ch. Stirkean's Astonoff Horatio'.

Sires of two champions were 'Ravelin Golden Boy', 'Ch. Don Carlos of
Progresso', 'Ch. Skyrona Blue Prince' and 'Ch. Buranthea's Saint Malachy'.

Yorkshire Terrier bitches who produced champions

As might be expected from their wonderful record in the breed, the Invincia
Kennels produced the top bitch with 'Ollie of Invincia', who produced four
champions. Next to her came Mrs Crookshank's 'Prism of Johnstounburn'
with three.

Yorkie bitches that produced two champions were: 'Woldsdene Blue Rose',
'Stirkean's Astolat Enchantress', 'Deebees Lillet', 'Astolat Nicolette', 'Jill',
'Lady of the Lake', 'Miretta Marianne', 'Pretty Paulette', 'Misty of John-
stounburn', 'Our Sue' and 'Beauty of Atherleigh'.

The smallest British toy breed

Much has been written advocating the mating of small Yorkshire Terrier males to much larger females. This in itself is breaking the regulations, as when a weight limit is set on a breed it is very bad policy to breed from bitches who are far removed from this weight limit. It is bad as far as the breed itself is concerned, and bad for the individual dogs. A tiny bitch produced from the mating of two such varied sizes could carry the large genes of her weightier parent, and so have great difficulty herself, when she is having puppies.

Older breeders maintain that any bitch that weighs less than 5 lb. should not be bred from. As bitches should not weigh more than 7 lb., this does not seem to give us much scope. The bitches of 3 ½ lb. and 4 lb. are quite capable of producing puppies and, as long as they are mated to tiny dogs whose pedigree is all under 5 lb., the result should be safe for the bitch. Of course, these tiny bitches will not have as many pups per litter as the bigger ones — this is Nature's way of making life easier for them — but any sons of these smaller bitches will have a strong reducing effect on their progeny and the daughters of such a tiny bitch will, if mated carefully in turn, produce small-type puppies whose birth will give them no difficulty at all. Care should always be taken to make sure that any bitch mated is carefully examined by a vet. before the mating to make sure that she is capable of having puppies — her pelvis is wide enough, she has plenty of heart-room and is in good enough physical condition to rear a litter.

It is the responsibility of today's breeders of Yorkshire Terriers to breed to the Standard, which means breeding to a size limit. Those who are only trying to breed puppies to be put out at wholesale prices and in wholesale numbers, should think well before mating bitches, as under the present law if one sells a puppy as a 'toy Yorkie' and it turns out to be 10 lb. or thereabouts, then one could be open to prosecution under the False Description of Goods (False Representation) Act, and quite heavy penalties could be recovered from you by the purchaser.

As the breeder of one of the smallest dogs this country has ever known, 'Emmrill Christmas Fuzz' who never grew heavier than 1 lb when fully grown I know just how adorable such tinies can be when they are full of *joie de vivre* and very vigorous. But, however adorable and desirable, and we were offered thousands of pounds for him after he appeared on the Blue Peter Programme on children's television, the responsibility of ownership is very great and not ever really compensated for by the anxiety and constant state of worry that is always present whenever he was out of my sight. I could never have left him and he was always at the back of my mind whatever else I was doing or thinking. I expect the same worries were part of the life of the owner of the tiny bitch Cody Queen of Dudley who in July 1968 was said to have weighed only 20 ounces at 16 months. The smallest Yorkie bitch I ever saw was a six month old puppy that weighed 1 ½ lb. I was judging at Brent and a lady

The author's 1lb Yorkie Emmrill Christmas Fuzz aged approximately 7 months.

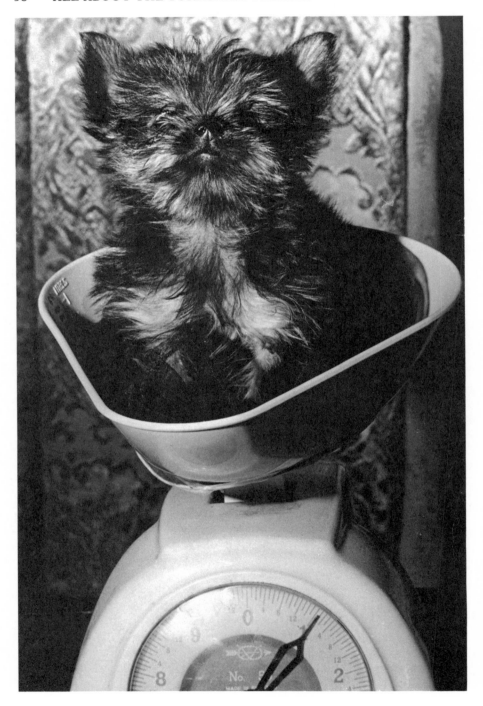

brought this tiny mite to the ring-side to show me — it was too young to be entered by two days. It was quite lovely — sweet little face, tiny upright ears, good mouth, which she opened and showed me and a firm little body and a lovely level back and top-line just like Fuzz had. She had brought her to show me because of Fuzz but as I had classes to judge I finished them all before looking round for her to have a proper chat to, but she must have thought I was not interested as I had to concentrate on my judging and so was not able to look at her again until I completed my task, so she walked away to my everlasting regret. Perhaps if she reads this she will get in touch as I would dearly like to know what weight she eventually attained.

The question of size in a Yorkshire Terrier is a very perplexing one to those outside the breed who are curious about it. How can one explain to an ordinary dog breeder of other breeds that don't have more than a half pound variation in a litter of six that Mrs Annie Swan, breeder of the famous Invincia Kennels advocates not breeding from a bitch less than 6 lb. in a breed that has the top weight of 7 lb. and that she quotes as being as true in 1958 when she wrote the book as in 1911 when Major T.A. Polson wrote the following in his long article that was published in Vol. 4 of *The Kennel Encyclopedia* and was under the general editorship of Mr J. Turner:

'The last litter bred by the writer (Major Polson) consisted of four puppies, their weights when fully grown varying from 3 lb. to 9 lb. and this experience is general.

Having regard to the foregoing it follows that the union of two small specimens will not, *per se*, ensure the puppies being small, and this being the case, we cannot too severely condemn the practice of breeding from tiny bitches. One occasionally sees advertisements to the effect that such a dog is at stud "to bitches not over 5 lb.". They display either ignorance or indifference to the positive cruelty likely to follow when the time for whelping is at hand and the poor mite of a mother is unable to give birth to the litter without assistance, and very often not even then, with the result that she dies after great suffering.'

'Tiny bitches are not profitable' writes Mrs Swan in 1958 and if she had to contend with the ignorance and bias of such breeders as Major Polson I'm not at all surprised that she was worried. What a divergence in weight in one single litter — 3 lb. to 9 lb. They could be totally different breeds and even different groups — Australian Terriers, a much larger breed and in the 'Terrier Group' weight 10 to 11 lb.; Tibetan Spaniels 'Non-Sporting Group' from 9 lbs. in weight, Shih Tzu, 'Non-Sporting Group' from 9 to 18 lb. I know for a fact that a Toy Poodle of 9 lb. is a big coarse creature and getting back to the 'Toy' Group the Silky Terrier is from 8 to 10 lb., the Maltese is under 7 lb., the weight of 4 to 6 lb. being preferred and the Chihuahua up to 6

Fairy Prince, owned by
Mr W. Bain of
Edinburgh, weighed
3 ½ lb.

lb. with 2 to 4 lb. preferred, Pomeranian dogs 4 to 4 ½ lb. and bitches 4 ½ to 5 ½ lb., Japanese Chins 4 to 7 lb., the daintier the better and Italian Greyhounds 6 to 8 lb. and lastly the other all-English Toy Breed that goes back in time centuries before the Yorkshire Terrier was ever thought of and that is the English Toy Terrier itself, which we are expected to judge at an ideal weight of 6 to 8 lb.

If the Yorkshire Terrier desires to retain its long admired title that every one of those early breeders we have mentioned before Major Polson, and Mrs Swan had striven to grant it of 'the smallest of the British toy breeds', then it can't afford to breed from greatly oversize bitches such as Mrs Swan believes are correct. I can assure anyone who is interested in this vexed question of breeding size in the Yorkie that a 6 lb. bitch out of a 9 lb. mother by a 3 lb. father will have far more whelping difficulties because of the 3 lb. size difference than a 5 lb. bitch out of a 5 lb. bitch who in turn was out of a 5 lb. bitch by a 4 lb. dog for the very simple reason that they are of equal size and Nature always intended the animals to be of equal size. I have maintained a like to like basis for my breeding for the past thirty years and I have bred tiny Chihuahuas from sound, vigorous and well-made 4 lb. bitches. In fact I bred a strain that by never retaining anything in my kennel for breeding myself from a bitch that had to be caesared, I had a wonderful strain in the end and that was over a period of twenty-eight years.

When I was a child we usually had a Yorkie about the place but they weren't 'toys' much to my mother's disappointment. She was always yearning for a really tiny one like the 3 lb. one she had grown up with, but when I was still a schoolgirl I bred Cairns that were much smaller than our Yorkie Muscha. I literally had them about the house as pets and show dogs for about ten years before starting to breed Yorkshire Terriers seriously. There were so many drawbacks to them — bad mouths, which I hated, roach backs, which were even worse, and slipping stifles and upright shoulders. Pop eyes, thick bone, short necks, huge floppy ears and a lot of the ones I judged in about 1958 and afterwards were very shy to handle, or so aggressive that they should not have been shown. All these faults before any consideration was given to quality of coat, texture, grooming colour of blue and tan etc. condition and show-worthiness in all the ways a showdog should be. My first Yorkie, 'Emmrill Paddie Wack', was a show-winner before I bought him as he was bred and shown by Mr and Mrs Morley of Pontypridd, in the Rhondda Valley in Wales, who did not have a registered prefix, so I added 'Emmrill' to his name. He was very pretty, under 4 lb. in weight with a lovely textured coat of good colour. Nobody ever said of him that he was too light or too dark, so I should say he was just right. He was no chance bred one either but his parents were bred by an elderly Welsh gentleman who only kept and bred from tiny ones. It was the regret of my life and of a lot of Yorkie breeders of those times that we didn't put him at stud much sooner as by the time we discovered that he was a 'potent' sire, he was getting old and I found it impossible to find bitches of a high enough quality to put to him. In the end, thanks to him I had a very successful Yorkshire Terrier Kennel and I owe every bit of it to Paddie alone.

I don't think I shall ever get over his passing — it was such a frustrating one. He had gone with a shoot in the New Forest and one minute he was there and the next he wasn't. Nobody saw him go down a rabbit hole, but he was quite capable of flushing out small vermin. When I heard he'd been lost I rushed down to the place where he had last been seen and called him by the hour. For weeks we hovered around there at every spare minute we could find and everybody around there, including the people on whose ground he had been lost, was on the look-out for him. I can't believe he could disappear so completely but no trace has ever been found of him.

'Christmas Fuzz' died, we saw his body and in time we came to accept it but for years afterwards I found myself listening for Paddie. We were amazed to find that he was fourteen years old when he went missing. He still seemed like a young dog to us and we could hardly believe time had gone by so quickly. He never lost a tooth, never lost his good sight or his wonderful hearing — or his tremendous zest and love of life. His memorial can only be a 'thank you Paddie' and his grand-daughters and great-granddaughters that come around to use our latest stud dog. One thing all the Yorkies I have owned have had in common is a great talent for disobedience. How people ever train them for obedience tests I wouldn't know. None of mine would be capable of it as they all have such minds of their own. This has often been their undoing as they will not come when they are called if they have got anything better to do and

Ch. Carmardy Little
Henry, sire of
Carmardy Little Jamie
of Emmrill and Int. Ch.
Carmardy Benjamin.

they are all so interfering.

My husband bought me a little show dog called 'Jamie of Carmardy' from Mr and Mrs Parkins. He was a younger brother to our Casanova of Carmardy and was small and had a better coat colour than his brother. I was always having to watch that he did not run out of the house as for the first time in our married life we had neighbours. Jamie very much wanted to chase the cat across the road and spent hours looking through the hall windows and barked and growled every time the cat moved. We had a fence across the top of the garden and he had to stay behind it. One day a policeman knocked at the door to say he and his dogs were chasing a burglar who had just been seen running across our grounds. The burglar alarm in a house in the next road was making a terrible din, 'Jamie' was barking his head off and wanted to chase after the police German Shepherds, which he thought were not nearly as bright as he was. He was down the drive after them and I had to run fast to catch him. If he could hear me calling him I do not know because of all the din going on but he took not the slightest notice. I got hold of him before he reached the road and with him under my arm went back indoors. The telephone rang, I put 'Jamie' out into the garden through the French doors, answered the 'phone then went to call 'Jamie' back in when his noisy barking wouldn't matter. He did not come, I put all the outside lights on and found the fence broken and bent to the ground and obviously 'Jamie' had gone through it. The thief had fallen across it while escaping from the police. It was early evening and very dark and I couldn't see my dog anywhere. I walked down to the road, it was a very quiet cul-de-sac and not usually any danger at all, but 'Jamie' had run across the road, been hit by a car that probably didn't even see him or feel anything because he was so small and light. I could only make out a slightly blacker spot on the road, put my hand down and found his warm little body quite still. He was rushed to the nearest vet who said he had been killed instantly so, although the burglars didn't rob us of any of our money they took our little pet from us as surely as if they had killed him.

To have a dog killed is very tragic indeed but in some sort of way it is better than having them stolen. Yorkies, I'm sorry to say are very stealable and we too have suffered this evil. Once two ten-week-old puppies were stolen while we were having lunch. A brick was thrown through the window of the 'dog room' and only the two pups were taken on that instance. There was a dog and bitch and the little bitch was being hard to wean and not taking too kindly to the new foods she was being given, preferring her mother's milk. Consequently I was hand-feeding her with bits of chicken, raw mince, pieces of lamb and hard-boiled egg – all useful dainties at such times. The police sent posters around the vet's surgeries and a vet over twenty miles away reported that he had attended a little tiny Yorkie puppy that had died. She had been brought in by a gipsy family that he knew and the police went to the camp and found the survivor which we had back on that occasion. The next time we were not so lucky as the robbery was 'cased' and very well planned. We had a high chain link fence all around our property and two whole sections of that were undone at two inch intervals. That must have taken hours, and they chose a very dark night but had to wait for a late television programme which kept lights on in the house quite late. The entry made – they could not have got in over the huge gates from the outside but once inside it was easy to climb over them. There must have been at least two people and they didn't throw bricks through the windows – they were much cleverer and quieter – they brought tools and unscrewed the hinges of the door. Once inside they chose the most glamourous coated and prettiest four and put them in carrying boxes which they also stole. Our favourite house-pet was one of them; he was down there having his coat in oil and mating one of the bitches (who was also stolen) and taken with them was a seven-month-old Yorkie bitch that had just started being shown and a silver toy poodle of the same age. Absolutely no information at all has ever been produced as to where these dogs were taken but that very same night a farmer only five miles away had ninety sheep taken and they couldn't be carried under anybody's arm. Opinion is that dogs and sheep could have been put into one of the big cattle moving trucks and whisked across the channel before daylight. No expensive clipping and drying equipment was touched, the radio was left and some ready for sale puppies that could have been flogged off at the first pet shop were ignored. Only very few breeders specialise in silver toy poodles and we would all recognise one another's breeding on sight and I am sure none of them are in this country. Cassie for one would try and get home I'm sure he was so much loved and usually went everywhere with my husband.

'Cassie' did a good job among my daughters' boy friends, he sorted them out in no time. At mealtimes he would sit under the table – handy for any scraps that came his way accidently as the rule in our house 'No feeding at meal-times' is sometimes followed. Anyway no Yorkie could sit still under a table while a meal was eaten and Cassie was no exception – he undid shoe laces. However tightly they were tied there was no knot we ever found that was proof against him and we naturally tried them all in our efforts to keep our shoes on. Short of buying slip-ons without laces he got to work on everything that came his way and the funny thing about it was that nobody ever felt him at work. The very first indication that they had no shoe-laces would be when they stood up. With both shoelaces completely removed they soon walked out of their shoes. This was the moment of truth for us. If they laughed and said 'What a clever little dog, I didn't feel a thing' when we explained what had happened to their laces, they were looked on as friends but if they got angry and lost their temper at 'Cassie's' little foible, they were never invited again. How could you not miss and grieve to lose such an important member of the family? Life has never been the same for us since 'Cassie' went. He was always with my husband, went in his car with him everywhere and sat at his side or on his knee like the perfect little companion he was. If my husband was away from home he stayed at the window watching for him and he knew the moment my husband started down the drive, long before he came in sight and would run to the door, jumping up all the time until he was able to hurl himself through it. Not all our Yorkies are as demonstrative as 'Cassie' was. Now and again we see his pretty, sweet expression on the faces of some of his offspring, but they don't have his character or single-mindedness of purpose.

When news of our loss was published we had 'phone calls from many people who had also had their Yorkies stolen. One was taken from the garden when the little bitch had just gone out to relieve herself. One lady rang to say she had had two stolen from her car while shopping and another lady left hers tied up outside a baker's shop with a collection of other dogs and when she came out the Jack Russell, the collie and the mongrel were still there but her Yorkie was missing. No amount of searching and advertising ever brought about her return.

I was telling my London hairdresser about my loss and he told me of the very sad story of another of his clients who had been playing ball with her Yorkie dog and small boy in Hyde Park. The ball went under a bush, the Yorkie went underneath to find it and was never seen again. They stayed there calling to him for some minutes before going under the bush themselves but there was no sign of the Yorkie or the ball, which of course is typical. Once a Yorkie has hold of a ball or any other toy he would not think to let go of it to bark at a stranger. As it was it was long enough before Smartie had gone under the bush before they realised that he was missing altogether for whoever stole him to have got clean away. There are plenty of parked cars all

Emmrill Christmas
Fuzz in his owner's
hand.

round the Park and nobody would notice one moving away. The police were
called and large sums offered for the return of this little dog but he was never
found. One of the most blatant cases of Yorkshire Terrier stealing happened
to a friend of mine in New York. When she retired from work she bought a
Yorkie bitch puppy from me as a present to herself, as she had always promised herself a little Yorkie for a pet. My youngest daughter took her out to
the States on one of her visits and needless to say that particular little bitch
was one of the most adored of all the Yorkies we have bred. One night the
apartment where she lived was broken into but the only thing the thief took
was the little Yorkie bitch. Because of the heart-break this caused her sorrow-
ful owner she was afraid to buy another one as she did not feel strong enough
to stand any further mental anguish of that nature.

Whatever the attraction of the Yorkshire Terrier of England and America
to thieves the ones in Paris are also affected. I was telephoned by Princess de
Crois, the President of the Society for the Protection of Animals in France to
ask if I could help to find a Yorkshire Terrier to replace one stolen from a victim of the dreaded multiple sclerosis. It appeared that the lady who owned the
Yorkie had been presented with the puppy by her fellow workmates when she
had to give up work because of her illness. The little dog was her constant

companion and did a lot to while away the lonely hours when she was confined to her home alone. When her husband came home from work he used to take her out in her wheelchair and walk the little Yorkie at the same time. One early evening they were in a crowded street and he had some difficulty getting her chair up on the high pavement. As he struggled someone got caught in the dog's lead. He let go of the lead so the dog wouldn't get hurt and before he could stop him the man had picked up the dog and made off around the next corner. By the time he persuaded someone to look after his wife's chair and ran after the man he found no sign of him or their little Yorkie. What type of person would do this and what could possibly be the reason anybody would sink so low as to rob a cripple of her boon companion? Greed for the money they think its sale could bring perhaps or are they filled with such wicked, malicious envy that they covet them so much that they will go to great lengths to get one for themselves, short of paying for one in the usual way. No other dog I have ever owned has been such an object of desire among the thieves and vagabonds of this world. I have had far more expensive dogs, far more attractive looking dogs and more obedient and docile dogs that would settle anywhere at anytime and always be most obliging. What happens to all these little stolen Yorkies? They can never hope to be loved again anything like they were used to and they would not settle to new surroundings if they were not to their liking and, if they did not like the people in charge of them they would certainly give a good account of themselves. Also, if they were near enough I am quite sure mine would have found their way home, they have that much intelligence. The only solution is for owners of Yorkshire Terriers to keep them close to them, never leave them in cars alone or outside shops. Not even to leave them in kitchens where thieves can find them and teach them young to come just as soon as they are called — demand instant obedience in this. Even at Cruft's Dog Show thieves have got away with stealing from the hall at Olympia where attendants guarded every entrance. The famous 'Royal Seal' who appears on the cover of this book and who was undoubtedly the greatest winning Yorkshire Terrier of our time was never left alone on a bench; somebody was always with him. Besides stealing it has been known for dogs to be given poison at shows. The dog clubs have sometimes set up vigilante groups to guard the dogs of exhibitors showing their other exhibits.

4 The Attraction of the Yorkshire Terrier

Looks, character and personality

Most people like dogs and all the people who like dogs have some sneaking admiration for a terrier, even if they have always owned and loved another breed. Most small boys' idea of a pet is a rough-haired little varmint, preferably dirty white with patches, holding tightly on with his teeth to the end of a piece of rope or wood while the boy tries in vain to tug it from him. Only the terrier is completely satisfactory as an opponent in this game. Many of them, too, have coats that have to be stripped regularly, and if this is neglected they leave hairs all over the clothes and upholstery of their owners. This may not be so bad, as I've no doubt their owners love them dearly and can quite easily forgive them for this failing, but it may not apply to visiting friends and family who get smothered in what they must look on as objectionable stuff.

The Yorkie, the smallest and most delightful of the British breeds of terrier, is to be commended in this respect as he does not shed hairs everywhere and the exercise he takes need not be of the marathon kind. Although he might wander off in search of his owner, he is far more amenable to being enclosed in a given space than most of the other terriers. One does not need a very large space to enclose him either!

If his coat is cut to a serviceable length, just below his elbow and half-way up his back leg with a pair of hair-dressing scissors, he will need very little time spent on his daily grooming. If his top-knot is cut short enough to part in the middle and keep itself out of his eyes, and all the hair immediately under the tail and on his bottom where he could soil himself, is kept very short he will look quite presentable and be easy to keep clean. No doubt his proud owner will be prepared to go to the trouble of making sure that the parting down his back is straight so that his coat hangs evenly on either side. If the brush used is dipped in a drop of baby oil before use, a very smart appearance will be assured, so that the pet Yorkie can look a well-kept little dog on his expeditions out of the house. If his owners are not all that fussy if he does look like an animated floor mop, a quick brush through with a good bristle brush and a finish through with a metal comb each day will only take a few minutes, and, even if he looks just as unkempt again in a very short time, at least there is the knowledge that his coat won't be carrying any tangles.

This sort of coat needs frequent bathing to keep it clean, as any sort of neg-

'Let me whisper in your ear.' The author's grandson with two special friends.

lect will result in hard little knots which are heaven's own job to remove. Nobody should acquire a Yorkie who is not prepared to spend this small effort on its care and comfort. If his coat is really neglected he not only looks a sorry sight but is made miserable and unhappy, driving himself and everybody else mad with his scratching.

If he is happy, healthy and gets his regular out-of-doors exercise, and so long as his diet is adequate (see chapters 4 and 10), the Yorkie is a hearty little eater, without any tendency to gorging himself and over-eating, as is the case with some toy breeds. He has few if any food fads. With his terrier mouth he should have good strong teeth and so be able to gnaw quite big bones, a pastime that will not only keep him happily occupied when he could be trying out his good teeth on his owner's possessions and furnishings, but will give him the added advantage of keeping his teeth clean, healthy and free from the unpleasant yellow tartar which makes the breath objectionable. This tartar is the prime cause of toy dogs losing their teeth or making them so putrid that they have to be removed by the vet. under a general anaesthetic with all the expense and danger that implies.

The Yorkie character is not devious. He is open-hearted in his affections, loving everybody that has to do with him, being particularly appreciative of those who feed and look after him. He is the ardent slave of anyone who will play with him. Without being asked to do so, he takes it on himself to guard his abode, which means his master's house and garden, car and other premises, from all intruders, whether furred, feathered or booted. If his temper is aroused — and even the tiniest one is capable of tremendous fury when occasion arises — he will fight for his rights without letting up. He is as brave as a little lion and has no fear of other dogs, however big, and will even see off

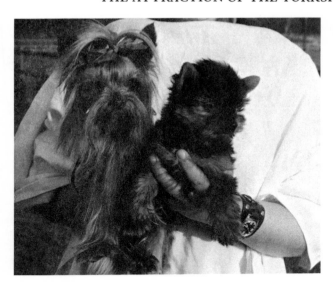

Relco and his baby
daughter Emmrill Jewel.

a horse if he thinks it is intruding. At the same time he is not himself aggressive as far as initiating a fight is concerned, usually waiting until the enemy
makes the first move. Once battle is joined, however, he is a fierce little
fighter, putting every ounce of his strength into the fray. There is nothing
half-hearted about him and he will go back time and time again. Once he has
decided he has found an enemy that enemy is there for life and he will fly at it
every time they meet.

As evidence of this our 3 ½ lb. stud dog 'Relco', has appointed himself as
'chief seer-off' of our neighbour's horses. Our property is bounded by post
and rail fencing which has wire netting attached to it to keep our dogs from
straying. The fencing keeps the horses next door from getting on our land but
does not prevent the tall thoroughbreds from stretching their necks over the
fencing and nibbling the tops of my conifer trees which also used to surround
our property. Whoever sees what the horses are up to usually shouts at them
or waves them away much to 'Relco's' concern. He dashes at them and if they
are a bit slow in moving their noses they are apt to get a furious little body
hurling himself at them and if they aren't quick his teeth also. It is very
amusing to see this tiny little mite rushing from end to end of this quite long
fence trying to keep his guard. If it wasn't for the danger I would welcome all
the exercise he is getting as he is one of my regular show-dogs and he is always
so well muscled.

None of my Yorkshire Terriers is in the least in awe of my huge wolf
hound — in fact they are most rude to her so that she has to be kept in her
enclosure when they are out. They sit on the wall of her run making nasty
faces at her and calling her very rude names when she has been given something that they want. We say they are doing their 'gargoyle' act. She is not a

bit put off by them and looks on them as her best friends, grinning at them and wagging her tail furiously. She also puts her large face down and licks them through the chain link with such force that quite often they are knocked off their perches.

My poodles are very easy going and they all get on well enough as a rule but sometimes the Yorkies will have a tease on, collect up all the toys and sit on them and growl at the other dogs. In retaliation the poodles will stand in the drinking-water so the Yorkies can't drink or they will upset the water and splash the Yorkies with it. They are great collectors and it is just as well to look in the Yorkie's beds if anyone loses anything from a button to a screwdriver, hearth brush or parts of the vacuum cleaner. No workman is safe from them if he leaves a tool-bag about. I warn everybody but they seem to forget and come grumbling that their belongings are missing. On these occasions the dogs rarely put articles in their beds but run out of doors and bury treasures quickly which is even more embarrassing. The oil delivery man no longer puts the cap down while our underground tank is filling and after the coal man has been any pieces he might have dropped find themselves in the middle of the lawn. They are able to move surprisingly big logs and have a lot of fun transporting them about. This however proved to be a dangerous pastime so the logs are now stacked away out of their reach, much to their disgust. The most worrying thing they have run off with has been keys — car keys and door keys. We have spare sets now and hooks on the wall to keep them on. One of our Yorkies, 'Kelly', has a partiality for the paper that comes off a certain kind of chocolate cake. However hard one tries a lot of the chocolate icing is always left on the cake paper. 'Kelly' must have found some and she always seemed to smell this when it was in the kitchen pedal bin and was determined to get at it. We put weights on the top of the bin to stop her pushing the top off and she knocked them off. She could put her foot on the pedal and lift up the lid and pull the liner bag out and she made a terrible mess looking for her chocolate paper. After she had licked the chocolate she had a go at crunching up all the egg-shells into minute pieces, she would tear up the tea bags and scatter all the vegetable pealings. However convenient we simply had to stop using the pedal bin because she always got to it before we emptied it. Her next attempts were much worse though as she could jump onto the pantry shelves and, if she ever managed to prise the door open she really had a 'ball'. Flour and sugar bags and spaghetti and noodles were her favourites — not to eat but just to scatter.

At one time 'Kelly' and 'Mink' had puppies about the same time. They always took a long time to settle with a new litter but my poodle 'Minnie' was also whelping and she was so good that I gave her 'Kelly's' two smallest bitches and 'Mink's' smallest dog pups so that they could get a good beginning. All went well and all three bitches lived in the kitchen in separate whelping crates. They went outside together and came back together after each exercise period and all the time 'Kelly' and 'Mink' wanted to look at their puppies who were still with 'Minnie'. At night we lit the floodlight so that the bitches would not fall into the swimming pool and we would call them from the back door and they would come running. One night 'Minnie' wasn't with them. It was very cold so I went out to look for her and heard a terrible gasping sound coming from the pool. It was poor 'Minnie' swimming away and she came to the side when I called her and I managed to pull her out. Now we had lived for two years with this pool and she had walked around it most nights and never gone in it before. I dried her with the big jet dryer and she was soon snuggled down with her puppies. The next night I went outside with the bitches, they were soon back in the house and it was several nights before I was called to the 'phone and left them outside. When I went to call them the two Yorkies came at once and I found the poodle swimming away in the pool but not seeming to enjoy it much. The next night I watched from the door as they came back after their final run. The Yorkies ran in as usual but the poodle hung back as far back from the pool as possible and seemed to dawdle in giving the pool as wide a berth as she could. Poodles are such clowns and love to show off and I am quite sure that if swimming was one of her things she would have dived in and swum towards me in order to have me pull her out and make a fuss of her. Those two awful Yorkie girls had pushed her in between them. After that we put her out on the other side of the house and she never went near the pool again, and those little Yorkie scallywags couldn't have their own back on the poodle who had taken on their babies. 'Minnie' has now gone to a nice kind home where there isn't a pool or any revengeful Yorkies!

The attractions of the Yorkshire Terrier

As a little person he is quite the extrovert and will pal up with anybody who is prepared to play his games. He is a great chaser and, if there are no birds or mice or rabbits to chase, he will race quite happily after a feather or piece of paper blowing in the wind. One of his most enchanting habits is the way he will ask you to play with him and the vivacious way he has of teasing. He has a very real sense of humour and, if allowed enough freedom, gets a tremendous zest out of life. He is probably the most agile of any dog and for his size jumps with complete ease heights you would hardly credit. Four-pounders can jump up on to a three-foot shelf without any effort at all.

I bought my first Yorkie because I was fascinated so much by this agility. It happened when I was visiting a lady in Wales some years ago. We were partaking of her Welsh hospitality with tea and cakes and all the time her little Yorkshire Terriers were running in and out of the room. One of them, a six-month-old dog puppy, ignoring the water put down for his convenience in the kitchen, kept jumping on a chair and then on to a quite high pedestal that held a single gold-fish in a round bowl. With only a few inches on the edge of the pedestal for his feet to gain purchase, he would stand on his little hind legs

Johanna at the
telephone.

and, with his face hanging right in the bowl, proceed to lap the water to his
heart's content, though I doubt if it was much to the content of the poor gold-
fish. He did this several times but neither my host nor hostess took any notice.
At last, unable to contain myself, in my fear for the poor goldfish, I called
their attention to what was going on. 'Oh,' laughed my hostess, 'he's always
done that ever since he first learned to jump up. The goldfish doesn't seem to
mind and he's over eight years old. I expect "Paddy" finds the fish's water
warmer than his own, which is always put down fresh on the kitchen floor.'

There are certainly 'no flies' on even the tiniest Yorkie baby and I found
myself completely captivated. In no time at all I found myself begging his
owner to sell him to me. Her resistance was quite formidable and I also
expected I would have to convince my reluctant husband that I had just fallen
completely for this little scrap and just had to have him. To my utter astonish-
ment I turned to find him nodding in agreement and smiling quite happily.
This was such a surprise that it has gone down in the family annals. My husband's usual attitude to my buying impulses had always been 'Don't buy if
you can possibly do without it', and if I still insisted that I wanted it he would
find every reason under the sun why it was unnecessary for me to have it. This
impulse was probably the most 'unnecessary' of all my husband had ever been
asked to approve, and I had — I don't mind admitting — been preparing to
do battle in the usual way. Consequently his easy acquiescence completely
amazed me. My family were equally amazed for they said it was the first time
they'd ever seen us in such complete agreement about dogs.

However, to get back to 'Paddy', I bought him with my husband's approval and he spent the rest of our holiday with us, visiting our friends and relations and behaving in an exemplary manner. By the time we returned home he was our dog in every way. The efforts we made to show our little pet and the lessons we learned as a result will, I hope, amuse you later on in this book.

We had 'Paddy' for some years and he'd found his niche among my other little heart-throbs. When he chose, he could jump higher and find himself a refuge high up out of their reach. He lived quite amiably among them, even in the same room as my champion Chihuahua, who was senior stud dog, knew his position, and was apt to be very aggressive at times, especially with the poodles who treated him with due respect. 'Paddy', however, just refused to kow-tow to the Great One. He didn't fawn or demur and they seemed to get on in perfect harmony until the Breeding Season started and 'Paddy' followed his nose straight to the bitch pen and there was stopped in his tracks by His Nibs. Sparks would have flown, I am sure, but we couldn't let 'Paddy' fight, especially when there was nothing for him to fight for. He was hastily removed and scolded thoroughly every time he was caught making for the bitch pen again. This might have deterred the poodles but had no effect at all on 'Paddy' who continued to visit the wired surround of the Purdah Pen at every opportunity.

We all felt sorry for him but, for some unexplained reason, never thought to buy a bitch, a Yorkie bitch that is, for his particular delight. When my husband appeared one day with a Yorkie puppy we thought at once that it was a splendid thing and just what 'Paddy' needed. However, to our chagrin, we found he had bought the puppy for a friend. Realising how disappointed we were for 'Paddy' my husband went back and bought another from the litter and she became 'Charm', our naughtiest Yorkie ever, a goose chaser of the first order, a killer of cats, if she could ever catch one, and 'Paddy's' first wife. A year or so later, when she presented us with our first Yorkie litter, we didn't know which one of the parents was responsible for the excellent type we got. 'Charm' has only ever been mated to 'Paddy' so always produces very much the same kind of pup, but subsequent litters from a variety of bitches have now proved that 'Paddy' is a unique little dog and leaves an indelible stamp on all his progeny, whatever their breeding. My years of dog breeding have shown me that a potent sire that impresses his good points on so many of his progeny is a rarity — and to think we so nearly never used him!

'Paddy' comes from some very tiny stock, and by mating him to our own little bitches we only ever get small ones. As the years have gone by we have acquired several bitches — in two cases from impulse buying on my husband's part quite as impractical as mine. As a result we own two four-pound bitches of no breeding potential but great attraction. Apparently my husband couldn't resist them! Which sounds very familiar to me, of course. Actually these four-pounders, being round, fat-bodied, looked quite sizeable to me compared with my other breeds and when I found them plenty wide enough in the pelvis I mated both of them to 'Paddy' without hesitation.

When I told some of my Yorkie breeder friends what I had done they were horrified. 'Never mate anything under 5 lbs.,' they said. However, 5 lb. bitches looked very big to me as I had got used to the tiny ones. Both tiny bitches whelped their puppies quite normally and made excellent mothers. I mention this only to illustrate that some small bitches can have puppies quite easily but it doesn't always follow and I am in no way advocating the practice. If those people who have been dealing with this breed for much longer than I say that the bitches should be over 5 lb. they will have good reason for saying so. The best advice anyone could receive if there is any doubt would be to consult a veterinary surgeon, and then to act on his advice.

As a family pet the Yorkshire Terrier is an excellent choice. Always ready for anything and still willing to sit and be companionable, if the mood is a quiet one. Very young Yorkies are a bit too lively for some ageing people, but they can be trained to stand still on a box when being judged, so it is really a question of putting up with the high spirits to begin with and then waiting patiently until they have learned to suppress them. The older Yorkies seem to suit elderly people very well as they don't have to be lifted up, being agile enough to jump on to laps, chairs and into cars and buses. They are light enough to permit their being carried but quite sturdy enough to do their own walking.

The best size for very young children would be the over-large ones, too large for show in fact. This way they should be cheaper and are less likely to come to any harm when romping with the youngsters. No dog, whatever its size, should be left to the tender mercies of a very young child. Their time together should always be supervised so that they learn to respect each other's frailties. The child could pick up a puppy and drop it, leave it on a chair to fall off before it had learned to flex its muscles for the jump and so break or injure a limb. It is possible for quite a tiny baby to inflict agonising pain on quite a robust puppy by pulling hard on its tail, tugging its limbs nearly out of their sockets, stamping on them and rolling over them. Eyes can be poked with fingers or more dangerous weapons and some small children (though the parents must surely be to blame here) are capable of kicking or hitting at a puppy. It is also obvious that a puppy need not put up with these things without retaliation and, when it uses its teeth, as its handiest weapon, trouble can start with a vengeance. With average care, however, these troubles can be avoided and a happy relationship established very early to the mutual benefit of both.

One of the happiest sights I have seen in this respect is that of a mother walking with her tiny toddler and the family pet in a quiet road in our local town and demonstrating an idea that could be put into general use — the dog was wearing a fairly wide soft leather collar with a metal ring slotted through for the lead. This allowed for room for an extra lead, so as they walked along the mother had one lead and the tiny girl the other.

No child should ever be allowed to be afraid of dogs. If he has been unfortu-

Jewel asking for food.

nate enough to be frightened by a particularly fierce one, and this can happen, he should be quickly introduced to one of the many docile sweet-tempered ones that abound everywhere. In my own mother's case she had, as a child of three, been jumped on and knocked to the ground by a ferocious dog trained as a guard-dog. So terrified was she by this experience that a doctor had to be summoned. After giving the necessary treatment this wise man (who must have been far in advance of his kind in matters of child psychology, since this happened nearly eighty years ago) advised her parents to get a tiny, gentle, very pretty dog for her very own. Her father went out to find such a dog and came back with a tiny Yorkshire Terrier. She was called 'Topsy' and never grew over 3 lb.

As a fellow sportsman

Everybody who meets the Yorkshire Terrier for the first time is amazed by his friendliness and courage. He will not be at all in awe of meeting other animals, or the larger breeds of dogs, even if he had never seen them before. In his tiny body is the heart and courage of a lion and this quality, if nothing else, attracts very many people, who without knowing him had hitherto thought him just a useless, pretty little toy dog, full of vanity and intent on keeping clean and preventing his lovely coat from getting ravaged. Quite the contrary. My tiny 'Fuzz', who at five months weighed only about 1 lb., was invited to appear on television to meet the biggest champion Great Dane in the country. This lovely dog was most amiable and his owner, Mrs J. Hutton, assured me that he wouldn't hurt my little one. However, it was with much trepidation that, on her advice, I held 'Fuzz' out so that 'Merry Deal' could sniff at him and fully realise that he actually was 'dog' too and not some animated sort of toy that he could be at liberty to frolic with. This, of course, was very wise advice. 'Merry Deal' was all of 38″ high at the withers and could have licked 'Fuzz' up like a fly and swallowed him whole. I needn't have feared, however, as 'Fuzz' was quite capable of showing what he was made of. 'Fuzz' allowed 'Merry Deal' to sniff at him and then calmly sniffed back at the Dane, stretching out of my hands to do so. We allowed them to become acquainted as much as we could before they actually had to appear before the cameras, which wasn't very long. As the show was going out 'live' and as nobody can ever know for certain how an animal, even a dog, will react at any given time, both Mrs Hutton and I had some misgivings as to its ultimate end as we were not ourselves wanted on the programme. Fortunately, the cast of the Blue Peter programme were well experienced with a very wide variety of animals, and it all went off very well with 'Fuzz', quite unperturbed by the occasion, sitting down companionably at 'Merry Deal's' feet and even drinking out of his dish. He was completely free and could, had he been afraid, run to me for protection. In his tiny Yorkie mind he saw nothing to be afraid of in just another dog, even if that dog's foot was on a level with his face. Although he was surrounded by dozens of strange faces, men on huge moving cameras towering over him and another man wearing headphones who kept dancing and waving his arms about in the most alarming fashion, these all left him unperturbed.

Everybody had been most kind and anxious to help and everything had been provided for our comfort by the large number of kindly people connected with the Blue Peter programme. The studio had been specially heated and strict orders given that doors should be kept shut to keep out draughts. 'Fuzz' was provided with an enormous wicker basket, car rug and hot water bottle as well as an electric kettle to keep the hot water bottle supplied. The lady star, Miss Valerie Singleton, relinquished her dressing-room for him and so he can be forgiven for thinking himself a most important little person — the fuss they made of him afterwards would have been the ruination of a dog of lesser character. He became a very celebrated little person — a T.V. Personality, in fact, which is the peak achievement of many in their climb to fame. He has a scrapbook of newspaper pictures and articles and a magnificent portfolio of photographs of which the ones reproduced are just examples. I am glad to say that fame didn't alter him a bit and at home he was still the lovable little imp he was before becoming the recipient of a fan-mail a pop star might envy.

Before his appearance on T.V. he had never been away from the shelter of the house. The four walls of the kitchen, with the ceaseless comfort of the AGA boiler, and with occasional visits into the drawing-room to receive fascinated visitors, had been his whole life up to this time. He had been so very tiny that I would not have him pulled on a lead or allowed him outside the door in case he felt cold. In fact I had been so anxious for his welfare that I had been afraid to have him inoculated against hardpad and distemper in case the needle hurt him. The foolishness of this decision was soon made apparent as my first thought when he was required to make these appearances away from home was that he could not possibly go as he had not been protected from distemper and hardpad and I couldn't therefore take the risk. It would take several weeks for the complete inoculation to take effect and while, in the ordinary way, there is no stronger advocate for prompt inoculation of all puppies with every possible serum than I am, 'Fuzz' was under 1 lb. in weight at that time and my vet. was as ready as I was to put off the vaccination until he was a bit bigger.

As on all problems of this sort I consulted my veterinary surgeon and his wise advice was to inoculate 'Fuzz' with the Measles Vaccine which would protect him from risk of infection for six months.

This we did and I'm glad to report that 'Fuzz', who was barely 15 oz in weight at the time, took the needle and the vaccine without turning a hair and had no ill-effects whatsoever. Anyone with similar problems would be wise to avail themselves of this wonderful new protection for tiny pups at the tenderest age. It does not give longer protection than six months but it is almost *complete protection.* At any time within the six months the puppy can be dosed in the usual way against Hard-pad, Distemper, Hepatitis and Leptospira Canicola, maybe the most important advance in scientific discovery for the dog breeder and veterinary profession as penicillin was for medicine.

The unconcerned and friendly way that most Yorkies greet strange people is one of their most endearing charms and many who have hitherto been firm adherents to other breeds have fallen completely beneath the spell of 'Fuzz's' adorable baby ways. So much so that it nearly became his undoing and I, much to my dismay, was the unconscious perpetrator of it all. It happened like this:

A press photographer who was so enchanted by the pictures of our tiny hero had requested permission to photograph him and this was granted. To his amazement he was able to get pictures of 'Fuzz' posing by himself in the most professional way (practice making perfect here, no doubt), also in close proximity to a variety of other breeds of dogs and much larger animals including our old house cow and the family's pet donkey, who has always accepted the dogs as part of her life and always treats them with rare good humour. This may have given him a completely wrong idea but when he saw 'Fuzz' sitting down and apparently having a *tête-à-tête* with such an apparently wild bird as a pheasant, he seemed sure that 'Fuzz' had some unusual powers. In fact, the pheasant was a favourite pet of my husband and had been hatched by one of our bantams. Later, therefore, the photographer

The author's pet pheasant with Emmrill Christmas Fuzz.

asked if 'Fuzz' would have his picture taken with an elephant. Now this sounded ridiculous and I should have refused at once but I had a very guilty feeling about 'elephants' in general, as I will explain, and so I said I would go.

The matter of the elephant had arisen when a reporter interviewing one of my daughters about 'Fuzz' had asked what her mother fed him on in order to keep him so tiny. Indignantly, for she did a lot of the feeding herself, anyway, she replied that we had never tried to keep him small. 'In fact,' she added in what *we* know is her usual humorous way, 'my mother brought him home some Elephant Meat to see if that would make him grow.' That was all the reporter needed. In no time at all our little Yorkie was known from end to end of the country as the little dog who ate elephants.

What had actually happened was that at a dog show we had been attracted by the appetising look of some large lumps of meat on the stall of one of our regular retailers. He was proffering them as 'Jumbo Steaks' and on enquiry he confirmed that they were actually steaks of elephant meat. On seeing our dismay he explained that over large parts of Africa since the elephant was now generally protected they were breeding too fast and using up too much of the vegetation. It followed, therefore, that the numbers had to be reduced and they were humanely destroyed and eventually found their way on to the pet food market, in much the same way as those other unusual meats, camel, kangaroo and whalemeat, to mention but a few. People who feed their dogs on tinned meat have been feeding such meats and others even more unusual for years past without knowing. There is nothing wrong in this as it is all good meat.

We jokingly decided to take some home and see if it would put any weight on our diminutive 'Fuzz' who was the tiniest little dog we had ever seen. This makes him very tiny because I have bred chihuahuas since they first became known in this country and have owned some extremely tiny specimens.

It wasn't clear how having his photograph taken with an elephant could do much to improve 'Fuzz's' image with those tremendous creatures but, in my innocence, I somehow thought it could. I was to be mistaken, however, for after the most harrowing time I had ever spent watching helplessly while little 'Fuzz' trotted fearlessly round the 2½-ton Colossus, ran under her foot before I could stop him and then, when being nursed by a stranger who appeared from I know not where, was suddenly placed right on top of the elephant's head. I nearly died and sprang to retrieve him from his precarious perch. Unfortunately I am not noted for my stature and even in the kneeling position she was then in I couldn't get anywhere near him. My frantic efforts so close to her eyes and my arms waving about so ineffectively must have frightened the elephant for she suddenly rose to her feet and there was 'Fuzz' high out of reach of the tallest among us. As the elephant obeyed commands in a foreign tongue only, it was necessary to find someone who could communicate with her, to persuade her to kneel down again. This all seemed to me to take years, simply years, and I could not imagine what poor little

The author's tiny
Fuzz rides high.

'Fuzz' thought about the situation. 'Burma' was a very tall elephant and 'Fuzz' was on the very tallest part of her. If he had fallen off in sheer fright no one could have been surprised. I could do nothing but get ready to catch him in case this happened. The brave onlookers had all scuttled out of the way when she had stood up and I was left there stupidly saying to the tiny mite 'Sit still, darling, and have a nice picture taken.'

I must be perfectly truthful here and admit that when he had at first found himself abandoned at such a dizzy height he shook like an aspen leaf and any picture taken would have shown about twenty little Yorkies. However, when I spoke to him he stopped and posed himself as he had got used to doing and those hard-hearted photographers even went on snapping with the result you can see. My knees didn't stop knocking for days.

After all these efforts and my resolution to improve his public image as far as elephants were concerned, the resulting picture which appeared across the whole middle page of the most widely read picture paper in the land, showed an evil-faced little stunted Yorkie with his coat ruffled to the extreme, licking his odious lips at the prospect of devouring the simply enchanting 2½-ton elephant that was lying placidly beside him. So much for newspaper publicity. People telephoned and wrote asking if his tongue always stuck out like that — it doesn't — and why his coat looked so unkempt. The last thing I thought of when he was returned to me from the elephant's head was to groom his coat back into shape. In the process of being fussed and fondled he certainly got to look rumpled but who was caring?

No mention of the exploits of the Yorkie would be complete without mention of the amazing little 4 lb. bitch, 'Smokey', who during the Second World War was found in a shell-hole in the New Guinea jungle just after the advance of American troops in that area into the Japanese lines. Corporal William A. Wynne, who was with the American Air Force in the photographic division of the Reconnaissance Unit, was offered this little pure-bred Yorkie for two Australian pounds. She soon became the mascot of the unit and accompanied Corporal Wynne on twelve air-sea rescue missions, went through one hundred and fifty air-raids and weathered a typhoon in Okinawa. At one time the Signal Corps were having difficulty laying a telegraph line under an air-strip. The wire had to go through a 9-inch pipeline and 'Smokey' saved the Corps a lot of time and trouble by crawling through the pipe dragging a tow-rope attached to the wire. No doubt her beloved master was at the other end calling to her and she would have gone to him willingly. He didn't have to be very clever to know that she could be relied on to go to him wherever he was, but it is a lovely illustration of their willingness to join whole-heartedly in any activity their owners are concerned in.

Some American Servicemen and their families told me this story when I was judging an exemption show at their base and shortly afterwards brought me a magazine article to prove the story. I remember it said that 'Smokey' lived on C-Rations (whatever those are) and was issued with vitamin pills with the soldiers. She had a particular fondness for Spam. When away from headquarters for any length of time Corporal Wynne bathed her in his helmet. The article went on to say that she became a 'star' turn on her demob. and appeared in an act where she jumped alone from a 30 ft. tower wearing her own little parachute. She performed all the stunts that big dogs did in her sort of act, such as walking a tightrope, jumping through hoops and waltzing, and was a tremendous draw wherever she went. For her appearance she wore a coat with the corporal's stripes and Service-ribbons. When she died she was mourned throughout America as the best and most useful mascot in the Services. My American friends had bought their Yorkies because of their admiration for 'Smokey'. They had wanted ones about 4 lb., but what they got was nearer 10 to 12 lb. They were bitterly disappointed as they had asked the English breeders for small Yorkies and were assured that the father, whom they saw, only weighed about 3 lb. They did not get to see the mother, which was perhaps a pity.

No one need be afraid that a Yorkie is not still game for the ratting and rabbiting sports he was supposedly bred for. My mother's brother continued her family's attachment to the Yorkie and big man though he was, he was rarely seen without his Yorkie, 'Mousha'. She was not very tiny, being about 8 lb. I should think, but she was a ratter par-excellence and could hold her own in any rat hunt, city dweller as she was. One nip on the back of the neck, over the head, and another dead one.

Our Yorkies dearly love to travel in the car and it is a case of physically removing them and locking them up safely before getting the car out of the garage on those few occasions when it is not prudent to take them with us. If left free they will chase after the car even on the main road. As soon as they see us make tracks for the garage they are there before us and almost before the car door is open they are up, over the back seat and down the well, a handy little carpeted compartment behind the back seat which the Yorkies have made their own. My husband uses a Dormobile for running about in — a most useful vehicle for holidays and the perfect answer to two-or three-day dog shows. One of my husband's special companions is a 4 lb. Yorkie called 'Maxine'. She is nearly always with him and alarms me by always balancing precariously on one of the cupboards. To make it more comfortable for her my husband supplies her with a cushion from which she surveys the world at large and travels for miles daily. In order to encourage her to sit on the seat beside him I moved her cushion there, but I needn't have bothered as 'Maxine' determinedly stuck to her cupboard. It was amazing to see how effectively she braced herself in order to stop from slipping off the shiny Formica surface when the car braked suddenly or swerved round a corner.

One family I know take their Yorkie whenever they go for a trip in their motor-cruiser. They fix her wicker basket inside a lifebuoy on the deck and until she gets her sea-legs she is quite content to sit in it quietly. However, it isn't long before she is pattering along behind them wherever they move and one of her games is making war on the mooring rope. She has only fallen in once and that was when she caught sight of her reflection when she was inquisitively looking overboard.

Acquiring a Yorkie need not involve you in such hair-raising experiences but you won't have another dull moment, and will certainly never find a more adorable pet.

As a show dog

As a show dog the Yorkshire Terrier is a most satisfying proposition. Small and compact, light to carry, content to stay quietly in his show basket or cage and amenable about all the brushing and grooming he has to undergo. A walk between the Yorkie benches at any show will be enough to prove this point. Rows of the little dogs standing placidly while their coat is being taken out of the rolls of paper or silk that have been used to protect it. Even when his owner is otherwise engaged a Yorkie will stand or sit on his grooming table. Other show breeds have to do this too but they don't take to it as quickly as the Yorkie and it often takes a long time to train them to stay put. Even so, it is best to hold them in place, for the first time you relax your hold they are off across the floor, under the feet of passers-by and causing no end of a commotion. When left alone in his cage for any reason the Yorkie becomes quite composed, unlike some small, spoilt dogs that scream and carry on until their owner returns. It is a great relief at a busy show to know that your little dog is not pining or disturbing the peace when he has to be left for any reason. Not

right A show dog of the present day.

A show dog of the past, Mrs Annie Swan's Ch. Delite of Invincia, 1939.

that there is a lot of time to be away as getting a Yorkie ready to be shown is quite a formidable task, as we will appreciate later on.

If there is an advantage in being kept well occupied at a show it is that the periods between the early arrival demanded and the eventual appearance of your dog in the ring may be long and tedious. To sit at your bench for hours on end with only your near neighbours to talk to can be rather soul-destroying. As you are usually benched near the same folk at every show, your bench being placed in alphabetical order, you soon learn all there is to know about them and their families, dogs, puppies, etc. It is very rare, in the ladies' groups at shows anyway, to hear anything discussed at shows other than immediate family or dogs. Being a rather tight little circle, whatever their interests outside the show world, no mention is ever made of it and you can have known someone for years at shows and have no idea that they are famous as musicians, artists or authors. It is a disquieting thought that you sometimes only find out these things when reading their obituaries. But, that's show business and you'll never alter it. There is no better place to forget completely the cares and woes of everyday life, all thought of which is banished altogether the moment you pass through the gates of a show. I cannot explain why this is so, but it always happens. Once you pass through those gates you shed your everyday life like a wet mackintosh and you are away in that peculiar atmosphere that I've only ever found at a dog show. It is the same in whatever part of the world you find yourself — the people will be different but the atmosphere the same, be it in America, Sweden, France or anywhere else. You will find too that after a time you will know hundreds of people by sight but will only really get to know personally the people in your own breed, and the ones you will know best are the ones with initials nearest to your own. Firm friendships are formed among these but, nice as they may be, a whole day of the same faces gets a bit monotonous. If you've rubbed your hound down with a grooming glove within half an hour of your arrival at the show at 10 a.m. and apart from the odd feeds and a spot of exercise, by the time you actually get him into the ring at 3 or 4 p.m. the day can drag a bit. Yorkies are a sure prevention of any sort of boredom. You will be kept happily occupied all through the waiting hours, and this is by no means a bad thing as you won't have much time for any back-biting gossip or spend a lot of money at the bars, which is how some people with little to do occupy their time.

Among all the glamour breeds of dogs there is none that pays so well for the efforts put into its preparation as the Yorkie. With his coat gleaming and trailing behind him, the lock of hair on his head (the fall in Yorkie parlance) and moustaches reaching to the floor, a top class Yorkie looks magnificent and, with the advantage of being shown on a raised box, he is more easily noticed than other toy breeds. Sometimes at an open air show the chihuahuas are almost lost in the grass and are often overshadowed by big dogs, especially if they have full coats. This doesn't happen to the Yorkies, however, for not only is their show box raised at least eighteen inches off the ground but it is

Emmrill Little Relco in
his travelling crate.

also draped with frills or velvet pelmets, so they are never missed. Their
owners also make a point of making a ring around them with their brushes
and combs and other equipment, thus keeping other dogs at a distance,
another advantage at a show. They still have their hair tied back with a
ribbon, which should match their drapes, and with a nylon lead to match,
they are about as show-worthy as any dog can be. It seems that only the
Maltese, sometimes the poodle, and the Yorkie share the common practice of
tying the top-knot in a ribbon. The poodle normally only uses a rubber band
nowadays and looks a little less glamorous as a result. This has a sure appeal to
someone looking for a breed to exhibit that lends itself to some window-
dressing. Make no mistake about this, the visiting public is greatly intrigued
by such foibles and spends far more time inspecting the toy breeds than the
more ordinary looking ones. I have asked them about this and they say that it
is a relief to look at all the pretty curtains and coverings that toy exhibitors use
after the miles of dirty looking ugly functional benches that most breeds are
placed on.

These then are some advantages that can be gained if, when choosing a
breed of dog to show, you make that choice the Yorkshire Terrier. Theo.
Marples puts it best of all in his very descriptive book *Show Dogs* when he
gives his opinion of the Yorkshire Terrier. He was the best one to know too;
as the founder of the world famous dog paper *Our Dogs* he had personal
knowledge of every breed of dog. Describing the Yorkshire he says — and I
quote:

'In my opinion the evolution of the Yorkshire Terrier reflects more
lustre on the British breeder than does that of any other breed of dog.

He is, with the exception of coat — which, of course can be regulated according to taste — a dog free from abnormalities and full of Terrier characteristics and intelligence, which he, of course, inherits from his ancestors on all sides. Beautiful to look at, active as a kitten, vivacious as the most "perkie Pom", the perfect Yorkshire Terrier is the acme of Toy Dog virtue and perfection looked at from every standpoint.'

Yorkshires are seen wearing ribbons in their hair still. Many men seem to be willing to show these little Yorkies so they are not put off by the titivating. Most ladies of course, if they have enjoyed dressing their little girls' hair for parties, will get the same sort of enjoyment. So we can safely say there is satisfaction out of showing a Yorkie quite apart from any wins that might be achieved.

One more advantage should be mentioned, although it is not always available nowadays, and that is the privilege of showing the Yorkie off the lead in the ring. So well-behaved are they and able to be trusted not to interfere with the other exhibitors that this could safely be allowed. The Yorkie exhibitors have always claimed that a lead disarranged the coat and spoilt its outline, so the breed went on for year after year being shown without the lead even after the Kennel Club rule was introduced forbidding it. Safe as this practice may be within the confines of the Yorkie ring it is a very different matter when competing in a variety class where big dogs and little ones are all shown together. One judge, with the foresight to recognise the danger, insisted that the Yorkie be led and this has gradually been enforced, although exhibitors held out for quite a time. Even today many of the older judges still give the Yorkie the chance to walk without the lead if he jibs with it on, but I have never seen them give this privilege to any other breed.

Among the show dogs Yorkies are about the cheapest to feed as they seldom evince the desire for specially expensive delicacies in the way of food, but thrive quite happily on any good wholesome food the same as most other breeds. They do, of course, eat much less of it so that you can keep a lot more for your money. It is not necessary to have kennels in order to breed Yorkies for show in a normal way. Of course if you intend making a commercial proposition out of it then it is a different matter and you will want much more technical advice than I give here. Many people keep anything up to a dozen, say, in a room in the house. A few can be accommodated in the kitchen and this is fine unless cooking is another of your hobbies, when it is more hygienic to keep your dogs elsewhere. Dog breeding and food preparation should not be carried on in the same confined space, unless you have a very large kitchen which can be divided up for both operations.

5 Buying a Yorkshire Terrier

BY far the best way to buy a Yorkshire Terrier, or any other puppy for that matter, is by direct approach. By this I mean getting in touch with the person who actually bred it and making a thorough investigation of its background. This may seem a grandiose description to give a simple matter of buying a household pet, but many people devote far more thoroughness to the purchase of a fridge or washing machine which will wear out and have to be replaced in a few years than they do to choosing a companion that will probably be with them constantly for ten years or so. If you engage an unsuitable house-keeper you can dismiss her. It is not nearly so easy with a dog. Temperaments do clash and a visit to the mother, will show what her pup may be like. A shy, quiet and retiring mother is quite likely to have children with the same characteristics, as is an over boisterous one. If you can see the father of the puppy as well that is even better, but don't think that a quiet mother and a noisy father will necessarily mean that the pups will be somewhere half-way between them. It is more likely that they will be either noisy or quiet. If the parents are nice and affectionate with their owner you can expect the same sort of feeling from the puppy when you eventually own him. Check that the parents are the right size. Another advantage when buying a Yorkie is that you will discover the exact size of the parents instead of receiving a vague description that they are either very tiny or 'a little on the big side'. It might surprise you to find just how big 'very tiny' can really be and also how very very big is covered by the 'little on the big side'. I have been shown puppies described as 'miniature Yorkshire Terriers' where the dam weighed all of 16 lb. and the so-called 'tiny' sire was a good 10 lb. Also a litter of 'Toy Yorkshire Terriers' where the dam weighed 15 lb. and the sire (which was not shown) was firmly stated to be under 3 lb. A clever bit of manoeuvring, which, if the breeder only knew it, is almost physically impossible.

Having decided that the Yorkie is the ideal pup to suit your particular needs it makes a lot of sense that a prospective purchaser will learn all it is possible for a layman to find out about the breed. A visit to the local library will show what can be studied on the breed. It will be well worth studying the basic standard of the breed and its characteristics before setting out in search of your puppy. If you write to the Kennel Club, 1–4, Clarges St., London W.1., for a copy of the *Kennel Gazette* you will find a list of breeders' names and addresses, also the dates of dog shows that will be held under Kennel Club auspices.

Wildweir puppies.

Sometimes breeders are hesitant to show off the mother although they are quite willing to bring in the sire of the puppies. Don't be put off but insist on checking the bitch for poor temperament and bad hereditary faults such as poor mouths, weeping eyes due to entropian, roach back, straight shoulders or straight stifles and a clicking or slipping stifle that denotes serious unsoundness in the hindquarter. Most breeders are only too eager to show off their stock so that any reluctance on the part of the breeder can usually be interpreted as a desire to hide something.

Collect your new puppy at a time when you are going to be free to spend a lot of time with him to offset the trauma of leaving his mother and brothers and sisters. He needs a lot of fuss made of him, tempting little bits of very interesting food and lots of toys and playthings to keep him happy. He can be introduced to his own bed as early as possible and made warm and very comfortable for the first night away from home. Don't shut him up on his own in a room all by himself and expect him not to miss his mother and family; put a loudly ticking clock in his bed muffled in a woolly and he will think it is the other puppies' heart-beats which to him will be a very familiar sound. Give him a drink of warm milk last thing and leave some paper down for him to use through the night. When he cries, as he will the first night, stuff cotton wool in your ears and leave him alone for quite a long time. If you listen and he is still crying give him another warm bottle and a small drink, then leave him as long as possible to start a sensible routine.

He will wake up before the family and probably howl from sheer loneliness but it is much better not to take him up to bed with you and to leave him until he calls at a reasonable hour.

When you do get up the very first thing to do is to put the puppy outside. It is best to supply him with a tray with some newspaper on it so that when he

Two Yorkie puppies
aged 8 weeks.

right A Yorkie at 12
weeks.

wets it the urine won't get onto the floor. The tray can be rinsed under the tap
and easily dried. Baby puppies can't hold themselves any better than babies
do and they don't have the advantage of napkins. Certainly drinking water
should not be left as he will drink out of boredom in the night and then to
relieve himself. A sort of playpen big enough to hold the puppy's bed, a tray
of newspaper for his toilet, some toys and a big juicy bone will keep a baby
Yorkie happy and out of trouble until such time as he is old enough to hold
himself. Early morning boredom and loneliness can get a puppy into all sorts
of mischief and make himself very unpopular with the first person to get
down in the morning.

Out in the garden, without the bed, the playpen will keep him safe when he
is put out to be clean for if his tray is used outside he will learn to use it very
quickly and always connect going outside with relieving himself. In this way
good house manners can be instilled with the minimum of effort on either
side. One woman took a three month old puppy home that had never been
allowed on furniture and had been house-trained by her mother so that she
always performed outside without any question. After the first night the
puppy was returned as she had wet on the carpet and the woman had been
unable to sleep all night as she had put the puppy in her bed and was afraid she
would roll over it and squash it or it would fall out of bed. From the time she
had been weaned and her mother had gone back to live with the family she had
occupied a puppy pen in the utility room and had just started going through
the night without wetting her piece of newspaper. She had a good routine and
went out about every hour. She knew what she was out for and scooted back
indoors when it was cold while her mother stayed outside. The new owner

was shown how clean she was and told that she was quite used to being on her own through the night. On her return she has gone back to being just as good as ever and it is doubtful if she will ever be offered for sale again. The buyer had had several dogs before so there is a lesson to be learned here.

A visit to a dog show, if held in your vicinity, is quite an enjoyable way of finding out what the show type Yorkie should look like. Even if you are not interested in showing, a picture of the breed, at its best, will enable you to find a pet puppy that, while possessing the particular virtues you demand for a household companion, will not look too far away from the true standard of the breed. A breeder who is primarily breeding for the show-ring or for other breeders to buy and show, will not breed whole litters of equal quality, many not complying exactly with the show standard. It may be many weeks before this is discovered and, in the meantime all the puppies will have had the best possible upbringing and every sort of dietary aid that that particular breeder is capable of giving to them and their dam. If one of these puppies goes over-size — over 7 lb. — it will not be show standard but will make a very handy pet and, should be cheaper to buy. An undershot mouth will not worry a pet owner any more than an overshot one. This is a bad fault for show but a slight one for a pet. Poor coat and colour also spoil the puppy for show but do no harm to the house-pet. Do not however, accept a puppy with a poor temperament. This is useless for a show dog and can be a perfect nuisance in a house-pet. Pick up a puppy gently and holding it under its forearms facing you look into its face. If it looks at you with its bright little eyes alert, puts out its tongue to lick you and works its little legs in an effort to get near to you, there is nothing to worry about. Don't be put off if the puppy has a fit of trembling — this is because he won't know that you don't intend to drop him. If, however, he opens his mouth and gapes at you and doesn't close it all the time you are looking at him, you will know he is suffering from a congenital nervous condition. If he also wets while you are holding him this will confirm it. Don't, whatever you do, allow a 'wetter' to be inflicted on you as you will regret it forever more. Excitement or not, any normal puppy will wait to be put down before wetting. A wetter will always be unreliable and most especially when you are visiting your most undoggy, wealthy relative, of whom you might, otherwise, have had hopes.

Puppies are usually sold at about eight weeks of age at which time they are likely to be properly weaned from the mother. I do not approve of puppies being forced out on to the world any earlier and at three months it is easier to assess the puppies ultimate character better than when they are younger. Good health and cleanliness go together in puppy rearing so be warned. A healthy puppy is full of life with bright eyes, shiny nose with no runny eyes or nose, is firm and round to touch with no bulging stomach — the evidence of indiscriminate feeding. Skin should be clean from parasites, scurf and dirt and should be loose, coat glossy and well-cared for and the puppy should have sweet breath. Make sure that its nails are cut as a new puppy however delightful can inflict untold misery by scratching everybody and everything and will soon be most unpopular.

The most outgoing uninhibited puppy will be the easiest one to cope with. Beware of a nervous mother as she could have nervous offspring and if there is a shy one that runs away to hide that could be the one.

The choice must be carefully considered as a misjudgement could cause untold regret. Dog and owner must be compatible in order to get the best out of their association.

Stand the puppy on a table facing away from you and quite gently place the balls of your thumbs on the inside of the hind legs near the knee joint. Press against the palm of your hand without any force. If you feel a click you can suspect patella luxation. Confirmation can be found by feeling the actual knee joint. Bend it slightly and make sure that the stifle cord is in place right in the middle of the knee. Any trouble here is big trouble and you would be very wise to leave any dodgy hind legs severely alone. This condition always gets worse and, although some very clever veterinary surgeons have successfully operated and remedied this condition in a few instances, I have seen hundreds walking about that have undergone expensive surgery and are even more crippled walking than before they were operated on. Many breeders do not or will not realise the seriousness of these slipping stifles and the fact that in most cases there is a genetic history, which means that it is passed on from one generation to another. It is found in many of the toy breeds especially where there has been any bantamising. I was extremely shocked when judging a toy breed at Crufts, where every entrant had to have won a first prize at a Championship Show within the previous 12 months, to find several lots of clicking stifles. It really is a great pity that the names of the judges that awarded such dogs a high award are not published. Whether through ignorance or sheer negligence, they do a breed immense harm in letting dogs with this serious defect win high prizes, as people will think them safe to breed from and use at stud.

However cheap the price don't buy a malformed puppy as you are bound to regret it. The Yorkie front legs should be straight. Nothing looks worse than a bow front, where the elbows stick out and the toes turn in. The dog will walk very badly and will look much lower in the front than behind — what is known as 'running up behind'. A roach back is ugly, and it often accompanies slab sides and other body malformations and I should imagine your enjoyment of any walk would be marred if you had to constantly see before you those horrible cow-hocks of the knock-kneed Yorkie. It is better to pay a little more in the beginning for a properly made dog than be forever apologising to people who will keep asking what is wrong with the poor creature. Don't buy out of pity, feeling that if you don't buy it nobody else will. There are far more people looking for Yorkies today than there are enough to go round. Let someone who hasn't been clever enough to study the breed beforehand get caught with such a dud, or, better still let the breeder find it on his hands so that he will have to learn from the economics of the matter that it is more profitable to try to breed sound stock that sells quickly for a fair price than dud stock that hangs on for long periods and then has to be sold at half price. Good advice to a buyer is to never buy anything that you have to be ashamed of. It is, after all the breeder of bad dogs that should bear the shame of them.

Drop ears, badly carried tails, a missing toe or hind dew claws are no reason for discarding a puppy as they will not be any inconvenience, and should have the advantage of a price reduction. Umbilical hernias, commonly known as tummy buttons, and missing testicles also warrant price reduction but are a much more serious matter and should not be accepted without your vet's approval. If the hernia is soft it might be harmless, however large, but if hard it will warrant a surgical removal with a general anaesthetic.

Complete absence of testicles will usually mean that a dog will show no sexual interest in bitches and so make a more manageable pet. On the other hand if one is present and the other 'floating' he can be much more embarrassingly persistent in these habits with bitches in and out of season and even other male dogs. This is obnoxious in a house-pet and the remedy is to have the dog castrated (completely unsexed) at the earliest moment. It is a simple operation and if carried out while the dog is young will not tax him in any way. What he hasn't had he will never miss, so there is no cruelty involved and, as these abnormal testicles often become cancerous, it will prevent the eventuality of a horrible and painful death.

If you decide that you want to buy a Yorkshire Terrier as a prospective top show prospect or in fact, a future champion, you are aiming high and should go straight to the highest authority viz.: The Kennel Club. This august body, which dominates the whole of pedigree dogdom in this country, have the names of every pedigree dog registered with them 'on tap' as it were and can turn up the name of any registered dog, of any breed in a matter of minutes. It is the function of the KC, as it is familiarly called, to keep the records of every dog registered with it and to add all the wins and stud particulars as they are achieved. Every show is authorised by the Kennel Club; all judges are passed by a special section of its Committee and all disputes are settled by the Kennel Club and its decision is always final. The Kennel Club sets us a code to manage dog affairs by, and every breed has a standard drawn up for breeders to be guided by — as well as for the judges to judge by.

The first thing a sensible purchaser will do will be to contact the Kennel Club and obtain the standard of the Yorkshire Terrier as laid down. Armed with this and the latest issue of the *Kennel Gazette*, which is only obtainable from the Kennel Club, you can plan your campaign to the best advantage. Find the dates of the forthcoming shows at which Yorkies are scheduled and visit as many as possible. They need not be championship shows, although these are the ones most likely to have the best specimens, as champions and dogs with challenge certificates towards their championship are barred from many local shows, which are held more for the benefit of novices.

Careful study of the breed points from the Standard and a note made of any tricky or indefinite point beforehand will be of great help when you meet the breeders and exhibitors.

If you are attracted to one particular specimen mark your catalogue immediately and, when the class has been judged have a word with the exhibitor and ask if there are any puppies available of a similar type. This is the most direct approach and the quickest and easiest way to start with a good one. You will have to pay a little more, it is true, but you have shown the breeder that you are looking for a good one and you won't have to waste time looking at all the unsuitable ones.

A walk around the show benches and a word here and there that you are looking for a show puppy will bring swift results and if several competing owners have something to offer you are in luck. They will try and outdo each other to offer you something better. This, of course, is to your advantage. Whichever one you eventually buy will need to be good enough to stand up to the criticism that will be bound to be made by the other disappointed sellers. The aftersales help and interest that you will receive from buying from a regular show-goer will be of inestimable help to you in enabling you to meet other breeders and exhibitors, and be shown and helped in the ring by the breeder of your dog so that you will not feel the nervousness that besets many novices when they arrive at their first show, and don't know whether their dog is good or bad. They wonder how the other exhibitors manage to make their exhibits look so well-groomed and have no idea at all how to go about presenting their own little Yorkies. They suddenly feel such a lack of self-confidence that this discomfort is transmitted to their little dog who, catching the mood fails to make the most of itself as a result.

If the puppy is only to be used for breeding and it is not intended to show it, the same careful forethought and study will pay dividends later on. Any knowledge gained about the breed is valuable, even if only one litter is planned. It might just as well be a good one. The difference between the price of an average stud fee and one to a champion is negligible when spread over a whole litter so any bitch not mated to a champion or at least a good winner, will cost as much as any other to feed and care for. A little care taken in finding a well-bred, typical bitch of good disposition and well within the bounds of the standard, will mean that the eventual offspring will pass muster. You can ask a fair price for the puppies and know that you are giving value for money — a satisfaction that must be sadly lacking from the consciences of many so-called breeders today who buy the biggest, even if it means the ugliest, in order to breed larger litters to swell the ranks of the mass of the really rubbishly Yorkies one sees about today. This is the inevitable price that the popularity of a breed exacts, to the great grief of genuine lovers of the breed.

It may not be necessary to get the very best and, if you are prepared to take a gamble then a glance at the advertisements in the Dog Papers will quickly put you in touch with people who have puppies to sell just when you want them.

I have gone into specific details of how to buy a show puppy or one suitable for breeding. If you want your Yorkie to be a pet only, you can still find your best buy at an established breeder's kennel. You will get better after-sales service, as the breeder will always have some interest in the puppy even after you have owned it for years. You will get specialist advice on how to feed and rear your pup and the chance to go back for any help in the early days, when this can be so valuable. The chance to meet the parents and grandparents of your puppy will enable you to see how your puppy will turn out for size and temperament.

Buying from a Dog Paper advertisement is a lot more hazardous, as it might not be possible for you to see the puppy if it lives hundreds of miles away. You will find that you will be told a lot of things in praise of the pup that fail to materialise after you have bought it. You cannot know the dogs on the pedigree and have to leave a lot to chance. Most breeders will expect payment and a deposit on the travelling kennel before they will send off the pup and then refuse to take it back if you are not satisfied. The papers have a scheme of holding on to the money, as a referee, until you are willing to accept the puppy, but this is still not a guarantee that the pup will continue to please and you are then stuck with it.

Buying from a dealer will probably give you a pup free from any infectious disease, as the dealers are knowledgeable about such things. He will not be an expert in Yorkies, probably, but will have bought whole litters at reduced prices and then sells them at slightly over pet prices in order to ensure his profit. If the pup is inoculated before you buy it that will be some advantage.

When you get your Yorkie puppy home, if he isn't inoculated he should be done as soon as possible, so make an appointment with your vet and get this done without delay. If you bought from a wise seller your pup should be covered with at least a month's insurance so that you have this time to get him protected and your purchase price is safe. It is strongly recommended that a complete inoculation is given — details will be found in the chapter on 'Rearing'.

You will probably find that the puppy has already been registered with the Kennel Club and is the owner of a long and important name. You don't have to call him by this, of course, and it is important that no time is lost giving him a name so that he can know you are calling him when you use this name. Use it every time you speak to him and look straight into his eyes as you say his name. Do this repeatedly when you feed him and he will connect his name with all the pleasant things of life and come quickly when he hears his name called.

He will need a bed to call his own and plenty of time during the day to enjoy complete rest and quiet. Make sure that the children and their friends understand this need for sleep. Carry out any training for house manners as soon as he wakes from these rests and immediately after feeding and drinking. His bed doesn't need to be very fancy. The new plastic folding beds are ideal for a Yorkie as they are too soft to damage his coat and not interesting enough to chew, like wicker and wood. They are easy to clean and can be rinsed under the tap and dried with a cloth. They will not scratch the walls and are useful to put under the seat in the car, or on the back seat. I find Yorkies very embarrassing car companions as they will jump about so. Trained to sit in their bed while the car is moving they would be much safer and less worrying to the driver.

Feeding routine is described in the chapter on 'Rearing' but the diet should not be changed too drastically even if you decide not to feed the same as the breeder did. Make sure the pup is already wormed and, if there is any doubt, discuss this question with your vet when he does the inoculation.

Your puppy will need a feeding dish and a heavy bowl for drinking. A double dish is available. A little plastic mat with a picture of a Yorkie under his food will save any mess on the floor and give him his own little feeding corner so he need not be a table worrier.

It is very important to give your puppy some toys and playthings that he can call his own. Hard rubber balls, rubber rings and bones are all good and some very fantastic toys are made like chops, cats, mice, etc., and some are even flavoured with chocolate or beef. Chewy toys made of beef hide supply a double purpose as they are good for his teeth and digestion as well as amusing him. He will play equally well with a few empty cotton reels tied together with nylon cord or some old nylon stockings tied into knots. Discarded gloves and old slippers are also much treasured.

For his grooming he will need a bristle hair brush, nylon or bone comb, cotton wool and mild lotion for daily cleaning of eyes and a toothbrush or some tooth cleaning material.

The Show Yorkie will need a box to stand on so that he can be trained for the ring at the same time as he is being groomed as, if his grooming is carried out on his own box, he will soon recognise that it belongs to him and respect it accordingly. A Yorkie standing on his box seems to have a great feeling of superiority.

It is very important that he has a collar with his name on it and a lead that can easily be attached when going for his walk. Nothing is more frustrating for both dog and owner than the lead clasp that is hard to do up. Make sure that the collar is tight enough not to let his head get through it but not tight so that you cannot get your fingers underneath it when it is done up. As the Yorkie front should be a straight one do not be persuaded into buying yours a harness. They are quite the wrong shape for this breed.

If his teeth begin to drop about the place alter his diet and make it easier for him to eat it. At the same time give him a large bone or a very hard chewy toy to make the cutting of his teeth easier. If he grows a double row, as many tiny toy breeds do, he should be taken to the vet for the milk teeth to be removed, as if these are allowed to remain they will affect his new teeth.

A show puppy getting used to his travelling box.

There was a time when a general anaesthetic was necessary for the removal of these little milk teeth as some are very tightly embedded. I have had a puppy quite unconscious for up to twelve hours after a few teeth had to be removed and this was most frightening. Nowadays a veterinary surgeon can give just a pre-med shot to take out the teeth and the dog will be round as soon as the teeth are out. What a relief!

A show puppy will need a travelling box in which to be carried to shows and the sooner he gets to like his box the better. Feed him in it a couple of times and let him sleep in it with his toys and belongings and he will soon learn to like going into it if plenty of good things happen to him when he is in it. A show puppy will also require a puppy play-pen to stop him getting into scrapes and perhaps spoiling his coat for show. His house training can take place in it. Make sure there is shade from the sun and protection from rain and wind.

If you intend keeping several Yorkies, or perhaps breeding or showing them in any number, you will need to keep records and these will have to be kept in some sort of methodical order. A large (8″ × 6″) strong envelope can be used to keep all his Kennel Club papers and his pedigree together. The inoculation certificate and booster doses records can also be put in and also any prize cards he may win. If a dog, a receipt of his stud service should go in and also a note of the resulting litter. The bitch should have her mating details and name of the stud dog she was mated to. A record of her litter and number of puppies born, etc. If the pups are sold the details can be put in the envelope

Ch. Blue Flash of
Streamglen.

but, if one of the puppies is to be retained he will need an envelope of his own.
On the outside give the dog's name in bold print and also his date of birth,
names of his parents, etc., so that you can fill in your show entries without
opening the envelope. A box file is as good a receptable as any in which to
keep the envelopes until such time as you find the need for a filing system proper. All show wins should be entered in a book or on a card which should be
kept in the envelope so that reference can be made easily when filling in show
schedules.

6 Training

House manners

GOOD house-manners are one of the first essentials in keeping dog and owner truly fond of one another. If manners are lacking the owner and his family are disappointed and no dog can be really happy in a house where he is always being scolded for his bad behaviour. Training to be clean in the house is one of the first and most important lessons a puppy should receive. Details are given elsewhere.

Jumping up with muddy feet is another habit which brings discredit on many a dog and this is a hard lesson for a friendly Yorkie to understand. It is as well to allow him to jump on a lap but care should be taken to wipe his feet clean first. If a towel is kept near the door for this purpose he will learn to wait for it to be used before going inside. Some can be taught to wipe their own feet on a mat. A special kind of mat is now available that takes all dirt and mud off feet, both animal and human, just by being walked on. Dogs are apt to monopolise these as they must be attractive to them. House proud owners would do well to investigate them as all Yorkies love to jump up to be petted and they are also fond of jumping on furniture. If this is to be disallowed they should be stopped doing it right from the start. Great persistence will be needed to win in this direction.

A dog should give the alarm and wake the household if anything untoward happens in the night. Persistent barking and crying are a great nuisance and he should not be allowed to indulge in these. He should also be trained from an early age to stay in a room by himself and not scream and bite at the door and furniture. Regularly leaving him in a room by himself when you are near to correct him if he creates a great deal of fuss, will help avoid his disturbing the neighbours when you leave him alone in the house for any period. He needs to be reassured that you will shortly return and then he won't be quite so unhappy when he is left. A good, big meaty bone will keep him occupied for some considerable time, and, if you have given him some active exercise just before leaving him he will be glad to sleep for a while. A carefully thought out programme and you should be able to leave him while you go out for the evening. No dog should be left on its own all night.

Postmen and 'paperboys are, like milkmen and bakers, very welcome callers. As he meets them regularly he should be taught to discriminate between them and total strangers. He should be stopped from biting and

Jewel learning to walk on the lead.

barking at people he will meet often. Yorkies are not as noisy as are some toy breeds but will make as much noise as any if encouraged to do so.

At about 10 to 12 weeks he should be introduced to a lead and walked about in the garden until he accepts it. It looks very unpleasant to see people dragging a frightened puppy along on crowded pavements and in the midst of noisy traffic. Carry him in crowded places for his own safety but make sure he gets daily walks on a lead so that he accepts it as part of his life. He is best carried away from the house to the bottom of the garden path. If one of his favourite people stands at the house door and calls him he will scamper to them as soon as he is put down. If this is done lots of times he will not notice he is on a lead, at first, and when he does just let him choose the direction and don't let the lead pull tight or be too restraining and he will forget it. If it makes him unhappy never pull him. He will only pull in the opposite way and you will have a fight on your hands. Make the lessons short, happy and end with his dinner in the kitchen which he will walk to on the lead, and he will soon connect walking on the lead as one of the joys of his life and not one of the tragedies.

Don't start teaching him kerb drill and staying down and other basic obedience tricks until he is over six months old. Whenever he is out, however, stop at the kerb and look both ways yourself and he will get into the habit of this waiting. To make him sit down just press him gently on his back just above his tail and hold him there saying 'sit'. Commands should only be one word and the same word should always be used for the same action. Don't say 'sit' one time and 'stay' the next thing for the same action. He will retrieve a ball from a very early age. If playing with children make sure he is not allowed to overtire as happens with very active children and young growing puppies.

When fully grown he will probably overtire the children.

NEVER take him out without a collar and lead even if he has learnt to walk to heel. The most dreadful accidents happen to dogs off leads so don't take any chances. However clever he is at walking close to heel, outside elements can occur over which you have no control and you may have to stand help-lessly by and watch your little loved one being run over because someone has tripped over him and flung him into the road, or he may be attacked by a bigger dog and bitten to death before you can get to him. If you have hold of the other end of his lead you can usually pull him out of danger.

Training the Yorkie for show

If you intend to show your Yorkie you can't start his training too early. He must allow his teeth to be examined, so early on make a habit of opening his mouth and looking at his teeth. They can be cleaned at the same time with a piece of cotton wool dipped in half milk half peroxide of hydrogen.

Give him lots of his petting on a table. If he is to have daily vitaminised chocolate or yeast tablets give him these on a table. When he stands on it quite fearlessly hold him in position for showing off his outline. Hold him under the chin with your left hand and under his tail with the other. Don't squeeze him but hold him firmly for several minutes at a time and tell him how beauti-ful he looks. If this is done after his daily grooming he will know he looks nice and, when he gets to his first show he will behave calmly on the table and let the judge examine him without a struggle, thus improving his chances of getting well-placed.

Yorkshire Terriers are shown standing four-square on a draped box or similar pedestal. As this takes a time to get used to, it is a good idea to let some of the grooming and training take place on this box at home and the dog must be trained to stand still for longer and longer periods. When the judge is pick-ing out his winners the dog must stand unaided and keep in the right pose until the judge has made up his mind. This can take quite a long time and, if the dog refuses to stand to the best advantage for all that time, his chances are reduced.

To train a puppy to walk as he will have to do for the judge, take him round in a circle, always keeping the dog between you and the judge. Then make him walk in a straight line, turn, and walk back to the judge then stand in a good pose before returning to the circle. Always use a happy voice and use his name. Tell him he is a clever dog and he will really enjoy his lessons.

The Show bench and travelling box

As exhibiting entails a lot of travelling and sitting in a cage or on a show bench at the show, the dog must get used to remaining in these for long, tedious hours. He will object to being left at first, but will gradually become philoso-

A Yorkie show box with concealed handle.

right Ozmilion Kiss Me Again at 8 months; owned by Mr & Mrs G.T. Buggins.

phical about the whole thing. Until he does so he should not be abandoned at a show as he will upset himself and all the people around. If show-going can be made a highlight of his life with special rewards like chicken breast and chicken livers and special foods that he only associates with a show, it is surprising how quickly he will catch on and always be ready for the next time. Many of my old show dogs look longingly at the show boxes and show bag and are quite envious of the youngsters starting out on their careers. On the rare occasions when some of the old ones go along to a show for the veteran classes and such-like, they go nearly wild with excitement at the prospect and, just like old soldiers they will parade up and down, showing the youngsters how it should be done. It is easy to see that they regret that their showing days are all but over.

There was a time when most show boxes were made of wicker — just oblong shaped baskets with the handle on the top. When the Yorkies had to be stood on their boxes for the judging a better type was designed that was flat on top with a wire front which opened as a gate. These crates were cheap and functional but as the long Yorkie hair could get caught in the wicker they had to be lined, then they had to be covered with velvet or similar to made an attractive dais for the little showman to be exhibited to his best advantage.

The next progression to this was wooden crates of the same size and shape and with handles at the side or sunk in the top for easy carrying but still flat to go under the show cover. These are rather heavy and not very attractive or as light as the latest fibre glass crates that come in any colour required. The snag with them is that unless the fibre glass is covered with material or very very thick varnish it is possible for threads of fibre glass to enter the pads and set up very bad irritation. For lightness, ease of carrying, smoothness and not rough on nylons as wicker these boxes have been very successful although rather expensive. If the exhibitor is only wishing to buy one crate there is another sort that is very suitable since a lot of shows are unbenched in the toy breeds. Because of the great expense and difficulties connected with benching firms and the astronomical price charged by firms with heavy week-end wages to pay, the Kennel Club has allowed even toy breed championships to be held unbenched on condition the show provides tables on which exhibitors can stand their own pens. As the object of shows is to show off the dogs to a paying public the Kennel Club's regulations state that the dogs must be seen so all over wire cages are the answer. These are placed on a long table provided and allow the public to have a proper look at the exhibits, which they could not do when the dogs were shut up in a wooden box. I bought some very smart gold coloured cages with green plastic removeable floors which I like because they fold flat when not in use. I take my dogs to shows in these in the summer time when they need plenty of fresh air, but in the wooden ones in colder weather. If more than one box is required for travelling in colder weather I put the show cover from the wooden box on the wire crate and this keeps out the cold and saves more crates or boxes being transported. As a mattress I have got a vet-bed to fit the floor exactly. This is white and furry and very warm and lets any moisture through, in the event of an unfortunate accident on the journey. The vet-bed is easily rinsed out and dries in no time too.

The above crates are very suitable for train travel as the wooden box has a very strong bolt as well as a hook and eye fastening that can be padlocked, while the wire crates have excellent strong fastenings that can also be pad-locked — an essential these days when dog thieves abound.

7 The Yorkshire Terrier Coat: its care and management

Present day breeders are forever delving into the past and searching out some of the old remedies and coat care preparations. One of the most important books on the old Toy Breeds was written by Lady Lytton in 1911 and I turned gleefully to her information on the Yorkshire Terrier in order to add some of her words of wisdom for this chapter. To my disappointment, however, she dismisses the breed scathingly as follows:

> As for the unfortunate Show Yorkshire Terrier with his unnatural existence as a "clothes peg" the less said the better.'

From my correspondence I know that there are a lot of people who would agree with this opinion but, luckily I found that Sam Jessop had written a really detailed and informative little book entirely about Yorkies called *The Yorkshire Terrier*' early in the twentieth century and he gives most detailed and clear instructions on the preparation and care of the Show Yorkie's coat with a long screed about how to bathe the coat which I include here to show how much harder such mundane and every day tasks became in the hands of the so-called experts:

> 'Washing need not be frequently if the dog's skin is kept in good condition by judicious feeding and exercise; but in the washing the best white curd soap should be used to bring the water into a foamy lather before the dog is put to stand in the bath. Spratt's FOMO is a valuable antiseptic shampoo for a Yorkshire. He should not be scrubbed. The soapy water is squeezed from the sponge on the part-ing along the neck, back and tail, leaving the head to the last. When the coat is wet carefully work the fingers through it, keeping the long hair extended. A thick absorbent towel should be wrapped about the dog and pressed with the hands and when the hair begins to dry, finish the process with a clean, long bristled brush (as pictured).

> If the coat is allowed to dry without brushing it will become wavy, which is a great objection. It is only by grooming that the silvery cas-cade of hair down the dog's sides and the beautiful tan face-fall that flows like a rain of gold from his head can be kept perfectly straight

Fig 3 Wide-toothed comb and long-bristle brush – the most suitable for the Yorkie coat.

and free from curl and wrinkle; and no grease or pomade could impart to the coat the glistening sheen that is given by the dextrous application of the brush. The gentle art of Grooming is not to be taught by theory. Practice is the best teacher. But the novice may learn much by observing the deft methods employed by an expert exhibitor.'

Exhibitors have often pretended that they use no dressing on the coats of the Yorkshire Terriers but it is quite certain that continuous use of grease of some sort is not only advisable but essential. Mr Jessop recommended the following:

'Take of hydrous wool fat 2 oz. Benzoated lard 2 oz. Almond Oil 2 oz. phenol 30 grains, alcohol (90 per cent) ½ oz. The first three ingredients are melted together upon a water bath; the Phenol dissolved in the alcohol, being added when nearly cold. The whole being thoroughly mixed together.'

Yorkie exhibitors used to have their own little secret and peculiar methods of inducing hair to grow. Diet was carefully regulated on the lean side not fat at all. Bread, mixed with green vegetables a little meat and gravy or fresh fish varied with milk pudding and Spratt's 'Toy Pet' biscuits. Bones were barred as gnawing them damaged the moustaches and beards. Sometimes the food would be given from the fingers and sometimes a kind of mask would be placed over the dog's head to stop the facefall getting in the food, etc.

The coat of the Yorkie is its crowning glory and from the earliest beginning of the breed this coat, its special silky quality and its length and particular colouring, have been the chief concern of its originators.

The surest way to get good coats is to breed for them. The novice breeder should spend some time at shows observing the breed, and it will then become apparent that some coats are of a very much better quality than others. The

Ch. Skyrona Blue
Victoria – Best Bitch at
the Northern Counties
Championship Show
under Ray Ryan and
owned and bred by Mrs
G. Sykes.

sleek, silky coats that hang close and straight, even at the bottom, with enough density so that no daylight can be seen underneath are a great improvement on those dry looking, wispy coats that fly about and refuse to settle, whose owners seem to be perpetually fiddling at them with a hair-brush and even so they still look as if they have never been touched. The ends too are uneven and disclose the fact that they are constantly breaking off. A slight unevenness can be expected in a puppy coat but at two years or so the coat should have reached its full potential. Only the lines which produce the better type coat should, therefore, be included in your own breeding.

Without doubt Yorkies' coats are a lot of work. Once started on the road to showing Yorkies there is no slacking or standing still. As daily attention is needed the amount of time available for this daily grooming routine will limit the number of show Yorkies kept in one kennel.

Grooming the baby Yorkie coat is quite easy and daily use of a good bristle brush will do wonders for it without any added aids to beauty. The diet here is of paramount importance and so long as the skin is clean and healthy and the right amount of fat and seaweed meal is included in the daily food the coat will just grow. Puppies will benefit from an occasional bath as they are inclined to get into a messy state during their romps and are prone to roll about in their milky food and dribble it down their fronts. For this reason the sooner the food can be given dry and the sloppy food stopped, the sooner the daily face washing can stop. Whiskers can get completely congealed with milk if not attended to daily. The long hair near the eyes is another part that gets congealed and the eyes should be bathed daily with a very weak saline solution to dissolve this before combing through. Do not brush the face close to the eyes for danger of injuring them with the bristles. Bath with a cream shampoo or Johnson's baby shampoo that doesn't sting the eyes. Dry quickly and keep indoors for the rest of the day.

It will be found helpful if, as soon as they are long enough, the hairs on the top of the head, known as the top-knot, and those on the upper lips and under the chin, are tied up out of the way. Start tying the hairs themselves with a piece of darning wool. This must be removed daily, the hair underneath washed or oiled with baby oil, and the wool retied. This can be done from about three months onwards. Care should be taken to see that no hair from the top lip is tied up with hair from the bottom lip. A bone comb is a good tool for this.

Once they are tied up regularly the top-knot and whiskers grow apace and soon it is possible to cover them over with paper before tying them up. Toilet paper, hanky tissue or tissue paper can be used and they can be fastened with little rubber bands. Get the ones used by florists and called 'flower bands'. They are so tiny that they only need one extra twist. Always check that no hairs are pulling underneath each 'tie' as this will cause intense pain. Nylon bands are stronger than rubber ones and are obtainable.

With so much handling the coat may need protection. Even the gentlest use of brush and comb tends to break the ends and split the hairs. The tip of the hair only should be worked between oily fingers before being tied up. Lanolin, olive oil, baby oil which has almond oil in it, coconut oil or some of the expensive oil mixtures marketed by Canine Beautician Specialists, can be used for this purpose. Contrary to the advice given by many people it is most unwise to rub oil into the skin itself under the mistaken impression that this willl promote the rapid growth of the coat. I am indebted to Mr David Stroud of the Macstroud's Yorkies and owner-breeder of the well-known Champion Macstroud's Sir Gay, for the information that oil on the skin of a Yorkie is much more liable to burn the skin surface and cause dandruff and a scurfy appearance than improve the coat. I experimented with my own dogs and found this to be a true fact so pass it on for those of you who are oiling the roots of your dogs' hair.

For the record fish oil, crude oil, engine grease and many other such substances are among the recommendations from various sources. No doubt lanolin in its purest form is of inestimable value. It is obtained from the skins of sheep so that the wool-workers in the mills of Yorkshire who took their terriers to work with them would, no doubt have wiped their greasy hands on their dogs coats or, their hands being often greasy they would only need to caress their pets for this grease to wipe off on the outside of their coats. It probably didn't even occur to them to rub it into the dogs' skin. Frequent applications in this way must have had a salutary effect and perhaps came into general use when dog shows started.

Breed expert, Mrs Annie Swan and Mr Theo. Marples advocated the use of oils. Mrs Swan advocated olive oil and coconut oil in equal parts and a little paraffin added, the whole to be melted together and stirred until the mixture thickens. When cool it will set and be ready for use. She also mentioned a mixture of marrow 4 oz., olive oil 1 oz. and caster oil 1 oz. to be melted together and stirred until cold.

In *Show Dogs* Mr Marples advised: 'The finest olive oil with the least drop of paraffin in it, being generally used but there are other preparations such as coconut oil and a very excellent pomade is recommended in Jessop's work on this breed which is sold by *Our Dogs* Publishing Co.Ltd. These applications not only keep the hair from getting matted, but act as a good hair stimulant. The dogs should be washed periodically with either a good dog soap or soft soap sparingly used.'

Mr Theo. Marples also tells us that the feet of the Yorkshire Terriers are 'stockinged' almost as soon as they leave the dam to prevent them scratching the hair off any part of them and the regular attention to their toilette now begins. They are combed and brushed almost daily and the skin kept in a soft and perfectly healthy condition. If there is the least suspicion of mange or eczema, it is promptly attended to by an application of some well-tried specific, which is always kept in the house. As the coat grows it is kept constantly in oil.

He tells us that Yorkshire Terriers must be kept and bred from in the house. One of the secrets of the success of Yorkshire Terrier breeders of the working-man section, who at the time he wrote his book he says were the most numerous, is the fact that the dogs are kept in the kitchen, where the housewife or children can give them constantly those little attentions which spell success. They usually convert the kitchen dresser into a kennel by taking out the drawers and making the interior into three distinct little houses, with little brass-railed gates. They are given woollen cloth to lie on, which is kept quite clean by washing and changing as required.

'Valuable Yorkshire Terriers are not given their absolute liberty. They are exercised (or should be) at frequent intervals, out in the open when fine and indoors when wet.

'In this way Yorkshire Terriers do lead a life of imprisonment, but not solitary confinement. They see all that is going on in the house (where they are well cared for) and their life is made happy in many ways, by the attention of the family, in a dietary being rigidly observed which is conducive to good health and accidents and death avoided which would, and do more or less, befall all Toy Dogs that are given their full and unrestricted liberty. Thus, although at times a cry has been raised by the humane against the system of rearing Yorkshire Terriers, where they are well cared for, as in the case of all good specimens which are too valuable to be neglected, the method and treatment together are a "blessing in disguise".'

In another of his very informative little books *Prize Dogs* Mr Theo. Marples tells us that to do justice to a Yorkshire Terrier, the owner must practically live with his dog. He requires almost daily attention to his toilet from puppy-

Fig 4 Boots (a) A little leather boot that can be bought to fit a tiny Yorkie; will prevent damage to coat by scratching (b) Simple pattern for a boot you can make yourself out of corded velvet or chamois leather.

hood up. This breed must be kept in the house — kitchen for preference — and, if the highest perfection be aimed at, the dog must practically be a prisoner for the term of his natural life. He requires a special kennel, made of wood and portable for preference, with a day and sleeping compartment, each of which should be about two feet square. Except when he is being fed, groomed or exercised, he should live in that kennel night and day after attaining the age of six months. The coat should be brushed daily from three months old, and a hair stimulant, such as coconut oil and kerosene, or linseed oil containing a little paraffin, applied about once a week. At six months old, or earlier, he should begin to wear socks on his hind feet to prevent him from scratching hair off his body. A steel or brass comb may be used for a Yorkshire Terrier, but a special kind of comb is made for this breed alone. Great care should be exercised in the combing and brushing, and specially after the dog is washed. He should not be washed oftener than once a month, except when going to a show, and should be dried very carefully before the fire. After he has been wiped well he should be combed out before the fire until perfectly dry. There is no breed which requires so much care and which entails so much constant attention and trouble as the Yorkshire Terrier.

'When the coat has grown to a good length, the hair on the head, called the "fall", must be tied up with silk ribbon, so that the dog may see where he is going. Care should be taken as to where he is allowed to exercise himself, any place where he is likely to get his coat entangled in anything being scrupulously avoided. In wet weather he should be exercised under cover and, if by any chance his coat gets wet, it should be thoroughly dried and combed out when the dog gets home before being put in his kennel.'

All foods of a heating nature should be avoided in the case of Yorkshire Terriers as that has a tendency to retard the growth of coat, which is the great thing to aim at, although soundness in colour of what is a clear blue back and good tan muzzle, ears, legs and feet is also essential. Straightness of coat is indispensable, waviness being a fatal blemish in a Yorkshire Terrier.

The best diet, according to Mr Theo. Marples, for a Yorkshire Terrier is rice pudding, bread soaked in gravy, occasionally boiled and mashed potates and gravy and a little raw, finely minced lean flesh meat, also arrowroot biscuits soaked in milk and pepsinated puppy biscuits.

I dread to think how many carbohydrates to the oz. this diet contains.

People who object to the tying up of the coat of the show Yorkie would do well to study this description of how the show Yorkie has been allowed to live. I hope only the most dedicated exhibitors would treat their little dogs quite so drastically. There might be some excuse in the bad winter months but dogs like children need sunshine and to deprive them of their rightful inheritance just for the sake of their show coats seems to me selfish beyond belief. It would seem that to tie the coat up out of the way and then let the Yorkie have his play is far more humane that shutting him away as advised by Mr Marples.

By the time the Yorkie is nine months old the black coat of his puppyhood will be giving place to a much lighter colour and the tan in his coat will get different shades of gold instead of the solid colour he started out with. If by the time the Yorkie is 18 months old the coat hasn't changed from black to blue there is very little chance that it will do so but the tan changes many times before the end of his career. A damaged coat will change colour — i.e., if a dog gets a wound or the skin is hurt when pulling out a tangle a black mark is likely to appear. If the ends of the coat are allowed to get badly split they will lighten in colour, so it is important that they are not allowed to become tangled.

Vitacoat makes a very good anti-tangle solution which is of great help in easing out the tangles if such a thing does happen. Failing this equal parts of water and eau-de-Cologne (the cheapest kind sold in the chain stores) if brushed through the coat has a similar effect. It can also be used as a brushing fluid and will help keep the coat clean. It is never wise to brush a dog with a dry brush as this can damage the hairs. Use the brush correctly too or you can do more harm than good. Always keep the brush with its bristles facing down as if you twist it up you will break the coat. If your thumb is kept along the handle of the brush it will help this action and be easier to control. A spray for the coat lotion is a good idea but I use a squeezy bottle as nothing ever seems to go wrong with it. Avoid the eyes when spraying by covering them with one hand and always spray from behind. St. Aubrey Coat Dressing is a famous brand make and mixed with half water is fairly economical. Their Royal Coatalin is an expensive but very beneficial coat grower. It comes in block form, and if the block is hollowed out and the hollow filled with Johnson's Baby Oil it goes a long way as it is best applied to the ends only. Johnson's make a very good grooming spray and the counters of the stalls at dog shows are, nowadays, crowded with aids to doggy beauty and they have all been prepared and packaged to the Nth degree. This explanation is meant for people

Ch. Dorrit's Susanne's
Treasure.

who haven't yet attended their first show or are puzzled by so many names and don't know which to use. I have used most of them and the ones I recommend are the ones that have proved most effective and easy in use and in getting easy reward from the coat when necessary. In U.S.A. I found the exhibitors using a 'Mink Oil' and this can be obtained in London.

For young puppy coats only the lightest and gentlest oil need be used and so there is nothing better than baby oil. Before starting to groom moisten fingers with eau-de-Cologne and water or a little spirit dressing and massage the skin in circular movements. This not only tones up the skin but the regular friction is very beneficial to the muscles. The coat will grow much faster if attention is paid to the skin. Then run a little warm oil on to the palms of the hands and rub them together then lightly pat the coat avoiding the skin. Take a clean brush and with the puppy lying on his back on a towel on the table or preferably from his point of view, on a grooming apron on your lap, give the coat a steady brush from the skin to the ends of the coat. Pay particular attention to the hair on the side of the stomach, inside the groin and under the forelegs. If little knots are found work them out with oily fingers or, if stubborn use the spirit dressing or anti-tangle lotion.

When all the coat has been treated and is quite free from knots and bits of grass, etc., take the comb and make a parting from the nose to the tail. Make sure it is even or the coat will look dreadful. Spray the coat well with spirit or grooming spray and brush from the partings to the tips until it is dry. Some people recommend brushing the coat from the tip to the root, but this needs care and can be as dangerous to the coat as back-combing if done by a novice. Tie up the fall (hair on top of head) and the dog is ready to go out.

If the coat is to be tied up this is the time to do it. Start with the head and tie as already described for the puppy but fold three inch wide strips of paper into three, place the hair to be tied on the middle panel and fold the other two folds over each other. Roll up under the coat as this way you can see better if any hairs are pulling and the coat will not be so wavy afterwards. The grease is better applied to the ends when taking off the wrappers in order to get them off easier. If too greasy when tying up the papers will slip off. Wool, tape or rubber bands can be used to hold the bands on. Rubber bands or nylon stay on longer but need careful watching as they hold dirt and dust and are hard to get off again. I like almond oil and it is pleasant to use.

If a dog has been ill, or has moulted badly for any reason especially when a bitch has reared a litter a much richer oil will be needed.

Before starting to treat the coat cut the ends to get rid of any split ends. A good inch or so is best as a short even coat will look much better than a straggly one. Oil the ends by working warm oil well into the coat and brush through with a fairly soft brush so as not to damage the coat further. Do this every other day for two weeks and on the alternate days spray with spirit dressing and brush from the skin out. A richer oil is needed — coconut oil and castor oil.

At the end of the two weeks bath the dog thoroughly with anti-grease shampoo. Massage the shampoo well into the coat and rinse well avoiding the eyes. The final rinse should contain a neutralising anti-static agent to keep in the natural oils and to make the coat more manageable — less likely to blow about in the air and take out the electricity that stops a Yorkie's coat from staying sleek.

A healthy coat would be ready for the ring after one or two treatments. The coat should be dried gently by patting dry with a soft towel — never rubbed. A Yorkie can be rolled up in several warm dry towels, allowed to shake himself well, then dried completely with a hair drier set at 'warm', which will only take a short time. Never brush dry as this is most damaging to the coat but take a wide toothed comb and comb the hair down the way it is required to lie. No oil or any other dressing should be applied if it is intended to show the dog. A good brush with a proper Yorkie show brush followed by a rub over with dry hands or a piece of silk or silk velvet will add the desired shine if any more is necessary.

If there is any skin condition such as dandruff, scurf or eczema, of course these conditions must be dealt with before attempting to put the coat in condition. Every chemist will have proprietary brands of dandruff dressing which can be used for humans and these will be found just as efficient for dogs. Regular use of a germicidal shampoo for inmates of a kennel who are not going to be shown, is very advisable. Fleas and lice, as well as ticks abound in the country at certain times and cause much misery, with irritation and scratching. If a show dog caught these pests that is probably the end of his career for quite a bit. In between baths a dusting with Gammaxane powder will keep dogs free. Today collars for dogs containing insecticide are excellent. In fact there are times when it is unwise to bath a house-pet or kennel dog, and, whereas it is difficult to show a dog unless he has been bathed first, the cold of winter and aftermath of illness are bad times in case they take a chill. They can be cleaned up quite well with talcum with a little Gammaxane sprinkled into the coat and then brushed out well. If they have got very dirty or muddy, warm bran rubbed well into the coat and then brushed out until clean and dry is another method.

Nursing bitches and very young puppies should not be bathed unless very necessary. 'Hyaline' is a safe shampoo to use in this case. All so-called soapless shampoos are extra efficient at getting out dirt but may possibly also take out the natural oil. Victims of eczema should not be bathed but treated with calomine.

My own method of growing and maintaining a show coat does not follow any of the foregoing lines as I have found many snags with most of them and great disappointment at times. Over the years I have evolved a system that is one hundred per cent effective, clean so that the dog is never too unpleasant to live in the drawing-room, very time-saving and improvement can be seen to be being achieved and the whole process is quite pleasant and acceptable to any Yorkshire Terrier that has been trained from babyhood to accept it. It also does wonders for coats and skin that are in a really poor condition after an illness or after rearing a litter.

I maintain a high protein diet — eighty per cent meat, twenty per cent good quality wholemeal puppy meal. They get milk to drink and raw egg twice a week. Each day a salt spoonful of SA. 37 which prevents any lack of vitamins or minerals, a teaspoonful of corn oil or sunflower seed oil or similar, some form of yeast and a generous helping of kelp (seaweed meal). They have plenty of clean water and a bone or hard biscuit or hard-baked rusk to chew to keep their juices flowing and to keep their teeth clean. Our dogs are housed separately for eating and sleeping so they always get 'fair shares', which doesn't always happen where the older bossier Yorkies are allowed to bully. Beds are kept clean with frequent changes of bedding and vacuum cleaning for thoroughness. Dogs are let out into their large run first thing in the morning and are left out to play, weather permitting until lunch time when they are put back for a rest. No dog will be in show condition if allowed to run its food off its back without adequate rest. In the afternoon they are allowed to play outside until feed-time at 4 pm when they are let out again until bed time

in the summer and just to be clean in the winter. They are all put out last thing at night so that they go through the night without soiling their beds and this is an essential in keeping their coats.

Show dogs are bathed with Vetzyme Shampoo each Sunday and put into oil in the following way — after bathing and rinsing, using Head and Shoulders or similar if there is any sign of scurf, then rinsing that out and then putting a cap full of Alpha Keri heavy oil in a deep bowl of warm water then standing the dog in the water up to its neck and leaving the dog 'in soak' as it were for about ten minutes. If a smaller quantity is to be used — half a cap full to a gallon of water — pour this mixture through the coat for about ten minutes. Leave this in the coat and when dry put up in crackers in the usual way and if oiled paper is used it can stay for a week without knotting at all. This oil is so heavy that it takes a lot of trouble to wash out, at least three baths of Vetzyme Shampoo will be needed and even then it will not be very satisfactory but it is a great time saver and if I am not campaigning a dog but wishing to keep it in good shape with the least trouble this is the way I do it.

If I am campaigning I bath the dog in the same way and use either a very good quality conditioner on the coat, such as is supplied by the Oster people, then rinse it out before drying the coat. This makes the hair more manageable and is a great beautifier leaving the coat sleek and glossy and quite within Kennel Club regulations, as there will be no grease on the coat as there is when an oily brush is used as a last minute gloss provider just before the dog enters the show-ring, which *is* against Kennel Club regulations.

If sufficient time is available to bath it out completely, the show dog can be immersed in a bowl of warm water to which a cap full of baby oil is added. This can be poured over and over the coat and will get every single hair coated with oil. This is by far the best way to apply oil to a Yorkshire Terrier's coat and if the hair is tied up in crackers it will save ends being broken and will prevent tangles that so often spoil a show dog's coat and also make it much harder

Care of the Yorkie coat.
(a) Equipment – mink oil, plate for comb and rubber bands, long-bristled brush, knitting needle, tissue paper, oil in saucer.
(b) Brushing oil onto the ends of the coat.
(c) Making a straight parting down the back with the aid of a knitting needle.
(d) Dividing up the coat and taking a suitable piece to be wrapped.
(e) Placing hair on the paper.
(f) Wrapping the hair in tissue paper.
(g) All the sections of hair wrapped.
(h) Wearing a special garment to protect wrapping.

to grow the coat to any great length. If I have to take the crackers out when the coat is in baby oil then I spray it with a very good quality conditioner such as is made by Brecht, Fabergé or similar. This is sprayed on thickly especially at the ends before brushing and the crackers are put on with hands dipped in oil.

The cracker papers can be oiled or tissue paper. If I use tissue paper I always buy the acid-free jeweller's paper. The black tissue is even better but not so easy to come by. I like a very wide cracker several inches longer than the coat so there is plenty to wrap around and plenty to turn up at the bottom. The coat is parted in sections about two inches apart, making sure that the parting at the bottom of the section is straight and the parting at each section vertically is also straight. Place the hair that has been sectioned off on the cracker, put it in middle of the cracker which has the top turned in about an inch. Wrap the paper over the hair, from each side and keep rolling the paper over the hair until there is no paper left. Fold the bottom of the cracker in half and then in half again and fasten with a rubber band. The smallest band is the best and it will need to be wound several turns until the cracker is fastened securely. Work the hair from near the skin so there is some play, this will make it far more comfortable for the dog to endure. Flower Bands No. 1 are recommended for tying up coats. Some exhibitors use very expensive nylon bands that were intended to be used to straighten children's teeth. I have used them but find them too strong and liable to damage the hair a lot. My favourite is to tie the crackers with silk-coated very fine elastic used for shirring. This is fiddley though and I found some useful bands when I was in America last, that are much gentler, but they break easily and have to be renewed each time, so although they are comparatively cheap they are dear in the end. All these bands should be stored in the dark as they rot in the sunlight.

I like to retie the coats about three times a week and when the bands are taken off and the crackers removed a good spraying with one of the new antitangle preparations really gets tangles out by brushing.

At a show I do not use an oil preparation as this is against Kennel Club rules but something has to be used to take the waves out of the coat that tying up leaves in it. For this I use a seven per cent solution of Eau de Quinine sprayed on and brushed until the coat is dry. All the waves will be removed and the coat will be ready for the ring hanging perfectly straight and shimmering like silk. If the ends of the coat are trimmed evenly each side of the parting it will give a much neater effect to the grooming.

I illustrate the beauty of the Yorkshire Terrier Coat with a picture of the little American Champion 'Cede Higgins', who I met in 1977 at Westminster Show in New York. I watched him in the show ring and was very disappointed that he did not win. When he came out of the ring I went to see his owner and told her that if I had been judging I would have given her dog top prize as I thought he was wonderful. His disappointed owner Mrs Barbara Switzer, told me that he had won Best in Show the day before at the Yorkshire Terrier

Championship that I had missed as I arrived from England too late to attend it. She also told me, and this I found hard to believe, that 'Cede Higgins' was her first dog and that she had bought him from a pet shop. This will be even more fantastic when I tell you that the very next year on 14 February he went Best in Show All Breeds at that top show of all in America that same show, Westminster, where he was thrown out the year before. The judge that recognised his merits was Mrs James E. Clark, one of America's most respected and knowledgeable judges, and one I have the highest regard for. As Anne Hone Rogers she handled at least four of the poodles I myself had bred to top placings, Best in Show and high awards at Westminster. She herself won Best in Show handling the toy poodle 'Wilbur White Swan' and 'Ch. Fontclair Festoon', full sister to one of my own poodles. This is equal to winning Best in Show at our Cruft's Dog Show and dogs that win this award are in a class of their own. The judge who had awarded him the Group was also world famous — the noted Miss Iris de la Torre Bueno, who I have watched judging and who certainly knows what she is looking for.

Barbara Switzer showed me how she tied 'Cede's' hair up — with oiled paper, such as she could buy from flower shops. The advantage of this is that it kept the oil in the coat and not in the paper and kept rain and dew out. I was very pleased to learn this useful tip as my show dogs have a grassy run and although they have a paved portion for wet weather, they prefer to run in the wet grass which, even if there is no actual rainfall, gets wet with dew and mist with the result that their paper crackers are saturated and have to be put in fresh several times a day. I could not find the same paper in any of the flower shops I deal with but found I could buy packets of white rather than the fawn Cede was put up in. This was waxed paper and although rather thicker, had the same effect of keeping the oil in the coat and the water out.

Another very useful tip that I had from my American friends was the use of quinine as a hair stimulant for the sebaceous glands that are the ones concerned with hair-growth used at the strength of one part of the quinine to seven parts of water. This solution can also be used to very good effect by spraying it on the coat before brushing and it will not only make the coat look clean and brighter, but when used at a show after the crackers are taken out, spraying the solution on the coat and brushing it out until it dries will remove the wavy look the coat will have taken on when tied up in crackers and will make the coat look thicker and much more alive. Some people advocate having oil mixed with the quinine but this is useless when actually showing the Yorkie as no oil is allowed. Not as much is needed as when water is used alone and so it dries much quicker leaving the coat with a denser look with a healthy gleam and well-groomed and sleek, having lost all signs of the static condition that gives the coat such a 'fly-away' look. In fact the coat looks as though the dog had been on a special diet for coat improvement. Such diets although most effective take many long months before much improvement appears in the coat. I feed unsaturated fatty acids in the form of corn oil, sun-

Ch. Chevawn Sweet Shonah owned by Mrs E. Layton and S. Chiswell. A beautiful brood bitch.

flower seed oil which are far easier for the dog to digest than a lot of the oil that used to be recommended, and have had a lot of success and been pleased with the result. Linseed oil is also a good old stand-by that is often mixed with food mixtures for dogs in the same way as it is for horses and cattle. All dogs need seven per cent fat in their diet to keep skin and hair healthy. Any lack will show as dry, itchy skin and it also flakes when it is too dry and this shows as scurf and dandruff which then need curing with a special medicated shampoo such as 'Head and Shoulders' which might have to be used several times before it is cleared completely but is worth persevering with as it really does affect a cure and was highly recommended by my vet.

8 Deciding to Breed from your Yorkie

The brood bitch

If you already own a bitch that you have bought merely as a household pet, and your vet advises breeding from her for the sake of her glands in later life, the best advice about whom to mate her to, is to study her pedigree and breed back to any champions mentioned in it, or their strains. This means that if there is a champion in the pedigree, he would be the best in it, and a return to the line that produced him would obtain the best puppy your bitch would produce, without knowing anything at all about her quality and any possible flaws in her make-up. If funds are such that a cheaper stud would seem more in keeping with your pocket ask the owner of the champion if they will take a puppy in lieu of a stud fee. Supposing he or she agrees to this, you can be sure that your bitch is of passable merit or they would soon tell you so. No breeder of repute wants to be landed with a puppy of very poor type as it will be difficult to sell and will do their stud dog's reputation no good. However bad the bitch the stud dog, unfairly, always carries the blame for any faults in his offspring. The honest opinion you will get from the stud dog owner, especially if the bitch was not purchased at that kennel, will be worth a lot of wasted time to you and you can well afford to part with a puppy.

For a first time you will almost certainly have to give up the pick of the litter to the champion's owner. If satisfactory and you wish to breed again the second time you may be allowed to keep the pick and give up the second best. It really depends on the quality of the puppies and the policy of the stud dog owner.

If, on the other hand you are starting to breed with a view to becoming an established breeder and you are looking for advice the same thing applies. Never use anything but the best stud dog you can find. Breeding and rearing toy puppies is hazardous enough and expensive enough so you don't want to have any discards. It costs the same in time and money to produce indifferent puppies as possible champions, and it is far more satisfying when the time comes to put them on the market to be able to offer well-bred, typical and well-constructed puppies. The friendly relations it will engender with your future customers will encourage you to try again and you will find that the first pups sold will be splendid advertisements for your stock and repeat orders will begin to come in.

If you do not already own a Yorkie bitch and wish to breed for a hobby or business I would advise that you buy two bitches of about the same age. Don't

buy more as it is better to breed your own and you will wish to keep everything you breed to start with. If one bitch is bought on her own and another
one at a later date there may well be jealousy and the new one resented. Any
such enmity will make for very difficult times for when they are nursing
puppies they will need to be kept apart. If, however, two of like age grow up
together they will eat and sleep better for each other's company, they will play
together and amuse each other when you have to leave them alone and generally they will bring one another into season close together so that you can
mate them about the same time and so both will be nursing puppies at the
same time. The advantages of this are manifold, especially if one turns out to
be an indifferent mother or if there is a shortage of milk. Being friends they
will usually adopt each others babies and, when you have run on some of the
bitch puppies for your future breeding they will accept them equally.

One word of warning here, though, however good two bitches are together,
they should always be kept separated when they have new puppies. If the
kennels don't have wire doors or any means of keeping the other out a good
plan is to obtain a wire crate supplied with a removable metal floor and a lid.
Mine are about 24″ × 18″ × 20″ high with a lid on the top kept secure with a
long stay. Inside there is room for a box to take the bitch with her pups and
enough room for her bed when she wishes to sleep away from the pups but so
near that she can watch them all the time. The fact that the bitches can see one
another and the puppies stops the snarling matches that often occur when
they are shut away from one another but know that they both have young.
Quite often this causes them to want to see the other one's pups and the outcome is often a bad fight or damage or worse to the pups. In their crates they
lie side by side near the Aga in my kitchen. We put a curtain between them for
the first going off, when they are naturally very puppy proud. They are lifted
out and put outside for their regular exercise together and they both scratch
the door together to be let in quite amicably.

When buying Yorkie bitches to breed from it is advisable to get them of a
reasonable size to start with, say about six or seven pounds. At 6–9 months
they will cost more but should already have been fully inoculated and over
cutting their second teeth, which are always good things to have over. Look
for sturdy, plump-bodied youngsters with plenty of heart room, level backs,
strong, sound legs, see that that they are bright of eye and their teeth are even
and cleanlooking. If the breath is bad, the ribs stick out and the backbone is
prominent they are probably wormy. Rheumy, watery looking eyes are also a
sign of these parasites. Make sure the skin is clean of dandruff or any bad skin
condition. Fleas and lice can be dealt with but are not necessarily found in a
well managed kennel. If the skin is tight, and stomach distended and the pups
dirty under the tail, look elsewhere as these are signs that the pups have not
been well reared or properly cared for.

The most important feature for future brood bitches is the width of the pel-
vic bones, for the further they are apart the better chance there is for any easy

Brood bitches in their special enclosure at the author's home.

whelping. Discard bitches that are droopy at the tail as these are often found to be badly formed in the pelvis and make poor broods accordingly. If in doubt about the condition of the bitches for whelping, a vet's opinion should be sought. In any case, when possible bitches are found it will save a lot of unnecessary worry later on if they are examined before purchase and a vet has a chance to go over them thoroughly. Any kennel worthy of the name will appreciate the care you are taking over the purchase and, as long as you hand over the money for the vet's certificate and not just promise to pay for it, there should be no objection from the seller. If there is, then you can suspect something is wrong enough for a vet's opinion to be an embarrassment and you are well out of it.

Make sure that the bitches have happy out-going temperaments. Remember that the friendlier the puppy the easier to sell and you can't expect shy, retiring bitches to have the most friendly puppies. Temperament is of utmost importance if your plan is to breed for show. It is sheer waste of time breeding shy puppies for this purpose, especially when so many wasted hours will have had to be spent preparing a Yorkie coat for show. A sensible choice in the beginning will avoid such a calamity. If you don't find the right temperament at first just shop around until you do. A Yorkie is a terrier, after all and was never bred, in the first instance to be nervous or shy. This sort of character, in my book, is a blemish of the first order.

I have made no reference to coat and colour and, while these are of very great importance in this breed, no novice can be expected to know how to differentiate, especially as all puppies are born black and tan and have so much changing to do. At six months the coat will be changing at the roots to a silvery blue and look for tan as bright as possible. I have found, however, that some tans don't come to their final depth of colour for nearly three years. The thin, silky coat is more typical than the heavy woolly one and will be a lot less trouble to look after. Avoid a harsh, wiry coat like the plague.

Although it is very difficult to choose correctly from between eight to twelve week old puppies it is better to take a risk or two and buy these than be persuaded to go home with 'older and proved' bitches. No breeder would ever part with a really first-class brood bitch as they are his bread and butter, and who wants somebody's throw-outs. I talk from bitter experience as I once got talked into buying a 'proved brood who whelped easily'. She did too, as easy as could be. What I wasn't told though, was that she ate the heads off all her pups the moment anyone strange looked at them. When I complained I was told that I wasn't feeding her properly. I gave her away 'not to be bred from' and wrote it off as experience. It taught me a lesson, though a bitter one, and I have never since bought anybody else's discards. If they are not good enough for them they are certainly not good enough for me.

When your bitch comes into heat for the first time you will naturally be very anxious to mate her. Some Yorkies come in at only seven months or so while they are still babies and it would be wicked to breed from them. While nature makes no laws that such is the case, experience shows that even if the bitch will be twelve months before the puppies are born, a first litter from so young a bitch is always a bit dodgy. She may suckle the pups right away but, on the other hand she may not and this could lead to her being a very poor mother for the rest of her life. 'Experts' maintain that at this early age the bitch's bones are more pliable and so assist easy whelping. The bones won't be much harder in six months and that extra time will have helped her to have settled down mentally. I have sometimes been called in to help a novice with such a young bitch on her first whelping and it is pathetic to see how helpless such a baby bitch is when faced with the onrush of several puppies at once. She gets frightened to death and even if bodily she is ready to become a mother, the mental strain is much better put off until the next heat. Besides, if it is intended to keep one of this first litter for your own breeding stock you may like to bear in mind the advice of many an old stockman in the cattle world which is: 'Never keep a bull for the herd from a maiden heifer'. Sound advice almost surely gained from bitter experience, and one we never dreamt of opposing. This may have been at the back of my own mind in deciding against first heat litters but I can honestly say that my bitches are a placid lot and make excellent mothers and they never want to leave their puppies of their own accord, but always have to be removed when they have done their work sufficiently. This would seem to describe a good brood bitch.

The first heat should be recorded and it will then be easier to foretell when the next is due. Most bitches have a regular six monthly interval but, as in all nature, there are exceptions, it can only be regarded as a rough guide. Some bitches only have a heat every 12 months and they can be safely mated every time. With others it is wise to limit the litters allowed. A small litter can be followed by another mating the next season then, if the litter is a reasonable size she should be rested the next one. Two large litters concurrently are too much of a drain on a toy bitch and after say four puppies reared she should be rested next time. One or two only and she can be mated again without much risk to her health. If a bitch rears four good puppies a year she is doing all right. Any more can be looked on as a bonus.

It is very wise policy thoroughly to worm the bitch about a month before she is due in season and fortify her normal diet with Bemax or wheat-germ powder sprinkled on her meat and a daily conditioning with a mixture such as Benbows, which I have always found excellent. Any comprehensive conditioner or vitamin supplement could be given to ensure that the bitch is in the best of health when mated.

The first signs will probably be that she constantly licks her vulva and on examination this will be found to be much enlarged. Swab her every day from now on and watch the colour of the discharge carefully. At the first sign of brilliant red inform the owner of the stud dog and arrange to take her in ten days time. This is only conditional and the dog's owner will understand this but will appreciate that you have let her know at the very first sign. If you have another bitch, your 'in season one' will begin to ride on her back and stand as if to be mated, with her tail to one side. This, contrary to what some very experienced breeders believe, is a quite early stage in the affair and it will be some days before she will allow a male to mount her back however steady she is for another bitch. Many matings are unproductive because owners of bitches will persist in taking them to the stud as soon as they will stand to another bitch. It may be another five days before she will accept the dog himself.

Don't take your bitch to the dog before the tenth day as this is only rarely successful. If you can wait until the 13th you are best but 10th or 11th, at least. As a beginner the stud dog's owner will probably rather you went too soon than too late though, as it is very frustrating to find that a bitch has 'gone off'. If there is still a show of colour you are quite safe. As this colour fades to pink warn the stud's owner. In actual fact when the vulva is very, very large the bitch is still very small inside. As it wrinkles so she opens up and a mating can take place. It is possible to mate a bitch in full colour and for puppies to be born as a result but this is the exception rather than the rule. Presuming that the bitch is normal she should hold to the service after the tenth day. If at the first try the mating is not successful you will be asked to bring the bitch back, possibly in two days, or maybe you will be allowed to leave her. This is for you to decide. If the mating was not satisfactory, and the stud dog's owner will tell you if it wasn't, then you must give her a second mating. As long as the dog penetrates, stays on her back for several minutes and then turns and has to wait for some definite time before the bitch releases him, you can be satisfied that you have had a good mating.

If, on the other hand the dog leaves the bitch quickly and has his penis erect and ejaculating, then the mating was probably abortive. If he rights himself quickly he can probably mate again right away and, if held in for three or four minutes it should be all right. On the other hand he may mate correctly the second time. A clever stud dog can get himself back if made to jump off the seat of a chair or, if the bitch is held aloft and he jumps for her. This is a trick that has to be taught when he is young and not a single second should be lost in getting him to jump. If several attempts are abortive the bitch, being a maiden, may want easing inside. If the stud's owner doesn't suggest doing this and you are nervous yourself, it is well worth calling for the vet. It is simple and quick and makes a world of difference. Another reason that mating is difficult is when the dog or bitch need to urinate. Make sure that both are able to do this before a start is made. They should not have been fed on the day of the mating and after it is over turn the bitch on her back, wrapping a towel round her and hold her so for a short while. If a lot of fluid runs out this is a sign she has been well mated. Don't worry if she snaps at the dog to start with. Hold her head firmly in the palms of your hands and press your fingers on her shoulders. If you can hold her safely it will leave the dog's owner free to help him and keep him steady.

If a fee is to be paid, this is the time to write the cheque. You should then receive a stud receipt with the date of mating and expected date of the litter. Most stud dog owners write a promise to give a free repeat in the case of failure. Ask about this, if it is not done. Get the signature of the owner on the stud receipt and keep this document safely as this is your proof of mating in the case of any dispute and the Kennel Club should ask to examine it. You should also obtain a copy of the dog's pedigree if you have not already sent for one to study previously.

Don't let your bitch pass water for at least an hour. Put her in her basket and let her sleep on the journey home and then all you have to do is wait patiently. Some vets can tell if a bitch is in whelp at the third week when they can feel the puppies in their fingers like peas on a string. Not all vets have this knack, however, and you may have to wait until the sixth week before any real physical change takes place. No extra feeding or change in the routine are necessary before this time, but by the end of the sixth week her condition should be noticeable and then she will need a completely new routine. The more gradually this is introduced, however, the better. To emphasise this important stage I will list her requirements:

1. Exercise should be limited to steady walks and ambling about on her own. No more romping with the other dogs and absolutely no jumping down off the furniture, etc. Jumping up is far less liable to cause miscarriage than jumping down but, with a first litter both should be discouraged.

2. Feed twice and even three times daily to avoid overtaxing the stomach making sure she gets sufficient milk, meat and roughage to feed herself ade-

A well matched pair —
Ch. Emslade Galahad of
Yadnum (dog, *left*); Ch.
Golden Button of
Yadnum (bitch, *right*).

quately and also be able to support the growing litter inside herself without putting any undue strain on her constitution; e.g.:

Breakfast: 2 parts Farex, 1 part Complan, Glucose to taste mixed together with warm milk. (This will supply all necessary additives for normal growth.)

Lunch: Raw meat fed at the rate of ½ oz. per 1 lb. body weight sprinkled with wheat-germ meal as the source of Vit. E., lack of which is the cause of some bitches not carrying their litter to full time. Teaspoonful of S.A.37, a complete vitamin and mineral supplement.

Supper: Cooked meat or fish with 1 teaspoonful chopped liver and a little Atora suet to make up the fat requirement in the most digestible way.

This diet can be continued all the time she is feeding but add another milk feed making four feeds daily with a bowl of milk and glucose as well as a bowl of water available at all times if the litter is a large one or if she loses condition during lactation.

A bitch will usually leave her litter in better condition than when she started, if this feeding is adhered to. Cereal is not used in any other form except as a dry biscuit which they will sometimes take and sometimes not. Bemax or wheat-germ meal supplies roughage and All Bran can be added with advantage if she has any anal gland trouble.

Raspberry leaf is very beneficial especially in the case of a fairly small bitch as it really does make the whelping easier. I use it in any case as I find it assists with the cleansing, helping the uterus to remain in a clean and healthy condi-tion. A retained cleansing or afterbirth is a very bad thing and has very serious consequences unless dealt with promptly and raspberry leaf does away with this contingency. Tablets can be obtained from Denes who are most understanding and helpful as to the needs for small dogs. Far from being a crank with my dog feeding, nevertheless when such remedies are found to be effective I think it would be crass folly to overlook them. For a small bitch one tablet a day for a toy breed is sufficient up to the last week and then I give two daily. If things are going slowly a double dose of these tablets will often quicken things up and, as they are only herbal, can do no harm. Vets are inclined to look on such dosing as just old gipsy folk-lore, but, if it works what does it matter. I can speak quite truly when I say that I have never had to have a Caesarean for a bitch who has been on them. When I have run out or omitted to give them for some reason I have often had trouble with whelping chihuahuas. Luckily my Yorkies have all been natural whelpers but it would be foolish to take any chances when the answer is so simple and so cheap.

The most important need for ALL Yorkie bitches, and I stress the ALL, is an adequate supply of Vitamin D. It has been proved, without any doubt, that Yorkies are most prone to an imbalance in the calcium in the blood-stream during lactation. This may be hereditary or just bad feeding policy where bitches have been deprived of calcium under the mistaken theory that it would make for coarse, large puppies and harden the bones of the bitch at the very time when she needs them to be pliable. Whatever the cause the fact remains that it is a serious condition in this breed and many good bitches are unable to feed through a whole lactation without falling victims to it. I have only once met with this condition in my other breeds and thought I knew the answers. It was a bitter disappointment and a great sadness therefore, to lose a Yorkie bitch completely only ten days after her puppies were born. Hand-rearing five orphaned puppies for the next four weeks was a strain also, but I have felt very badly about the bitch ever since. She had the usual fortified diet as all my other bitches but, in her case there must have been some deeper need. She was given several injections of Calcium Gluconate as soon as the symptoms were discovered and before she went into any sort of eclamptic fit. My vet put some into the vein and another lot under the skin to act more slowly. At 12 o'clock she seemed quite normal again and was sleeping peacefully in a bed not far away from her pups in case she fretted for them. At five o'clock when we went down to look at her she was quite dead.

This was bad enough but only two litters later, despite all prophylactic dosing, another bitch went down with the same symptoms. She had received all the usual dosing to avoid such trouble but, on going down to look at a bitch that was waiting in the kitchen for an expected litter I happened to look at the Yorkie who should have been sleeping peacefully. She seemed to want to go out so I picked her out of her crate and as I did so noticed the funny trembly feeling in body which is always present in eclampsia. It was after 2 in the morning but I rang my vet and he was round without delay. This time, I'm glad to say we saved her life but my vet said she would have been dead by the morning if I hadn't noticed her starting. Her two pups were hand-reared from then on and as she is a great family pet she went back to her rides out in the car and village shopping and never looked back. She is not a prolific breeder and in four years has only had two previous litters of one each time. This time she excelled herself and had two.

My previous answer to this trouble has been Roche's Sterogyl Dragees. I used to give one 10 days before whelping, one at whelping time and one 10 days later. This kept my bitches quite free from eclampsia; even a chihuahua who had it at her first whelping before I used any prophylactic, never had it again and she bred for a full life and had two litters of six. None of her daughters suffered from it and I think if I could have treated the Yorkies in the same way they may have been all right. Unfortunately Roche's Laboratories have discontinued marketing this product. When I wrote to them they sent Sterogyl Liquid in phials — enough in each one to give a child every six months. The correct dose for a 5 lb. bitch was beyond my mathematical powers but I gave half a phial to a basset-hound bitch with 10 puppies and she reared them without any harm to herself.

I had bought a large supply of Calcium and Vitamin D tablets from my usual doggie chemist and had dosed according to instructions. On the advice of my vet I am discontinuing their use and changing to Crookes Collo Cal D which he suggests my dogs may find more easily assimilated. Apparently calcium can be given in such a form that it is not absorbed by the body at all and it is necessary for the Vitamin D to be present in a large enough quantity for the calcium to be of any use in the bloodstream. It is rather technical but I trust clear enough to show that some such extra need is present in Yorkie bitches of some strains and it is best to be prepared. Naturebone and Stress are two other excellent products. The importance with tiny toys is that a large enough quantity is present in small quantities. If the feed is about 4 oz. in weight and synthetic additions are about ½ oz. the little creature's stomach content will be like a block of cement. The same applies to the puppies' own diet which will be explained later.

For the last week especially in warm weather the suet can be dropped from the feed and the bitch given two teaspoonfuls of olive oil daily.

9 The Stud Dog

Booking the stud dog

FINDING the right stud dog is the answer to most breeding problems and one of the biggest problems is that his influence is not nearly as strong as that of the bitch and, however good a stud dog as to his own points, it is rare indeed to find a dog that can transmit these points to his offspring without losing the majority of them on the way or getting so overshadowed by the faults that the bitch might carry that they cease to exist.

Choosing a stud dog for a first litter must be a very hit and miss affair and if genes and chromosomes are going to be taken into account there are so many permutations that it would make your head spin. I have stated earlier that a dog of the same strain as your bitch, preferably a champion is the best to use.

In a breed where size is of such importance as in the Yorkshire Terrier it is essential that not only a tiny dog should be used, but one who has a very small mother and father also, so that whichever one he throws on to his progeny they will be less likely to be huge puppies. If the grand-parents can be shown to be small also you are even safer still. Of course, if there is a hidden monster in the back of your bitch's pedigree or in the dog's, this is quite likely to appear, and no blame can be put anywhere, for this kind of thing constantly happens. You will have to breed many generations from fairly small stock before you can begin to fix a type of your own but you can't begin too soon trying to fix any desirable feature.

The policy of mating large bitches to tiny stud dogs in the mistaken belief that the progeny will come half way between the two is one fraught with danger. The result is more likely to be some enormous pups and some very tiny ones. The big greedy ones will stamp all over the tinies and rob them of nourishment and the little ones will probably die by being pushed out unless they are taken in hand and given separate feeding. In such a situation by far the best policy is to take the big ones away and hand-rear them and let the tinies have the mother to themselves. This, of course, belongs to another chapter.

One very firm piece of advice to a beginner in any breed is not to buy a stud dog to begin with. However good the dog you buy (and stud dogs good enough to found your own strain will set you back many hundreds, even thousands, of pounds) after mating to all the bitches you own, he will be redundant

Ch. Macstroud's Sir Gay owned by David Stroud; a very important stud dog and sire of champions.

for you won't want to start breeding him back to his own daughters at this early stage.

Use the best dog you can afford or offer a puppy in lieu of stud fee and you won't go far wrong.

When you have decided that you favour one in particular write to the owner and make a definite booking for his use. Do this even if you see the dog's owner every day. There will then be no excuse for refusing to let you use the dog of your choice when your bitch is ready to be mated.

As soon as she comes in heat write to the stud dog's owner again and give a tentative date for mating her. This can be altered by telephone if her proper time is on any other day.

The owner of the stud dog will appreciate it if you give your bitch an anti-insecticidal bath before taking her. Leave some in her coat so that if you are unlucky and the dog himself has fleas or lice or worse, your bitch won't catch them from him. Surprising as it may seem even champions have fleas sometimes.

If you can't take your bitch to the dog yourself make arrangements to send her by train. Get a sound travelling box with a strong lock and put a white sheet or towel for her to lie on so that when she arrives it can be seen at a glance if she is still showing any colour.

She will be better rested in her strange quarters the first night and mated the following day. It might be wise to ask for a second mating before she is returned. When sending the stud fee remember to include the return carriage, which should be the same as you paid to send her.

Warn your local station master that you are expecting livestock and he will see that you are informed as soon as she arrives. Warn him that she is in season and must not be let out of her crate.

Remember that she will still be matable and carelessness now could cause a misalliance. Keep her carefully secluded for the whole 21 days.

When using a young stud dog for the first time many people wonder what is the best time to start. The answer to this from my own experience and many other toy dog owners is that unless they have at least one bitch before they are a year old they are often very slow to get started. After the first bitch another about thirteen months and another at fifteen months and everything should be all right. They can have more if needed but I give the minimum to get a dog properly started. If left until two years old some dogs are frightened of the idea and others don't make the slightest attempt to mate a bitch. Sometimes with patience these can be persuaded to try and they have ended up good stud dogs but it is not always the case.

A good stud dog is worth his weight in gold — a dog that goes straight for the bitch and is not put off by her temperament but knows if she is physically ready. Some dogs know this and will not mate a bitch on any but the right days. Others will mate a bitch if she just stands still for a scratch. A toy dog must be taught that he must expect to be held on to a big bitch. It is no good him not wanting to be touched as some of them do. Without help he could fall over backwards and possibly injure himself. It saves time and temper if he can be trained from the start so in the beginning don't let him have his way with any bitch he fancies, as is sometimes done. Chose a steady, old bitch, who knows the drill and hold her for him. He could probably manage her quite easily himself but don't let him or he will get too independent. When he has mated the bitch don't let him turn but hold him on her back for 10 to 15 minutes to let him get used to the position. Turn him after a time but keep on holding him until he is released. Make a fuss of him and let him see that you are pleased and if later on you get a difficult bitch he will let you help him without question. A dog that is regularly helped with his matings will wait and look for this help and this can often avoid complications. Once an understanding is established between stud dog and handler make sure the same person is always available to help him.

When helping a tiny dog to mount a much taller bitch always make sure that whatever you use to raise him is absolutely firm. Many such matings go wrong because the dog is nervous of falling rather than of the size of the bitch. See he doesn't slip with his hind feet.

If he misfires train him to jump quickly. If he can't find any furniture to jump off one of my stud dogs jumps against a wall to withdraw himself.

After serving a bitch it is a sensible piece of routine management to pour a

Richard Haynes' super
champion Ch.
Eburacum Paladin,
another well-known and
excellent stud dog.

jugful of a very mild solution of TCP, Cetavlon or similar antiseptic preparation over the exposed parts of the male or alternatively immerse the whole in
the solution. If used fairly cool it will help things back quickly.

Some dogs have a poor sense of direction when mating so it is politic to
guide the bitch's vulva. If a dog seems eager but misses every time shut him
completely away from the bitch and summon help. There are very expert
people who specialise in conducting difficult matings and many good dogs
have been saved from extinction by their help at the right time. Once they
have learnt their job no further help is necessary, but many frustrating and
abortive hours can be saved if their help is available before the poor little dog
exhausts himself completely.

A stud dog should not be fed on the day of the mating until afterwards. He
will need extra meat, raw for preference and extra wheat-germ meal and a raw
egg on top are found helpful. He should be allowed to rest quietly for about 12
hours after a mating. It might take him 48 to renew himself enough to be able
to mate again. Two matings a week are usually enough for the average Yorkie.
Some can do more but it shortens the life-span considerably to mate too often
as the strain on the heart is considerable. Many dogs faint during copulation
but usually recover quite quickly with no ill-effects.

Although it is much more satisfactory for the male and female to 'tie' during
mating, this, in fact, is not really necessary for conception to take place. Some

Fig 5 Sexual organs of dog and bitch.

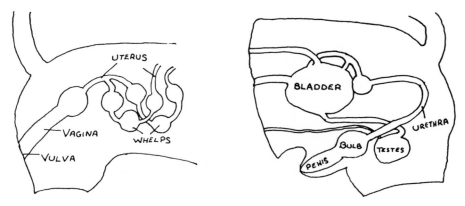

matings are successful when they have been nothing more than a 'stab' as long as that 'stab' was in the right direction. Some years ago the owners of a champion bitch went to mate her to quite a well-known champion stud dog. The stud dog owner put a blanket on the table put the pair of Yorkies together on the blanket, she held the bitch's head, the stud dog jumped up on the bitch's back, wriggled about a bit, worked his back legs about twice then got off the bitch, walked to the edge of the table, jumped down and pushed open the door and disappeared.

'That will be twenty guineas, please' said the stud dog owner.

'He only stabbed at her' said the bitch's owner in a shocked voice. 'I'm not paying twenty guineas for a stab.'

Unfortunately I do not know if this bitch had another mating, if the mating was effective or if when it proved abortive this Yorkie breeder got a return service. It is true that so long as the sperm stays in the bitch long enough to fertilise the bitch's ova or eggs the mating will be successful. As this episode illustrates some stud dog owners are only interested in collecting the stud fees and doing the minimum to earn them. While it is true that the stud fee is paid for a mating and not the resultant litter, anyone with a conscience should be anxious to know that his stud dog has been virile enough to have sired a good litter, and not just collected a lot of money in fees for services with no resultant puppies. There is all the difference in the world from such as these and the more genuine stud dog owner who looks after his dog's virility with the correct care and diet, offers a second mating two days later and if the whole procedure was a disappointment, offers a repeat mating the next season with suggestions as to how it can be improved. It is most likely the bitch was brought at the wrong time in her season and only experience can improve matters. Perhaps an explanation of the mechanics of mating will be of some use to those who are ignorant about what really happens during a mating. The diagrams above are self explanatory as far as the differences between the sexes but what actually happens is that when a bitch is presented to a dog when she is at the correct period of her heat he will sniff at her under her tail to make sure that she is at the stage best suited to his liking, and this is all done by smell. When she stands still and presents herself to him by turning her tail to the side, pushing her enlarged vulva at him and standing perfectly still the dog mounts the bitch from behind, forces his erect penis into her vagina by working spasmodically. Once inside he will work his back legs much more vigorously and after doing this for a time he will start to eject spermatozoa inside the bitch. The bulbous part then gets very swollen at the base of the penis and, when it comes in contact with the female's vagina it causes a violent reflex action as the penis becomes engorged with trapped blood because of a valve which cuts off the normal flow of blood. The bulbous part then gets very hard and this causes the 'tie'. The mating pair are then unable to release each other for some considerable time. This then is Nature's way of making sure that as many ova (or eggs) as possible can be properly fertilised.

It is a very good idea as far as Yorkshire Terrier stud dogs are concerned to make sure that the long coat of the 'Show' Yorkie is tied up out of the way for the mating. Many use lengths of nylon stockings for this purpose but I find a better grip with the ribbed sleeve of an old knitted jumper.

Sometimes the bitch decides to be awkward and snap at the dog — even the mildest tempered bitch can do this and in order to save their valuable dog being marked for life or thoroughly frightened off his job, they often tie the bitch's mouth with what is known as a 'tape' muzzle. Bitches simply hate this, especially those that live as pampered pets. It also makes a poor impression on her adoring owner. When I was in America some years ago I found very tiny little plastic coated wire-framed baby muzzles made in such tiny sizes as 0, 00 and 1. They are very comfortable but at the same time are one hundred per cent safe for the dog. The most harm she can do him is to prod him with the wire cage but as this is coated with soft plastic it is only very gentle — a lot less harmful than teeth.

10 The Brood Bitch

Whelping

UNLIKE some other breeds the Yorkshire Terrier seems to go most of the 63 days of the Gestation period. This simplifies matters considerably as there is less likelihood of the puppies arriving unexpectedly about a week early as they do in some breeds. It is best to be on the safe side and have everything ready at least two weeks before and, if the bitch is introduced to her whelping box about this time she will not need to be searching round the house to find what she considers to be a suitable spot. Her ideas and yours are not likely to coincide as she will most likely choose the best eiderdown or the drawing room cushions. One problem that affects a lot of Yorkshire Terrier bitches when they are getting ready to whelp is the great discomfort of the greatly increased temperature that she must get accustomed to. My Yorkies are a hardy lot as far as heat is concerned and they love to play out of doors what-ever the weather. They never hug the fire as some breeds are apt to do and when they are put under an infra-red lamp or close to a radiator or boiler, they make a terrible fuss, panting away and getting in a state. Somehow they must be made to accept the extra heat that is essential for the well being of the new-born puppies. They have come from a very warm place and any suspicion of chill anywhere and you have a case of hyperthermia on your hands. Unless care is taken to see that a comparable temperature is maintained on a par with that temperature which might be as high as 95% for puppies who have no mother and need artificial heat and at least 85% for new born pups. For the poor mother though this can be most uncomfortable. A lot of Yorkshire Terriers get themselves into a state just because they don't like the heat, especially if they aren't used to it. The sensible thing to make her get used to enough heat to keep the pups thriving and constantly warm is to get her used to the unnatural heat gradually so that when the time comes she is able to put up with it without losing her milk or getting into a highly nervous condition.

Although I advocate the use of infra-red lamps it is imperative that great care is taken with them for if they are too near they will scorch the pups and make the mother so uncomfortable that she will leave her litter completely. On the other hand if placed too far away the air directly above the pups will get chilled and so is equally dangerous.

There are excellent but expensive pet beds on the market that have a built-

Fig 6 Whelping table

Served Jan. Whelps March	Served Feb. Whelps April	Served March Whelps May	Served April Whelps June	Served May Whelps July	Served June Whelps Aug.	Served July Whelps Sept.	Served Aug. Whelps Oct.	Served Sept. Whelps Nov.	Served Oct. Whelps Dec.	Served Nov. Whelps Jan.	Served Dec. Whelps Feb.
1 5	1 5	1 3	1 3	1 3	1 3	1 2	1 3	1 3	1 3	1 3	1 2
2 6	2 6	2 4	2 4	2 4	2 4	2 3	2 4	2 4	2 4	2 4	2 3
3 7	3 7	3 5	3 5	3 5	3 5	3 4	3 5	3 5	3 5	3 5	3 4
4 8	4 8	4 6	4 6	4 6	4 6	4 5	4 6	4 6	4 6	4 6	4 5
5 9	5 9	5 7	5 7	5 7	5 7	5 6	5 7	5 7	5 7	5 7	5 6
6 10	6 10	6 8	6 8	6 8	6 8	6 7	6 8	6 8	6 8	6 8	6 7
7 11	7 11	7 9	7 9	7 9	7 9	7 8	7 9	7 9	7 9	7 9	7 8
8 12	8 12	8 10	8 10	8 10	8 10	8 9	8 10	8 10	8 10	8 10	8 9
9 13	9 13	9 11	9 11	9 11	9 11	9 10	9 11	9 11	9 11	9 11	9 10
10 14	10 14	10 12	10 12	10 12	10 12	10 11	10 12	10 12	10 12	10 12	10 11
11 15	12 15	11 13	11 13	11 13	11 13	11 12	11 13	11 13	11 13	11 13	11 12
12 16	13 16	12 14	12 14	12 14	12 14	12 13	12 14	12 14	12 14	12 14	12 13
13 17	14 17	13 15	13 15	13 15	13 15	13 14	13 15	13 15	13 15	13 15	13 14
14 18	15 18	14 16	14 16	14 16	14 16	14 15	14 16	14 16	14 16	14 16	14 15
15 19	16 19	15 17	15 17	15 17	15 17	15 16	15 17	15 17	15 17	15 17	15 16
16 20	17 20	16 18	16 18	16 18	16 18	16 17	16 18	16 18	16 18	16 18	16 17
17 21	18 21	17 19	17 19	17 19	17 19	17 18	17 19	17 19	17 19	17 19	17 18
18 22	19 22	18 20	18 20	18 20	18 20	18 19	18 20	18 20	18 20	18 20	18 19
19 23	20 23	19 21	19 21	19 21	19 21	19 20	19 21	19 21	19 21	19 21	19 20
20 24	21 24	20 22	20 22	20 22	20 22	20 21	20 22	20 22	20 22	20 22	20 21
21 25	22 25	21 23	21 23	21 23	21 23	21 22	21 23	21 23	21 23	21 23	21 22
22 26	23 26	22 24	22 24	22 24	22 24	22 23	22 24	22 24	22 24	22 24	22 23
23 27	24 27	23 25	23 25	23 25	23 25	23 24	23 25	23 25	23 25	23 25	23 24
24 28	25 28	24 26	24 26	24 26	24 26	24 25	24 26	24 26	24 26	24 26	24 25
25 29	26 29	25 27	25 27	25 27	25 27	25 26	25 27	25 27	25 27	25 27	25 26
26 30	27 30	26 28	26 28	26 28	26 28	26 27	26 28	26 28	26 28	26 28	26 27
27 31	28 1	27 29	27 29	27 29	27 29	27 28	27 29	27 29	27 29	27 29	27 28
28 1	29 2	28 30	28 30	28 30	28 30	28 29	28 30	28 30	28 30	28 30	28 1
29 2		29 31	29 1	29 31	29 31	29 30	29 31	29 1	29 31	29 31	29 2
30 3		30 1	30 2	30 1	30 1	30 1	30 1	30 2	30 1	30 1	30 3
31 4		31 2		31 2		31 2	31 2		31 2		31 4

in heating element in the bottom of the bed which has to be plugged into the mains. These are very good and if a piece of 'Vet-Bed' is cut to the same shape as the bed the pups are extremely comfortable on it, and there is no fear of them being lost in the blankets and subsequently smothered. The Vet-Bed (or similar as this is a brand name for quite a variety of porous synthetic fur which is sold by most of the pet supply agents) lets the moisture through so the whelps stay dry as well which is a great and very convenient advantage over the old methods. One other is that the pups are always warm and dry and the surface gives even the most tiny ones plenty of purchase which they don't get from a shiny one.

I still prefer to whelp on masses of newspaper because my little bitches are used to it and get a lot of satisfaction from digging deep into it and consequently these vigorous labour pains are much better for the little mother and she is able to make far more progress than a bitch that hardly digs up at all, who will often go into primary inertia and have to have veterinary help before

Fig 7 Bed for mother and puppies inside the safety of a wire crate. There is room for the mother to lie away from her family.

Fig 8 *right* Whelping box used under infra-red lamp.

she can produce her litter. I get a strong grocer's cardboard box of a suitable size for the bitch and put in a thick wad of newspaper. I place the box on a sheet of very thick plastic, to protect my floor, and between the box and the floor insert a Petnap Pet Bed Heater which, at under £10, will be the best value for money of anything else I can recommend. With a fully tested metal panel of only 10 watts, and a extra strong flex, it uses only about 7p a week to run constantly and there is no chance of a puppy getting chilled and it is never uncomfortable for the mother. My room is a good constant heat but in warm weather the heater is also very useful as it never gets too hot to stand. Vets, pet hospitals, catteries and all the breeders I have spoken to who use it swear by it. I will give the full address. :-

> PETNAP
>   Spinkes Works,
>   Section G2,
>   The Causeway,
>   Chippenham,
>   Wilts.

Give her a box large enough for her to stretch right out in but not so big that she can mislay a puppy. A grocer's thick cardboard box is ideal and the best bedding is newspaper. Put several copies of the *Financial Times* or similar in the box and leave the rest to her. I find a special new piece of blanket put in the box when first introduced to her will make her use it as they love a new bed. About the seventh week carefully clip or trim off all the hair on her tummy so that the puppies won't have to suck hair, not forgetting the teats at the very top near her armpits which often get clogged and very sore if hair is forgotten on them. Go carefully around all her back parts and under her tail so that it is easy to get the puppies born without the hair interfering. Keep these parts washed with plain Windsor soap and water or a very mild Cetavlon solution. A little warm olive oil gently massaged over a very distended tummy will help to ease it and, apart from smearing the vulva generously with Vaseline when the whelping seems imminent there is nothing more can be done for her until labour actually begins.

She should have several short but purposeful walks every day right up until she is due as this will keep her circulation going and her muscles in order. Slack muscles are one of the causes of inertia to which some fat and lazy bitches are very prone. This is often the prime cause of a bitch needing a Caesarean and should be guarded against.

Yorkshire Terriers as a rule are too active to get inertia as the result of slack muscles and they are seldom greedy eaters but the bitches that are house pets or show specimens can play you up no end just like the veritable little prima donnas they are. One of ours goes off her food completely, has morning sickness which can only be helped with helpings of glucose or honey in her saucer. She refuses all food out of her normal dish and has to be finger fed with the tastiest morsels. We call it 'The Chicken and Turbot Syndrome' and my husband is a great big sucker and always falls for it, far more than he ever did for me when I was in a similar 'delicate condition'. Known as Blue Mink (Minkie to my husband) she likes sitting on laps, riding in the car and watching Wimbledon on the TV and in fact she much prefers indoor sports to the more healthy outdoor ones and shirks walking and all the things that will do her good. She insists on jumping up on chairs, which she knows she's not allowed to do, only so she can jump down again. I went to a series of lectures and learned what dreadful things can happen to unborn pups who are jerked

Fig 9 Whelping box with infra-red lamp removed and perspex top in place.

Fig 10 *left* Whelping box with run attached.

about in the womb in this way. Mink is a prime subject for inertia and she gets it nearly every time she whelps. She doesn't make any milk for days after she whelps, she's afraid to miss something so she sits up and her poor puppies can't reach her to pull any milk into them. I spend days trying to squeeze out enough of the first milk to be able to give these miserable little brats the very necessary first milk with all the essential antibodies for their protection and as soon as I can I take the line of least resistance and give them to another bitch to rear and their recalcitrant mother goes back to her usual life of pleasure. The only time she ever brought up a litter of puppies properly was when she got herself mated to a silver toy poodle, after being bred to a Yorkie. At birth all the pups took after their poodle father and were quite odd, but Mink thought they were wonderful, lay flat down for them to reach, ate and drank all the correct things, made lots of milk and fed them all five of them, showing us that she knew what to do when she wanted to.

The day the pups are going to be born the bitch will probably go completely off her food. I say probably, as I have had bitches eat a large, hearty meal and straight afterwards retire to their beds and produce their litter.

Her temperature will drop from the normal 101 ½° to below 100° and she will be very restless, shifting around in her bed and scratching intermittently. If she has to be left on her own place her box in the wire crate, as suggested, and then there will be no chance of her starting to whelp and running round the house with a pup attached, banging its poor little head on the floor and making no end of a mess everywhere.

When labour actually starts she will be madly attacking her bed with tooth and nail and there will be no doubt that something vital is happening. This is the time to leave everything and clear everyone and all other dogs out of the room and sitting patiently and watching. Leave her completely alone but have her box where you can see all that happens. Don't talk to her as it will distract her. She won't mind you being there but she will have forgotten all about you. The more she scratches, digs and bites at her bed the better. This is her labour period and her way of working off the pains. The harder she works the easier will be her delivery. You can best spend this time checking that you have all the necessary equipment you are likely to need. I list as follows:

1. A cardboard box at least 12 inches deep containing either an electric heated pad or hot water bottle at a comfortable heat covered over with a piece of flannel or old woolly jumper, folded over envelope fashion to make a nest for the puppies. Keep this at the ready and at the same temperature so the kettle must always be filled.

2. Scissors and thread for cutting the cords and tying them if necessary.

3. Roll of Cotton Wool.

4. J Cloths made by Johnsons are ideal for whelping as they are soft and thin enough to be able to get a good grip on the 'trying to be born puppy'. They will wash and will stand sterilising with Milton or bleach, unlike paper

towels which are a bit too thick and than disintegrate when wet and work out very expensive.

5. Bottle of Hydrogen Peroxide.

6. A few surgical clamps. These are invaluable if the afterbirth does not come away at once and the cord breaks, as their use will prevent the cord disappearing back into the vagina.

7. Small quantity of Brandy or Whisky for the bitch's use and your own.

8. Thermos flask of coffee or tea at hand for your own use, as she shouldn't now be left while you make it.

9. Portable Radio (the all-night programmes are a real boon), book, knitting or pack of cards in case of a long wait.

10. Clock or watch.

11. Pail with lid for afterbirths and messy bedding.

12. Plenty of fresh newspapers and a fresh cardboard box or bed if the first comes to a sticky end.

13. Pad and pencil to record times of straining and birth of first and subsequent puppies.

Make sure that the fire, stove or other heating is constant and let the bitch wander about as long as you are there to watch her. She will want to go outside to relieve herself and then come in again without doing so. Don't let her out of your sight and make sure she does not actually pass a puppy while crouching.

She will whine and even scream but the time to really drop everything and concentrate completely on her is when her tail starts to stiffen. This is known as 'straining' and careful note should be taken of the time when the first one is noticed. Things could now start to happen quite quickly; she will lick herself and work her bedding into a dreadful mess. If a clear bladder appears at the vulva, this will be the water-bladder. If she can get around to it she will break this with her teeth but don't do it for her. It can stay there for quite some time and is nothing to be alarmed about. A dark, shiny object appearing is the puppy and, if all is well she will expel it in one big heave and by the time you have bent over her she will be busy licking the membrane off the puppy's face and biting the cord off with her teeth. If she just leaves it alone, and remember this is her first litter as well as yours, gently wipe the bag of skin off the nose yourself so that the puppy can start to breathe. Don't cut the cord at this stage but leave her for a short while to make up her own mind what to do. If she is going to be sensible she will eventually start to lick the rest of the membrane and so on to biting the cord herself.

If she accomplishes this satisfactorily this is a big hurdle over for she can be safely left to cope with the others as they come. If however the dark tip of the puppy's nose appears at the vulva but does not pop out when expected, then you must take the cloth and hold on to as much of the puppy as is poking out. Sometimes this is help enough and you can feel the slimy mass come away in your hands. If it doesn't you will have to ease it out gently, keeping the bitch lying on her side and pulling gently towards the bitch's head. Never pull to the back of the bitch as this will strain the cord and probably break it and leave the afterbirth behind. If the puppy appears but the afterbirth is left behind wipe the film off its face and put two clamps on the cord as near as you can to the bitch's body. Cut the cord about two inches from the puppy's tummy and give the pup to the mother to occupy her attention, then back to the clamps. Hold the cord tightly with your cloth and with your other hand holding the bitch's body pull very gently. If she thinks about it in the excitement of giving birth, she will give another strain and, if you can get the afterbirth away with the strain it will be a much cleaner and more efficient operation. Don't forget to remove your clamps before disposing of the mess. These can be obtained at any wholesale chemist. Boots will obtain them for you, and once you have had to use them you will never want to be without them.

The question of whether to burn the afterbirth or let the bitch eat it is a matter for you to decide. Some say it gives her some necessary aid but I have found it more likely makes her sick.

The interval between puppies varies with each bitch. The next puppy may appear before you have finished dealing with the first or may be an hour or two. If the bitch starts to squirm round her bed and seems to be less interested in her first pup, take it away and put it in the bed you have prepared for it. Before doing so take a careful look at it and see that its body is filled out and it is breathing regularly. If it had made straight for a nipple soon after being born and managed to hang on right away there is nothing much wrong with it. If, however it looks a bit flat, is still cold and clammy or is gasping for air you must get busy at once as all is not well. Usually the bashing about the mother gives it when she is beaking the cord and licking him dry is enough to start him breathing well. If not rub him gently all over with a piece of warm towel starting at his tail and working up his back towards his head and then turning him over and rubbing from his stomach to his heart. Pass him quickly from hand to hand in a kind of rolling action and then, with his head firmly held between two fingers swing your arm from over your head in a downward sweep, making sure you don't drop him, and then wipe his nose and mouth free of any mucus that this has dislodged. Hold him by his back feet and let him hang like this for quite a while and it will be found that moisture drops out of his nose and mouth. When this has cleared itself he will start to wriggle his head up and he should then be all right. Check his breathing from time to time and, as long as it is regular and his mouth is closed you can safely leave him in his little warm nest while you attend to his mother.

While my bitches are whelping the pups are taken away while she is actually producing and the pups are kept warm in a tiny box with a Petnap heater under a blanket which is folded like an envelope so that the pups can be popped in there and kept warm and out of harm's way. As they are warm and comfortable they don't need to cry and worry their mother, which is another blessing.

Some breeders use the shredded dog bedding but it is a bit dangerous for Yorkies as being so small a shred can get wound round a pup's throat and strangle it. If paper is shredded by hand (this makes excellent bedding) and torn the way of the grain it will tear very easily and small pieces can be cut too short to do any damage.

Nature always arranges things so well for in the natural state the bitch would dig herself a hole in the ground where she would keep the bed warm with the heat from her own body. They would stay there in the dark until they were old enough to follow their mother outside. That is why you are better off with an infra-red lamp with a dull emitter as a strong light above them keeps them awake when they should be sleeping.

It may take her a couple of hours to produce the second pup in a first litter. My first bitch went from 5 o'clock to midnight and, although I called the vet there was nothing he could do. This taught me not to lose my head again and, unless there is any sign of distress I usually wait as patiently as I know how. When the second one appears leave this with the mother until the third one starts to make his presence felt. The puppies will be quite safe on their hot water bottle as long as you have kept it filled or on their electric pad.

When all the pups have arrived she will start to get anxious about her other ones and will probably start getting out of her box. Try and get her out to relieve herself before putting the puppies back with her. While she is out clean up the bed, put fresh newspaper in and tightly roll up the top sheet before spreading it out. This will allow the puppies' feet to find purchase and not slip all over the crumpled paper when they are feeding.

When the mother returns, feel her tummy carefully in case there is still a puppy left and offer her a warm drink of milk and glucose with a few drops of brandy or whisky. This will help to settle her down and after putting the puppies back with her, shut and bar the wire crate and drape a curtain over most of it so that she can be quite private and help to keep in the warmth that she will generate from her own body. If you are using an infra red heater this is the time to put it in position. Remember a dull emitter is best as it doesn't keep the bitch awake with a strong light as do some infra red lamps. Start the lamp about 3 ft. to 4 ft. over the bitch's bed. Don't leave it until you have been able to test after it has been in this position for half an hour. If uncomfortably hot for your hand held immediately over the bitch raise it a little. If not warm enough lower very carefully as she mustn't be too hot or she will leave her pups to get more comfortable.

It is also a wise precaution to give her a double dose of Collo Cal D two raspberry leaf tablets, S.A 37, and 5 drops of Adexoline. S.A 37 is an excellent product and I have used it successfully since my vet recommended it to me when it first came on the market. The great merit of this product is that it was formulated specifically for small animals — puppies, kittens, mice, hamsters, cage birds and by increasing the doses at times of stress and need every vitamin and mineral that a dog can possibly require is included in its formula. I give them S.A. 37 whenever puppies need extra sustaining at the time they are growing the fastest, when they are cutting teeth and when they are recovering from worming etc. The Adexolin is an extra protection for the Vit. D to act on the calcium in the blood and prevent eclampsia. If you have been unfortunate to have had a pup with a cleft palate or any other serious deformity it should really be taken away before this. If it is your first litter, however, leave things as they are. They won't hurt until later and you can ask your vet to cope with things, as this, to my mind, is the worst part of breeding. In all my years of breeding I have never been able to bring myself to put anything down and I cannot honestly advise anyone else how to do it.

The above has been written with the expectation that the whelping will have been fairly normal. If all is not quite as straightforward, however, it is just as well to have some idea of what can happen. Whenever I have found myself with a problem at this time and have run to my dog books for guidance it is most frustrating to find that nobody ever seems to have any sort of troubles like mine, and there is no information to help me. Over the years, one way and another, I expect I have experienced most of the trials and tribulations of breeding dogs but it is still surprising how many new problems there are still to be faced. Here are some of the ones to be met with, placed under headings and in alphabetical order, for easy reference:

AFTERBIRTH: This is a soft mass of horrid looking goo that arrives attached to the other end of the cord from the puppy. Its technical name is 'the Placenta' and it is really very important as it has held the puppy to the wall of the uterus with blood vessels passing from the placenta into the body of the embryonic pup through the navel. Through these blood vessels in the cord the unborn pup receives its life-blood.

Although the mother receives definite nourishment from eating the placentas and in the wild these would need to sustain her until she can again forage for her own food, in these days of care and attention the bitch is more likely to vomit or have diarrhoea. As some schools of thought maintain that eating the placenta and bag acts as stimulation to the uterine contractions let her eat one — preferably the first one and take the others away.

It is most important that the afterbirths are counted carefully. Make sure there is one for every pup. If they can't all be accounted for get your vet at the latest within 24 hours to give an injection to get rid of one that may be retained. A bitch should be examined after whelping and, if a lump like a puppy can still be felt through the wall of the stomach and it is not thought that she still has a pup to be born, seek advice as soon as possible.

ANAESTHETIC: Most of the present day anaesthetics are very safe or, at least as safe as such things can be. A bitch near whelping who has not eaten for some hours is a good subject. Never give an anaesthetic to a toy bitch if she has been injected with Ergot or Pituitrin which is often given for uterine inertia or to speed things up. The contractions caused are often so violent that they put a serious strain on the heart and then the bitch is at a great disadvantage if she later has to be Caesared. Don't let a vet tell you that these injections are harmless and do not cause pain. I know better than any vet that the agony they cause is terrible as I have been given the stuff myself. My doctor explained that it is very difficult to get the dose down small enough for a human being and the dose they have to give is large enough for an elephant. What price our little Yorkie bitches!

I.C.I. have put on the market Fluothane which has been found efficient.

ARTIFICIAL RESPIRATION: This paragraph only applies to apparently still-born and very weak puppies just after birth. After clearing the nose and mouth of any mucous and getting the breathing to start, hold the puppy in the palm of one hand and with the fingers bent clap the palms almost together with the puppy's ribcage in between. The presses should be about 20 to the minute. The fingers and thumb pressed on the lowest rib and pressed in about half way is another method but rather tiring if kept up for an hour or so which it takes to get the breathing really starting. Never leave a puppy with 'the gapes' to try and recover by himself — he may not.

BRANDY: A most useful stimulant and reviver. Give at the rate of one teaspoonful of brandy (or whisky) to two teaspoonfuls of hot water with ½ teaspoonful of glucose. Sips of this can be given during a protracted whelping and if the finger is dipped in it and then placed on a limp puppy's tongue it is often possible to get them willing to live.

BREECH BIRTH: When the puppies are born feet first instead of the normal way of head first. A large percentage of Yorkie puppies are born without any trouble but, if they don't come within five minutes help must be given. If feet are seen to be sticking out of the vulva they must be held on to at all costs. No pulling need be necessary but, if they stay just an inch or so in sight for five minutes grasp them both firmly with a piece of thin rag. First you must push upwards in case the head or shoulders are wedged or in case the forelegs are caught in the passage over the head. Make sure you have plenty of Vaseline as thick as possible round and just inside the vulva and then pull down between the legs. If the body comes away but stops at the shoulders change your grip and grasp the body firmly in the palm of your hand, get your finger and thumb on top of the shoulders, if possible, or anyway as far up as you can, then pull down as hard as you can, always pulling towards the bitch's stomach and not behind her as this will surely overstretch the neck and possibly cripple the bitch. If you can only get a little away at a time don't give up but keep changing your grasp and move higher up the body. You can't afford to wait for the bitch to contract properly as all the time part of the pup is exposed to the air it could start its breathing going and then its lungs could fill with moisture and its chance of survival be very poor. You will probably be surprised at the sudden force with which the puppy will suddenly arrive and you will have to act very quickly. Wipe away the membrane yourself, if it hasn't already been broken. Give the placenta to the bitch to keep her occupied and rub the pup with a rough towel all over being careful not to damage the skin on its face which doesn't need rubbing anyhow. Rub the back from the tail to the head and the chest towards the heart. Throw it from hand to hand, hold it tightly in your hand and swing your arm up over your head and down several times.

Hold the pup by its back feet and let it hang upside down for several minutes. If the mucus falls out this way the pup will soon bend up of its own free will and your battle is won.

For limp or still-born pups see 'Resuscitation'.

CAESARIAN SECTION: If the bitch goes into second stage of labour and stays for over two hours straining without result the vet should be consulted and he will know if a Caesarian is necessary. If it is, the sooner it is performed the better for the quick recovery of the bitch and the chance of a live birth. In these enlightened days many women avail themselves of this operation to save themselves the discomfort of getting into proper labour. Many are known to have had five or six births quite successfully with no after-effects. The same should apply to bitches and I would always prefer a tiny bitch to be Caesared than to let her struggle to produce pups if she is not cut out for easy whelping.

The operation consists of the removal of the pups through an incision in the wall of the abdomen. The horns or 'arms' of the womb will have to be cut into also to get the pups out of them. Sometimes two pups try to get born together and so get stuck in the horn and in this case a Caesar is very necessary.

CLEFT-PALATE: Puppies should be examined for this at birth. Open the mouth and take a look at the roof. If there is a gap this is a 'cleft' and will inter-fere with the sucking action. It has been known for an operation to be per-formed to close this gap but in the only case I knew of, the pup lived only a short time. A hare lip is an even worse deformity and will be very obvious and is seen as a gash or two in the lips. The vet should be asked to confirm your suspicions, in case you make a mistake, and he should take them away. Although born fat and husky they soon start to whimper and whine because they can get no milk and will drive their mother mad.

CORD CUT TOO SHORT: If the bitch is too vigorous at the birth she often breaks the cord close to the puppy's body. Tie tightly with white cotton. If you cut the thread closely she will not notice it. At all costs you must prevent the hole from bleeding as a toy sized puppy will quickly die from loss of blood. To heal quickly and stop the bleeding if cut too close to the body to tie, dab with neat Hydrogen Peroxide, or Gentian Violet, or Friars Balsam, or Iodine.

DISCHARGE: It is normal for the bitch to discharge blood for some time after she whelps. As soon as this reaches the air it turns green which, although alarming to see, is not harmful. If, however there is a bad smell from the discharge consult the vet at once.

ECLAMPSIA: This is also known as Milk Tetany. The bitch is most likely to have this within the first three weeks but it needs to be watched for. Symptoms are rapid breathing, restlessness, panting, crying and when walking she will be seen to stagger and tremble. Later if help is not quick in coming she will go into convulsions — known as an eclamptic fit. Get the vet immediately as death is imminent. Give Collo Cal D as suggested previously and continue through lactation. Prevention is better than cure in this case. Inject calcium gluconate.

If your bitch gets eclampsia take the puppies away altogether. They will have to either be given to a foster mother or you will have to rear them by hand. (See hand feeding orphan puppies page 149.)

MASTITIS OR INFLAMMATION OF THE MILK GLANDS: If the bitch has a small litter she will probably make far more milk than they need. For the first few days, until things get properly balanced it is better to restrict her intake of food and especially fluids in order not to put any extra strain on her. You may find her with hard, hot, congested breasts that make it impossible for the pups to break down and get any milk from and so they could die in the midst of plenty.

Rub the udder with warm olive oil or butter and squeeze out just enough milk to relieve the congestion a bit. Remember that the more milk comes out the more her body will make, so great care is needed. Give a sedative but do not allow your vet to give a hormone injection or thyroid tablets as these could upset her bodily functions later on.

Give a tablespoonful of honey-water morning and night and do not leave any drinking water down. If her mouth feels dry wipe it over every hour or so with wet cotton wool. Give two teaspoonfuls of Milk of Magnesia and watch her temperature carefully. At the sign of any alarming increase in temperature your vet will give antibiotics; it may be days before she can give her puppies much attention.

Her nipples should be examined every day in case one of them gets caked with dry milk. Watch the 'blind ones' too.

LACK OF MILK: This is a rare condition but one I have met with once when the bitch although quite willing to mother her litter made absolutely no milk for a month and then, when the litter had been hand-reared for all that time and were then being weaned on to raw meat she suddenly produced milk in abundance. This bitch had whelped once before and made plenty of milk and reared her litter quite successfully.

For a poor supply of milk or to encourage a bitch with a big litter to get more milk give cotton seed cake. 'Lactogen' is the trade name and it has remarkable results.

METRITIS OR PYMETRIA: Inflammation of the womb. Suspect if temperature remains very high. Prompt attention from the vet can usually avert tragedy but if neglected may need complete removal of the womb, otherwise known as a hysterectomy. Strict attention to disinfecting and sterilising and spotlessly clean conditions for the little mother at all times are required. My answer to this problem is 'Cetavlon' manufactured by I.C.I. and the best and safest germicide I have ever used. A small bottle diluted to the correct proportions goes a very long way.

After whelping is completed and the bitch has been outside to relieve herself wash her back parts with a very mild solution of TCP or Cetavlon and wash her tummy over with white Windsor soap. Rinse and dry well before returning to her nest.

Her daily management will mean that she must be lifted out from her puppies at regular intervals every day, and put outside, as she is unlikely to leave them of her own accord for the first few weeks. She will want feeding in her bed, and as soon as her milk supply has settled down see that she has a plentiful supply of water at all times. If she is in a crate a water container that hooks on to the wire is an excellent one. A parrot's plastic drinking bowl hooks on and holds a day's supply of water.

No visitors should be allowed to bother the little mother for several days and then even the most immediate family must be introduced gradually and, if she appears upset by the visit, keep everybody away as long as possible.

Care of puppies in the nest

At three to five days the puppies will need their tails docked and their dew claws removed. As the puppies don't have real bone at this time, only a jelly-like substance like cartilage, this is not such a painful operation as it sounds and if done expertly the puppies rarely make a sound. Left to the second week, however, their cries will be loud and clear, so get them done as quickly as possible or learn to do them yourself.

I know breeders who do them as soon as they are born but, with such tiny pups, it is very difficult to see what you are doing especially with dew claws, and often they hardly show at all on the back legs to begin with.

These dew claws are rudimentary 'thumbs' and useless for walking, but no doubt of great assistance if the dogs had to climb trees! They are nothing but a nuisance, however, and it is essential that they be removed as they catch in grass, get wound round the leg, if neglected in later life, and have been known to grow right into the flesh of the leg, causing great agony. Don't use the docking scissors for this operation on a toy puppy as it is far too clumsy and not sharp enough. Curved nail scissors will be much more efficient.

Hold the pup on its back on the palm of your hand and hold the foot in your finger and thumb. Cutting from underneath, go into the leg a fraction to remove the root completely or they are liable to grow again. Press into a little pile of powdered permanganate of potash and hold it there quite firmly for a few seconds, pressing quite hard. This will seal up the cut and prevent any loss of blood. If the mother licks it, even though her tongue may turn quite black, it will do no harm. Not all Yorkies have dew claws on their hind legs but, if they do, remove them in the same way. Sometimes they will just look like an extra toe and sometimes be quite high on the leg. They must be removed completely. Make a note of the pups with these hind-dew claws as some European countries will not accept breeding stock with even a scar left from this operation. They look on these dew claws on the hind legs as a physical deformity and are not allowed to breed from them. Holland and Italy are very particular in this respect.

Much controversy appears in the dog press from time to time as to the cruelty of docking tails. It is compared with the fact that the R.S.P.C.A. has abolished docking in horses and therefore something similar should be done about docking puppies. Anyone who has watched or even read about the way horses are docked will soon realise that the operation on pups is a very mild affair especially sealing up the wound with permanganate of potash or friars' balsam. Horses are cauterised with a red-hot iron.

While it is readily admitted that most of the breeds docked would look quite awful with long tails — imagine the smart fox terriers and the poodles undocked — the method of cutting off the blood supply with a tight rubber band is advocated as being far more humane. Who is it supposed to be far more humane for, the dogs or the people who are afraid of using the scissors or of spending the extra money to have it done by the vet? This method is very, very dangerous and not in the least humane for the poor pup. A quick cut of the jelly-like substance and one small cry and in two minutes the pup is sucking its mother or snuggling down with its litter mates and all forgotten. The rubber band method takes weeks to mortify the flesh and sometimes turns septic or gangrenous into the bargain. I have seen two litters ruined by this method. One a litter of boxers where gangrene set in and the vet had to cut behind it so that there were no tails left. Each one had to have three or four stitches, the pups cried day and night in agony and in the end the tails fell off at the root. A litter ruined for show or even for sale as they were later sold for a nominal price just to cover expenses. The other was a litter of poodles and these didn't get gangrenous first but fell off at the root.

The advocates of this 'painless' method do not tell us how to take the dew claws off with the same technique, so if scissors have to be used for these far better to use them on the tail also. I have done hundreds of puppies' tails and, while I can't pretend to enjoy the job, I still prefer to do it myself than to have to stand and watch someone else do it. Also I can be sure that it is being cut in the proper place as this is essential for a correct dock. Wrongly done and a good show pup may be ruined for the ring.

Under the tail of the Yorkie pup will be found a patch of tan marking and the tail should be shortened to this mark. Tie a piece of strong white thread quite tightly at this place. Get someone to hold the pup or place it on the table. With a pair of sterilised surgical scissors (curved ones are better and use the curve on top), cut the tail from behind just under the thread. If the tail is cut from in front it will encourage it to grow too gay as this will shorten the tendons on the wrong side for correct tail carriage in the Yorkie. Promptly press the cut end in permanganate of potash crystals, very firmly for a few seconds. This will seal in any blood and assist healing. It will be found necessary to crush the crystals well before starting. Use a thick newspaper. Pour the crystals on the paper, fold the paper over and roll hard with a rolling-pin. Keep moving the crystals and crushing until they are very fine. Coarse crystals drop off and let the blood through.

Make sure the mother is well away from her pups while all this is going on or she will be very worried. When she returns she will fuss and prod them as she will know something has been going on. When she finds that the pups are sleeping quite peacefully she will settle down quickly.

Take the opportunity of cutting the sharp little nails at this time as they tear the mother's under-carriage to pieces in no time. Use the small nail scissors and cut to the hook. An easy way to avoid cutting below the quick is to place the scissor blades at the root of the nail, run them up towards the tip and, when they stop of their own accord at the curve, cut.

This nail cutting should be done at least once a week while the pups are suckling and at least every month throughout the dog's life if it doesn't wear them down of its own accord. Regular cutting will avoid the fuss that they make if they only have them done occasionally. Too long nails will interfere with correct movement besides being very painful.

Puppies are born blind and find their way by smell. By the end of the second week if the eyes haven't opened of their own accord make sure they are not stuck up with matter. Swab them with cotton wool dipped in warm water and they should be all right. If matter is found there two days running it is a sign that all is not well and there may be an infection.

Penbritin is an excellent antibiotic for very tiny toy puppies and does away with many of the causes of 'fading out of puppies'. It must be given for the full course of five days as otherwise a definite level of the drug won't be maintained in the bloodstream to complete the treatment.

This drug will be found useful for bowel infection, kidney infection (recognised by a milky appearance to the urine), snuffles and any respiratory troubles that might arise.

If the stools of the pups appear to be greenish and curdled, suspect acid milk. Test for this with litmus paper (too acid will turn blue paper red). If it remains mauvish don't worry. Dose the bitch with magnesia at the rate of one teaspoonful per day and then half every other day over a week. Take care with her diet and make sure her temperature is normal. A pinch of bicarbonate of soda in her drinking water will counteract this tendency.

Cut the side of the box down to a couple of inches and line the remainder of the crate with newspaper and it will be seen that the pups will clamber over the side and relieve themselves on the paper there, thus keeping their sleeping quarters clean. This is the first manifestation of that instinct for cleanliness in the sleeping area inherent in all dogs and the wise breeder will give puppies every opportunity to express it. A pup that is ready to crawl out of his bed at three weeks of age can soon be persuaded to use paper in any suitable place and from that a good basis for clean house manners is laid down right from the start.

At about three to four weeks the teeth begin to appear and it is quite understandable if the mother begins to find her feeding duties arduous. Even before they break through the skin these teeth can hurt quite a lot, as you will find if you put your finger in their mouths.

One of the first signs that she has begun to feel her pups should have supplementary feeding is the fact that she will vomit her own food into the bed to feed her young. This is known as 'regurgitating' and all good dams do this. Make sure that she gets another feed and is kept away from her pups for some time, otherwise she will starve herself for them. The pups can be safely left to eat this as she will have partly digested it for them. If weaning hasn't been started before this, now is the time to begin as this is Nature's way of saying so.

After-care of the brood bitch

Before returning a brood bitch to her own kennel she must be very thoroughly dosed for worms. The vermifuge I recommend is an 'expellor' not a 'vermacide' which is a 'killer'. The reason for this is that in a tiny system the vermacide could be too drastic in action as a 'killer' drug must be used. There is a danger too that the worms can die and not be expelled but remain in the intestines, blocking them and causing terrible colic pain and death. Unless promptly dosed with liquid paraffin they will be in great trouble.

In dosing an adult Yorkshire Terrier therefore it must be borne in mind that this can happen and, although a worm killer would seem to be the sensible answer, thought should be given to the condition of the bitch.

As worm eggs can live for a long time in any suitable temperature, it is essential that great care is taken to destroy not only the worms but any eggs that could possibly be passed by the bitch. Make sure that she is shut up in a concrete run or kennel entirely away from all other dogs. Dose her early in the day so she can be watched and everything she passes burnt at once. As puppies usually get round worms we will deal only with these in this instance.

Fig 11 Types of worm

Wash her mouth, feet, underneath and back parts with a strong solution of salt and water and scrub the kennel or run with a solution made up of 1 ½ lbs. salt to one gallon of boiling water. Any kennel she has used and her eating and drinking utensils should be treated as well.

Naturally you will have burnt any worms that you saw the puppies pass but she is sure to have eaten some and certainly would have licked the eggs off the pups during her cleaning-up operations, so she will almost sure to be affected. The life cycle of the round worm from the egg is only a matter of days. The female lays simply thousands of eggs and these are passed out in the motion of any infected dog so that it is very easy for dogs, with their habits of sniffing, to take these eggs into their own bodies. The eggs very quickly hatch into tiny worms and, not content with remaining in the stomach or intestines, they break their way into the blood vessels and soon arrive at the heart, liver and lungs. If they crawl up the windpipe they get swallowed down into the stomach again and soon are producing eggs by the thousand. For this reason a second good dosing a week to ten days after the first and the same care and attention with the boiling hot salt water is most necessary.

Puppies and, in fact, all dogs badly infected with worms have dull staring coats, weepy eyes, bony bodies and will look generally unthrifty. It doesn't always follow, however, for I have found lovely fat, firm little pups with sleek, shiny coats who seem to be thriving splendidly but on dosing are found to be 'loaded' with worms.

While round worms are the usual worms found in puppies any adult can get tapeworms and these are very difficult to kill completely because they can be yards long, but the head, which sticks well into the wall of the dog's inside, is smaller than a pin-head and so very difficult to eradicate. The medicines for this kind of worm are very drastic and should only be administered to a toy dog under veterinary supervision. The action is to dissolve the worm and expel it. If the head comes away all is well, but if it doesn't the worm will grow again. Symptoms of tapeworm are hard, dry segments found around the anus and sometimes a wriggling flat white thing is seen in the back-passage. This will only be a segment, however, and the dog will keep passing them. It will cause him to drag his rear on the ground in an effort to rub them off.

Hookworms are another parasite and quite as dangerous as round worms as they are also called 'heart worms'. Unless you bring dogs from the American continent, however, you are unlikely to be troubled with these, but they are very prevalent over there.

Never return a brood bitch to her own kennel without examining her thoroughly to make sure that her milk supply has dried up and she has no hard places or caked teats to trouble her.

If milk is still present and all her pups have been sold, rub her over with camphorated oil, remove water bowl and feed a very little honey and water. Dose for three mornings with enough Epsom salts to cover a sixpence or a dime. If this does not work consult your vet.

You will find that the pups have played havoc with her coat and the best way to cope is to cut it off short, give it a good oiling on the tips and then a conditioning bath. Give her a double dose of seaweed-meal or seaweed tablets, and boil some linseed meal in her food.

Keep up the Collo Cal D or S.A.37 for a month after she has left a litter and then any deficiency she will have after lactation will be compensated.

Orphan puppies

Perhaps the biggest tragedy that can befall a breeder is to lose her bitch during whelping, or while she is feeding her young. If there is a reasonably sized litter to cope with there is, luckily, little time for self-condemnation about mating the bitch, etc. Every minute of your days and nights for many weeks to come are going to be fully occupied and in between times you will be too tired to think. This will determine the more sensible reader to make sure he has a fostermother to call on in case of such an event. Most bitches will take orphan puppies if they are rubbed over with her own milk before being put with her and allowed to lie with her own pups for a while during her absence.

If no foster is available, however, no time must be lost in working out a routine and getting down immediately to rearing the litter by hand.

As I have successfully accomplished this a good many times I feel I can best give the methods I used. Other people may have found different ones successful also, but I write here of my personal experience.

The first thing to be decided is the time schedule. As the pups need feeding every two hours it is a great help if another member of the household can take on two consecutive feeds otherwise you will feel very tattered by the end of a month. My helper and I work it so that I stay up and give the two o'clock feed, then retire till eight. She gets up at four and six. After a few days we change round. The formula we have hit on after much trial and error is one that does not seem to upset tiny tummies or distend them but keeps them content for the two hours. Some feeds filled them up to bursting point but they were hungry again in less than an hour. We found that hourly feeding although sometimes necessary with a very weak puppy was not nearly so successful as two-hourly. We considered a feed successful when the pups seemed replete and slept soundly without whimpering and their bodies remained firm and well-covered. The more evenly covered the body the more successful we thought we were being.

It is very important that regular intervals are maintained between feeds so we feed on the hour exactly. As it takes about twenty-five minutes to complete the mealtime routine we started with the smallest first and the biggest last. After a couple of weeks our approach would be heralded by great excitement from our orphaned babies and the fact that they would look on us as mother figures was very gratifying.

Everything needed for the whole routine should be kept on a tray, to avoid delay. Once they knew we were getting ready to feed them the noise would be deafening and hard luck at night on light sleepers.

The feeding method is one I am quite proud of as it overcomes most of the difficulties we found with feeding bottles — even the kitten bottle which at one time we used with difficulty.

The feeder is illustrated in Figure 12. It comprises a long dropper-like tube with a valve on one end and a tiny teat on the other. The tube holds one teaspoonful of liquid and has a half-way line.

The advantages of this over feeding bottles and droppers is that the pup has to suck the food out. The valve is not depressed but regulates the flow. It can be squeezed to clear the teat if it gets clogged and used to clean the tube. After each feed and sometimes before if the pup has been slow the food can be emptied quickly and a fresh supply drawn in. This avoids the colic that they can get from taking food too cold and it is so much simpler to see how much has been taken, so no danger of overfeeding. With the bottle method it is very difficult to see just how much food a pup has taken and feeding has to stop all the time to check. It soon gets cold and all has to be emptied out to warm up and the whole process started again.

The formula used is as follows: Sherley's Lactol, Virol, Glucodin, Welpie.

Mix the Lactol according to the instructions on the tin and the number of pups you are feeding. Allow a bit extra for wastage. Use an eggcup to start with and afterwards I found a teacup without a handle went into a slop basin of hot water to keep warm. It is important that the eggcup should be in a cup of hot water and the cup in the basin and the water should not be allowed to get cold.

Into the Lactol mix one teaspoonful of glucose to one tablespoonful of Lactol and half a teaspoonful of Virol mixed with the hot water before the Lactol is mixed.

It may take some time to get the puppies sucking properly but if a tiny drop is placed on the tip of the tongue they will generally be willing to swallow it. It is better to wait for them to decide to suck than to squeeze the liquid in. Open the mouth by pressing gently on the cheek-bones. If this doesn't work open the jaws and place the teat between them. Then wait.

Never hold the head back but always slightly forward.

It will help to keep them a bit cleaner if a paper hanky is wrapped round their necks before starting to feed. In any case you will have to give them a good wash all round their mouths and down their necks when you have finished. If you have a motherly old bitch she might do the cleaning up for you, but, in any case, do all the feeding first and the cleaning up last. While washing the face you must wash the organs and massage them enough to urinate and use their bowels. This must be done before they are put down. A bitch can be a god-send here but if it is your first litter you won't be able to call on one.

If the pups are very weak when you start to feed them the first few feeds can be two parts water to one of brandy and half a teaspoonful of glucose.

Very weak pups can also be kept alive by licking honey, Virol or Nestlé's milk off the finger. These thicker substances are safer than the milky liquids where there is danger they will get down the windpipe as this will cause pneumonia.

Few achievements have ever given the satisfaction of seeing a healthy litter of pups ready weaned and ready to face the world and know that you have made it possible. Still it is a satisfaction that most people can well do without.

Don't be in too much of a hurry to put new born orphan pups on milk. A few days of glucose and water until the tiny digestion is ready and able to cope with milk. The stools will show when this is so.

11 Rearing the Yorkie Puppy

ONCE the puppies are docked and their dew claws removed there is not a lot that need be done for them as long as they have clean bedding and the mother has regular care and attention. She will do all that is necessary as far as cleaning them and pushing them around to keep their circulation going. The licking she gives them stimulates their bodily functions and she licks everything up.

At this time she should be allowed outside about six times a day and her food should be highly nutritious without containing too much stodge as she will not be using much energy or need to keep herself warm as she should be kept in an atmosphere 65°–70°F. Carbohydrates are not much value in these conditions but food high in protein and plenty of milk and raw meat are very necessary. Contrary to many breeders' advice goats' milk is not of more value than cows' milk in dog feeding. Its Vitamin D content is very low and children who have been fed only goats' milk became rickety, but became normal again when cows' milk was given.

At about four weeks of age the puppies, whose eyes will have opened at the end of the second week, will be moving around their bed and will start to investigate the dish containing their mother's food. Some of them will take a lick and, if they are not getting as much food from their dam as they can take, they will make quite a meal. It is important that her food should be such that it is small enough or liquid enough for the puppies to be able to cope with it. This is the first sign that the pups are beginning to be ready for weaning and their own food can now be introduced.

Before starting to wean, however, it is important to dose the puppies for worms. This is better done while they are still completely with their dam as they are bound to go back a bit when new food is introduced and this is not the best time to dose them. The mother will lick up the worms they pass, unless you are very quick, but this is better than leaving the tiny mites to cope with the worms in their insides. All pups seem to have worms and the sooner they are expelled the better.

Dose as soon as possible after the third week and give a second dose ten days later when the dose should be increased.

There are quite a few satisfactory substances on the market for this purpose.

For many years I have had safe and very satisfactory results with Coopane, which is Piperazine as are most of the present-day remedies put out by such well-known firms as Bob Martin and Sherleys, etc.

The advantage of using the modern drugs over the old-fashioned Ruby and oil of chenapodium mixtures is that the pup doesn't have to be fasted for twenty-four hours before dosing, but rather fed normally and dosed right after a meal. This is a far kinder and safer method, and I have never lost a pup through worming with it although in the past I had many very bad cases of colic in toy puppies with the oils. The tablets have a wide margin of safety and as long as the puppy is weighed carefully and dosed according to its weight all should be well. The tablets are one for each ten pound of body weight; one-quarter for a 2 ½ lb puppy. I have dosed quite sickly looking pups this way if I have suspected worms were holding them back, and results have been amazing.

Yorkie pups need highly nutritious feeding and it is bad economics to feed such expensive food to the worms.

Weaning

Having got over this very great hurdle in the life of so small and helpless a little creature, it is time to start introducing the first items of the diet that must be given for at least the next three months. For the first going off, introduce a little scraped beef and let the puppy lick it off your finger. This is more sustaining than milk mixtures and after a good feed of meat take the mother away for an hour or two. This will give her a rest and the chance to get some of the much-needed exercise that she has been missing for so many weeks. The best time is the 2 p.m. feed and it can be kept at this time every day and she can have her afternoons off for the rest of her time of duty. When she returns at about four she will then give them a good feed to start off with but as her supply diminishes they will take a milk feed at that time and then can be left until 10 p.m. when they can take another meat feed to see them through the night.

When puppies are still sleeping with the dam I find that they are less willing to take breakfast than any other meal, probably because they have been able to get all they wanted from her during the night.

These feeds can be introduced gradually with a few days' interval between so that the pups can get used to the new food gradually. If the bitch's milk seems to be drying up, of course, hurry things on until at the end of the week they are taking four feeds as well as any milk the mother still has available.

Cows' milk, although excellent for calves, is not nourishing enough for puppies and, as goats' milk isn't the answer either, it is better to fall back on one of the excellent substitutes for bitch's milk now being marketed. In this age of science we can be thankful that our dogs have not been forgotten and, by using these very carefully formulated products, know that we are giving the puppies the essentials that they need.

We must bear in mind that the size of the Yorkie puppy's stomach is so small that it would be impossible to give enough cows' milk to nourish the pup properly without blowing it out alarmingly. This is one of the main causes of the pot-bellied youngster so often met with in kennels where there is no real understanding of the correct way to feed toy-sized puppies.

It is necessary, therefore, that even his milk food should be fortified to make sure that no necessary vitamins are being overlooked. The main advantage of cows' milk is that it is fresh daily and so many vitamins lose their value if stored for any length of time or do not withstand the great heat necessary to dry them into powder form. While many of the synthetic vitamins are better than nothing, it is much better for the dog if as many as possible are fed in with the food we give. This is especially so with any toy breed where a 4 lb dog needs ½ oz. per lb. of bodyweight daily. This means 4 oz. only for an adult dog. I know people who can't envisage such a small amount of food being any good for anything and the dog will be given three times as much, to his great detriment, alas.

Any growing creature needs far more nourishment than an adult, so we can safely feed our pups quite a lot more than they will need when fully grown. Any milk mixture that has been stored in a tin may be lacking in Vitamin D and, although the pups will have received adequate supplies of this with their mother's milk, it is essential that they should get sufficient to convert the calcium in the milk in such a way to prevent them getting rickets.

It is true that too much can actually cause rickets so care must be taken. It is also true that if not enough Vitamin D is present to convert the calcium in the body to do its proper function, it will be expelled without doing any good at all, as it only remains in the body for a limited time.

Many breeders give cod liver oil and think that they have given their pups all the vitamins necessary. Others give halibut oil and feel the same, especially as this is more expensive. The truth is that neither on their own are adequate at all. Dogs need a mixture of both to derive what they actually need. Always remember that all vitamin oils lose their vitamin quality if over-exposed to light. Only very small quantities should be bought for small dogs like Yorkies unless you have a large kennel with many dogs to dose.

Vitamin A is essential for bone and muscle growth in young puppies and is helpful in resisting disease.

Vitamin E is also essential for all breeding stock both male and female and can be found in wheat-germ meal or oil. It has been proved that it keeps better and is more easily assimilated in the meal. It is not so necessary to include this in a baby puppy's diet unless the meat fed is going to be horseflesh. As this meat is lacking in Vitamin E breeding troubles may be met with in later life if the diet is completely lacking. The Yorkie needs extra Vitamin E as it has been found to be particularly useful in growing coats and in giving them extra good condition.

Vitamin B is called a complex vitamin as there are Vitamin B1, B2, B6 and

B12 included. The dog's organs take their normal requirements and expel any surplus and, as most of the foods that can be offered to a dog are rich in most of these vitamins, it is possible that the daily food ration will contain all the essentials. If more are needed, then Vitamin B1 or Thiamin is found in Brewer's Yeast and this can be safely added to a daily diet. One tablet of dried yeast for 4 lb. bodyweight. Any more is wasted. Lack of this vitamin can cause disturbances in the nervous system and it aids growth and muscular energy and is useful for bitches under stress.

Vitamin B2 or Riboflavin is found in most foods especially liver, kidneys, eggs and milk products, the whey of sour milk and in cheese. It deteriorates if exposed to the light and, if puppies are poor doers, prone to diarrhoea and liver disorders, they are often lacking in Vitamin B2. Serious deficiency causes dry, scurfy skin, hair becomes dry and brittle, liable to fall out, and bare patches appear, especially round the eyes and mouth.

Nicotinic Acid is another factor of the B complex and dogs fed almost entirely on cereals often suffer from a condition similar to pellagra in humans. Introducing sufficient amounts of lean meat soon remedies this.

Vitamin B6, otherwise Pyridoxine, is essential for renewing the blood supply and nervous system for ensuring normal growth in young puppies. Any shortage is shown in loss of weight, stunted growth, anaemia and convulsions.

Vitamin B12 is probably the most important of all the B Complex in the feeding of young puppies as it is the essential factor for increasing growth. A regular dosage can have a miraculous affect on growth and is often added to a large dose of iron and given as an injection. In certain cases it has made all the difference between life and death to fading pups.

Folic Acid, Inositol, Pantothenic Acid all belong to this group and are needed for the prevention of blood, skin and hair deficiencies.

Vitamin C is said to be manufactured in the dog's own body so that adding fruit and vegetables to include this vitamin is unnecessary. Most fruits and vegetables are rich in iron, however. Extra Vitamin C should always be given daily in cases of broken bones or any slow healing condition.

Phosphorous is as important to the dog as calcium. It is essential for maximum bone calcification and the utilisation of Vitamin D.

Other minerals necessary are salt, sodium chloride, potassium, and the dog also needs such trace elements as iodine, iron, copper, cobalt, manganese, magnesium and zinc.

It is important that a diet be formulated to include all the above in the daily intake. Some of them, like salt, can be stored in the liver for about a month but calcium needs to be renewed every twenty-four hours in times of stress and for normal growth in the young. Dogs do not approve of salt in their diet but a small amount does no harm and seems to be easily disposed of in the urine. If a tiny pinch of iodised salt is added instead this takes care of the Iodine requirement which is miniscule.

Iron is very essential and any lack leads to anaemia, a regular killer of infant puppies. Meats such as tripe, udder and slaughter-house waste are short of this vital mineral so also is milk. Raw liver, kidney and heart are rich sources and should be fed daily. It has been discovered that a new-born puppy's liver contains enough iron to supply the little body until it leaves its mother. Afterwards it must be fed some daily to maintain good health. For iron to be properly absorbed a minute trace of copper is needed but, as this is present in good meat, it should present no difficulty. Lack of copper can sometimes be detected in the brown stains found on the underneath of white coated dogs from the urine and round the lips from the saliva.

A magnesium deficiency can cause eclampsia and hyper-acidity but this element is rarely missing in a well-balanced diet and, if carbon is added any acidity is overcome. Charcoal is a useful preventive.

It is a concrete fact that a dog's main diet is meat and the better the meat the better fed the dog. For instance, a dog fed on the well-muscled rump of a bullock would be much better fed than one that was only fed on the tripe, as this is of very inferior quality. Meat's chief property is protein, which is made up largely of amino acids. There are twenty-two of these and at least ten are needed to be added to the dog's daily diet and the others are formulated in the dog's own body. Various meats are excellent sources of amino acids and while the protein found in muscle meat is better than that in tripe, liver and kidneys and other glandular tissues have an even higher value.

Milk contains a particularly high class of protein but, unfortunately its good qualities are destroyed by excessive heat.

Eggs are of high value and the yolk contains more amino acids and protein goodness than the whites.

A dog's body is not designed to deal with large amounts of bulky, fibrous foods and, as these are mostly carbohydrate in nature, they are not as essential to a dog's body as protein.

Yorkshire Terriers, with their tiny stomachs need more protein than bigger dogs, i.e., working dogs and sporting dogs who can use more carbohydrate food for energy and body-heat. Too much bulky food makes a toy dog fat and unhealthy and it can really be suffering from malnutrition. Too many synthetic mineral and vitamin supplements can also take up too much room in the stomach so it is wise to use these in the most concentrated form and if they can be found in the natural foods so much the better.

The product S.A.37 which contains the highest analysis of added vitamins and minerals I have yet discovered can be obtained from a vet and is well worth investigating. I have used it ever since it appeared and my vet and I find it excellent for toy breeds.

A diet that seems to suit my Yorkshire Terrier puppies is as follows:

From weaning to 3 months of age four feeds daily are given. If early weaning five or even six feeds may be necessary to keep the puppies evenly fleshed.

Yorkshire Terrier puppy diet chart

For the milky feeds use a formula from 2 packets FAREX, 1 packet CASILAN, ½ packet GLUCODIN. Mix these ingredients together in a jar.

BREAKFAST: Take enough of the above mixture to feed all the puppies and mix with warm milk. Feed until stomachs are full but not hard like tennis balls. Increase amounts with growth. This feed should be continued until full second teeth are through and is useful for expectant and nursing bitches.

LUNCH: Take a piece of good raw beef, very lean, cut into strips and with a pair of kitchen scissors cut into very tiny pieces. This is more easily digested than mincing and gives the teeth more exercise. Small pieces of liver in addition each day.

Mix one teaspoonful of ATORA SUET to each tablespoonful of lean meat. This will mix more thoroughly with the lean meat than ordinary suet and it is an essential need. Minced meat is also acceptable.

A spot of halibut/cod liver oil mixture can be added if other vitamins are not being given. Sprinkle a little seaweed powder over the meat. A wonderful additive for coat growth and colour.

TEA: A small dish of milky tea with glucose. A few good quality puppy biscuits fed dry. If these are started when the puppy is young it will encourage the chewing of hard food which is necessary for healthy gums and teeth. I use Lactol Biscuits. Baked rusks with margarine are also useful.

SUPPER: Cooked meat or fish, cheese or offal, preferably liver. This food should consist of two-thirds protein and one-third cereal which can be in the form of a puppy meal or baked brown bread, or a cereal breakfast food. A fresh herring cooked until the bones are soft (use a Pressure Cooker if available) and then mashed up, bones and all, makes a good, nourishing feed and is excellent for putting weight on a lean dog.

Brewer's Yeast is best given in tablet form and can be given as a reward in training. Do not give more than 1 tablet per 4 lb bodyweight.

Reduce feeds to three omitting teatime one at four months and when fully adult one feed daily should be sufficient or two if preferred. Mostly meat with a little roughage. Such as Bran or Bemax.

Cold water should be available at all times for drinking. Rusks or biscuits during daytime for sake of teeth.

This diet chart should be handed to new owners of puppies when they are purchased and, if adhered to you will be sure that any puppies you sell will be properly nourished.

Keep the puppies' whiskers clean by washing and combing after meals.

Fig 12 Feeder for orphaned puppies

12   Care of the Yorkie Puppy

EVEN before they have left their mother you will find your baby pups getting up to all sorts of activities. They may begin by gently patting one-another on the head, but this will soon develop until the bigger ones are actually dragging the smaller ones in the litter around by their ears or tails. The little bully will soon manifest himself and long before they ever learn to bark they will learn to growl.

The first thing they will need is a bigger play area. Special play-pens for puppies are made which are most useful — fitted with a lid over the top they prevent the most adventurous from climbing up and falling over. They can badly damage themselves doing this, but, most litters contain at least one such adventurer.

At about five weeks they will appreciate a few rubber toys, especially ones that roll such as a ball or rubber cotton reel. It is surprising how quickly they will learn to jump on them and push them with their noses. This will give the tinies a respite from bullying but, if it is found that they suffer in this respect split the litter into two play-pens and let the rougher elements stay together. At eight weeks they are better in pairs anyway. About five weeks we like to take our babies on to the lawn, in fine weather and let them have a really good scamper. Those breeders who don't play with their puppies are missing the best part of breeding. We get a laugh a minute with ours and I guarantee half an hour watching a litter of baby pups will chase any blues away.

This is the time to note the individual characteristics. The bully we have seen, but now one of them will indicate signs of a squirrel instinct. One little fellow will collect up leaves, stones and bits of grass and hide them in a corner. Along will come a little tease and scatter the squirrel's handiwork, who, if he's made up of the sterner stuff will just gather them all up again and keep on doing so. The perpetual 'mummy's boy' will soon show up. Left to his own devices for a minute he will howl for attention and keep it up until he gets it. He will not want to run off with his brothers but will stay close to us or to his mother. The little roamers will be 'off like shots' and will have to be searched for if we don't notice them quickly. Every one will be different and the interesting fact is that the personalities they expose at this time will still be there for the rest of their lives.

When selling pups as pets it is important that the buyer gets one with a suitable personality. I use these times to assess them and sort them out in my

A litter of puppies on their vet-bed in their breeding cage.

mind so that the right dog goes to the right person. A very boisterous noisy puppy would be no good to an old lady living in a block of flats. In the same way a shy, retiring one would be all wrong in a family of robust youngsters. The clinging ones are ideal for childless ladies or those who have brought up a family that has left home. They soon dote on the cry-babies, which is a lucky thing.

Choose country homes for the ones that need a lot of exercise — the little roamers of the litter — who will suffer from claustrophobia shut up in a town flat. Let a man buying himself a pet have an active little jumper who will be able to fly into a car and jump about without hurting himself. He will soon get bored with one he has to keep lifting up and holding safely.

Mothers with several young children appreciate a sensible little dog who will train easily, keep close to heel when out shopping, and enjoy riding in the pram with the baby. There are such dogs and Yorkies seem such a wide mixture that there is nearly always the right pup for each of these in every litter.

Yorkie puppies are, perhaps the most adorable of all puppies and it is always very hard to have to choose just one. Try to find out from your customer what sort of temperament they prefer before bringing in a puppy for their inspection. If they don't seem to have much idea, make a quick assessment yourself and choose one for them. Bringing just one or two will greatly reduce the selling time as, with more to choose from you will find that they will be ages deciding. As all Yorkies look alike as regards colour, they will not be able to tell them apart but, if you tell them that one is being reserved for your own use, they will only want that one. Don't show them a faulty pup to start with but, if they seem very suitable people and the price is really above them, suggest that they may like to take one without such a good mouth or with the wrong coat or colouring. Explain that these points go against it in the show ring but make no difference to its value as a house-pet. This way they will go away well satisfied that they have got a bargain, and your faulty pup will have a good and loving home. If you try to overlook any faults or ignore them completely, asking the same price for a faulty pup as for the rest, they will soon be pointed out by someone else and your customer will have just cause to resent you and maybe the pup that they will feel they have paid too much for. Selling pups, if some little trouble is taken, can lead to many lasting friendships. It does, of course, put a lot of responsibility on the seller so great care must be taken to give as accurate a description of your puppies as you can. Never guarantee anything — if you assure your buyers that one will be a particularly tiny one, that could be the one to spring up and end up well over the standard weight. Rather show the mother and any grandparents. Give full details of sire's weight as truthfully as you can — get the owner to put his weight on his stud card if possible. Leave the buyer to assess the possible size of the puppy and, if they have made the guess themselves they will be well satisfied whatever size it eventually turns out to be. Give the new buyers a card with birth weight, weight at each worming and weight when pup is sold. Also give a diet chart and full information about inoculations, if these haven't been done. A copy of the pup's pedigree must also be handed over. You will have to make this out yourself. Obtain enough pedigree forms for each puppy and fill in the stud dog's pedigree in the top half where it says 'sire' and your bitch's ancestry where you see 'dam'. You must sign these as true to your best knowledge.

If the puppies are already registered with the Kennel Club you will hand over the Registration Card and sign a transfer form which will arrive with the cards from the K.C. In view of some of the disastrous sales that have taken place lately where 'pet buyers' turn out to be agents for unknown foreign buyers, it will make things harder if you fill out the transfer form completely with the buyer's name and address. Get the buyer to sign it and send it to the Kennel Club yourself with the necessary fee. This will obviate the unpleasant shock of finding your name listed in the *Kennel Gazette* as having sold stock to someone that you would never, normally sell to.

The question of registering a prefix or suffix at this early date is a matter you should consider carefully. If you are going to breed at all regularly the sooner you do this the sooner will your mark in the breed be made. If you are going to exhibit or export it is essential. You register your choice of prefix, etc., with the Kennel Club and pay a yearly fee or you can pay a lump sum and compound for life. The choice of a title should be one you will be pleased to hear later on and not a name you dislike. Places you have lived in or house names are acceptable. Some people have very clever combinations of christian names, etc. As the Kennel Club needs to hold meetings to discuss your choice and also to publish a short list in the *Gazette*, you should allow about six weeks to get your registrations through. You could of course, register your *prefix only* before the pups are born.

If the papers have not arrived when the pups are sold you must send them on as soon as you receive them. Make a point of this as it is very important. No puppy can be shown unless registered at the Kennel Club and the new owner must have the dog transferred to his own name.

When playing with your puppies you should make a point of starting their grooming. Start with a soft baby brush but change to a bristle one as soon as the coat starts to knot. The comb should only be used after the brush. Brush the hair on the head backwards and part the coat in the middle of the back to train it in the way it must grow.

While many Yorkie pups seem to keep their ears erect all the time, many are born with them down and don't start to put them up until their first teeth are through. Some don't get up until they have cut their adult teeth and then they go up and stay up.

It will be found helpful to ears that are half inclined to go up to strip the hair off the edges with a finger and thumb. Chalk the fingers and take just a hair or so at a time. This can be done to about half way down and will often help a bent ear to stay up. Yorkies should have small neat ears and the ones that are too large are the most difficult ones to get up. When buying a puppy always choose one with the ears up if you can or at least that look as though they are on the way up. Although, according to the standard these hanging ears are supposed to be acceptable, they are not nearly as attractive as the erect ones.

If buyers insisted on strong erect ears when purchasing puppies it would induce breeders to be more careful about this point. So many of them shrug their shoulders as if it doesn't matter a bit. They will tell you that the ears never go up before the second teeth, or that judges don't in the least mind them down. There are many other tales told to unsuspecting buyers who find out too late that they have been misled.

If 'soft' ears are fixed as sometimes they are, it must be borne in mind that the fixing only applies to that particular dog. He will still carry the gene for 'soft' ears and is therefore dangerous to breed from.

Before the mother leaves her puppies it is a good plan to let them go outside with her every time she is put out to be clean, once they are over five weeks old. If the weather is bad put a cover over a play-pen in the garden and pop the whole family in at regular intervals. The bitch will train them more thoroughly than you can and you will not be vexed by new owners ringing up and saying that the pup stayed outside for ages and then came in and wet the carpet. Before the pups leave you they should know outside from inside and then they are less likely to get their 'lines crossed' in this way.

Male Yorkies that haven't had some rudiments of house-breaking can be the very devil to train and many people despair to the point of wanting to return them to their original home. Great patience is needed and a constant watch must be kept so that they can be intercepted the moment they start going round in circles. They will want to go immediately on waking and within five minutes of eating and drinking. Puppies going to new homes should not be left with water at night for the first few weeks. Let him have all he needs to drink in the day. At night, when left alone, he will drink out of boredom and then won't be able to hold on until relief arrives. A baby pup has little control but, as he grows older and he knows that you like him to do everything outside, he will aim to please you by holding on. Bitches are better at this than dogs, but give him time as you would let a human baby stay in napkins until he is able to cope. This is a great bother to some people and no trouble at all to others who claim to have trained their pup within the first week. Never smack or shout at a pup as this will only make him nervous and wet more. Praise him to the heights however when he pleases you by going outside or even standing at the door and waiting. Pups who are left on their own at night need an old tin tray with newspaper put on it. Sprinkle it with Sherley's puppy trainer and he will then use it and not the floor. If this tray is put down in the day for a recalcitrant pup you will hear him on it and, if it is close to the door you can easily whip him outside before it is too late. Common-sense, patience and a lot of love are the best answers to a dirty puppy.

Once the pup is eating four good feeds a day, has had two wormings, his coat checked for parasites and, if found, powdered with flea powder or bathed in anti-insecticidal shampoo, with a basic knowledge of house-manners, you have done all you can and he is now ready for sale.

Eight to ten weeks is a good time to sell a Yorkie into a pet home. He will forget his family much quicker at this age and will settle all the better for it. A few noisy nights can be expected but if a hot water bottle and a cuddly toy are placed under a piece of blanket in a small bed he will soon settle down. Don't give him a large bed to start off with as he will feel lost in it. Pack-a-beds are round plastic beds that come in very small sizes and a tiny Yorkie pup will just fit into the smallest size. As he will chew most beds he starts off with you can afford to let him outgrow this one as it is hygienic and soft and won't catch on his coat like wicker. If a puppy cries despite these precautions a ticking clock wrapped in an old towel will often do the trick. It will sound like the heart-beats of his brothers and sisters that he has been used to hearing.

Pets are best sold locally as it is a great worry to send such tiny mites on long journeys. A few well-chosen descriptive words in your local paper or a card on the notice-board of your newsagents or pet-shop will usually achieve results. Selling them off lock, stock and barrel, although probably giving the least worry, is not the way I advocate. I like to meet the people who will live with my pups and I'm afraid my conscience would not let me send them into the

Emmrill Tiny Jewel at 8 weeks . . . . .

. . . . . 4 months and . . . . .

. . . . 6 months.

blue without knowing where they will end up.

People do set up 'puppy factories' to do just this, but I am not writing this book with them in mind.

While we all hope that the puppies we breed will make a name for us in the show-ring, time will show that most will be sold for pets and companions. There is, after all, a great deal of satisfaction to be gained from this as, if we have made a good job of bringing up our little pups their new owners are going to remember us with kindness and even affection. One day, when the sad time comes when their little pet has passed on they will come back to you again and always send their friends and relations.

Always be willing to see your customers again, even if they think they have cause for complaint. Be prepared to listen to their problems, help them if you can and, if not, send them to a reliable vet if their troubles are health ones. Don't just tell them that your puppies are never ill or that they have been neglecting it. The fact that they are troubling you is proof that they are anxious. Do all you can to put things right and, if the pup turns out to have a hereditary fault, replace it at once. This is the only way to build up goodwill. After all, you bred it and so are responsible.

Selling and assessing value

If your brood bitch and stud dog have been chosen as carefully as we suggested, it is possible that some, if not all of your first litter will be of show quality. You will probably have got your eye on one that you feel is better than the others and have made up your mind to keep for yourself. Let the owner of the stud dog take his pick of the litter before letting yourself be carried away or you are going to be disappointed at the very beginning. If your favourite isn't chosen don't be delighted that you can keep it but rather, have a good look to see if you can see why it was discarded. If you can't see anything wrong, ask. The answer you receive will be part of the education that you must have to become a breeder of 'experience'. If the answer is that a certain sex or certain size was required, then your pup can perhaps be run on. Ask for an honest opinion and listen carefully to the judgment. Again ask the breeder who sold you your bitch to look the litter over and assess it for you. You may not get the same opinion — you probably won't — but you can then form your own ideas. If they both find faults in your favourite then sell it and keep one that they may both have agreed was the 'pick'. After all they should know more than you at this stage. When you find that you are able to pick faults and see good points in your various litters then you are beginning to get 'an eye' and shouldn't need anyone else's advice much longer. Unless you develop this 'eye' you are best just breeding pups for pets. It is essential, if you wish to breed for show that you are able to differentiate. If all your geese look like 'swans' to you, you are in for a rude awakening.

Study the standard and try to see what shape your puppies' heads are, for instance. If too round or apple, they should be fairly flat on top. Look at the teeth and see if they all fit scissor-like or if some are more prominent at the bottom. Examine the coat to see that the black doesn't run into the tan. Test the limbs as explained before and decide if the puppies all please you when they move or if some look 'cow-hocked' or otherwise. Let them walk towards you and watch to see if they look 'true' or plait, which is another way of saying 'cross their legs in front'.

Any pups that pass muster can be advertised in the weekly dog papers. Your newsagent will send the adverts up for you if you don't know how to work out the prices. It may take a couple of insertions for the whole of the litter to go but, if you are running one on for yourself it won't matter if you are left with a pup or two for a while. If the stud dog owner or the bitch's breeder or both offer to buy any or all of the puppies let them have them. They are paying you a compliment and will be able to do far more for a show pup than you could. If the stud dog owner offers to buy all the litter it used to be considered fair for her to pay the value of the stud fee for each. In these days of high values, however, this would not be enough for a show prospect and more like double would be a fair price.

If the pups remain until they are three months old then they should be inoculated against hardpad, distemper, hepatitis and leptospiral jaundice and parvo virus. The cost of this can be added to the price of the pup and, a little extra added for the extra care.

If stock is sold before it is inoculated it is a good idea to give the new owner a month's free insurance cover. This is better than advertising as it will help your sales as new owners will be relieved to learn that the expensive puppy they have just bought is fully covered against these terrible diseases as well as any accident, death or any cause and being stolen or straying. The cover books make admirable reference books and full details of each pup are left on your counterfoil. They also have a form of receipt which saves your printing costs. Explain that the customer has a month in which to get his puppy inoculated before the period of cover expires.

13 Showing the Yorkshire Terrier

THE advantage of a hobby is that it takes up time that might otherwise be wasted and is a relaxation from the tedium of one's daily work. Dog breeding is to me and the majority of dog fanciers, an all-absorbing pastime. The aim of breeding to any real purpose is to produce the best possible example of the breed which has merited our enthusiasm. There is no point in producing something good, be it animal, vegetable or mineral, unless it can be displayed to the world at large for its admiration. It is also necessary to be able to compare our unique production with others of its kind to make sure that we have been so clever to outshine them all. This is how the biggest part of us think when we start this kind of hobby. We read books, visit kennels, ask advice and sometimes take it and the whole thing is child's play. So mediocre were the results that everybody seemed to be getting that we could surely show them a thing or two. The only way to do this in the case of dog breeding is to exhibit at one of the innumerable Dog Shows. The minute you step into that ring, however, your fate is sealed, for you will be lucky if you ever get away from it again.

Your first shock will be that the end-product of all that book-work, kennel-lore and acting on advice, does not resemble anything in any way the perfect picture you thought your Yorkie made before you left home. 'What has happened to the wonderful bloom you saw on his coat?' you ask yourself. 'It doesn't shine nearly as much as the other coats do and how can it look so short?' It had seemed that there couldn't be a dog living with a longer or more beautiful looking coat than yours. If we are very lucky we may get called out by the judge for a second look but the chances are that our inexperience, coupled with the nasty surprise we have just received will send us away cardless. Two ways are now open to us, we can either pack up our belongings and with our little vanquished hopeful tucked under our arm vow never to enter a dog show again, in which case perhaps we will have had a lucky escape, or, wait until the judging is finished and the judge is free to talk, ask what advice he would give you as a newcomer; if it is worth persevering with the dog you have, and what you can do to improve his chances. This is accepted procedure and one that no responsible judge will deny. You have done him the courtesy of entering under him and although you didn't win, you are quite at liberty to ask his opinion. Hide your disappointment under a pleasant manner, for after all he must have far more experience than you to be

Yorkshire Terrier Club's Show, December 1980. (*left to right*) Mr O. Sameja's Ozmilion Story of Romance, Best in Show; Mrs B. McCawley's Camley's Continuation, Best Opposite Sex; Best Puppy in Show, Mrs Buggin's Ozmilion Kiss Me Again.

in his exalted position, and listen carefully to what he has to say. Even if he doesn't happen to be a specialist in your particular breed, he will know dogs and dog shows and you can learn more from five minutes with him than all the books you can read and all the biased remarks you will no doubt receive from fellow competitors, whose opinions can sometimes be biased.

The next time you show your dog, supposing you have taken his proffered advice, you might find that you will remember to walk your dog on the side nearest the judge, to hold the dog firmly while the judge looks in his mouth, to stop moving your dog when the judge tells you to, and keep your dog standing on his toes when the judge is making his final appraisal instead of letting him loll at your feet. Such small matters, maybe, but important enough in a busy judge's eyes to lose the day for a quite passable little pup like yours. If on the second try you manage to win even a lesser award it will be a step in the right direction and you will probably have caught the bug and be anxious for the next show to see if you can do even better.

This is how it starts with most of us. We just can't wait for the next show, and even when those three elusive green cards which denote a champion have been hard won after no end of struggle do we give up? 'No fear.' There is always a Best of Breed to be won and then Best in Group at a Championship Show, which is always such a boost for your breed in dog showing circles. A very, very good dog can carry all before him and win Best in Show. This would appear to put an end to one's ambition but not so. There is, at the end of every year's showing, a special award for the Supreme Dog of the Year. This is the dog that has won more Best in Show awards at the Championship Shows over the year, and naturally carries with it a very high degree of glory.

Ch. Fascination of
Daisydell

It follows, of course, that such a dog would be worth a considerable amount of money, figures in the region of £10,000 have been spoken of in connection with some of the most outstanding. It may surprise some uninitiated people to know that to my certain knowledge such a sum was once refused by one of our doggy fraternity, who, although she more often than not found it difficult to make ends meet, must have received sufficient gratification from owning such a dog for the money to be of secondary importance. It may be, of course, that she was just too fond of the dog to part with him for even this formidable sum.

Some people obtain complete satisfaction from simply breeding the odd litters and selling the pups on the pet market. Providing the pups are strong, healthy and typical of the breed they are said to represent, nobody will quarrel with this. Many people cannot get to shows at all but at the same time wish to breed show stock. This is much harder for them to do, for, unless they attend at least some shows at regular intervals, they are in danger of losing their 'eye'. This means that fashions change in dog showing almost as quickly as in the *haute couture*. Depending on the popular stud dog of the moment, the show entries, especially in the lower classes, are constantly changing even if imperceptibly — fine, narrow heads can give way to wider, coarser skulls in no time at all, if a potent stud, who is in much demand for his quality of coat and good colour, also happens to carry a gene for heavier bone. Similarly, in Yorkies particularly, should the reigning dog possess a shorter back than usual it is surprising how quickly a majority of the older entries not bred from him start to look long and low in comparison. This is a major difficulty facing

HAIR BEHIND HEAD KNOWN AS "THE FALL"

ERECT EARS
Y-SHAPED NOT TOO FAR APART
COVERED WITH SHORT HAIR OF DEEP RICH TAN

FLAT HEAD

EYES, MEDIUM
DARK & SPARKLING

LEVEL BACK
SQUARE SHAPE

GOOD LOIN

BLACK NOSE

MOUSTACHE

TAIL
SLIGHTLY HIGHER THAN
BACK WITH DARKER HAIR
UNDERNEATH

BEARD

COAT LONG
AS POSSIBLE FINE & SILKY
TEXTURE & PERFECTLY
STRAIGHT. COLOUR
DARK STEEL BLUE
FROM OCCIPUT TO
ROOT OF TAIL

FORELEGS
QUITE STRAIGHT
COVERED WITH
GOLDEN TAN NOT
HIGHER THAN ELBOW

FEET AS ROUND AS POSSIBLE
NAILS BLACK

Fig 13 Breed Standard of the Yorkshire Terrier.

the breeder who aims to breed for the show market but never attends a show. They have to be very clever indeed to be able to get a true picture just from studying the show reports, as some of them are reported to do. They need to be psychic as well, to understand some of the show reports. It is also important that there are always judges available who have known the breed over a long period and can recognise the dangers that might arise from too much progress away from limits of the Breed Standard. This is a sort of 'blue-print' for the breed which is set up by the Breed Council, or 'Societies' if no such Council exists, and lodged with the Kennel Club, whose responsibility it is to maintain this standard in the Breed and to uphold it as it stands until such times as an alteration in it is deemed imperative. Any such alteration of the standard is looked on with very great concern and only after most careful investigation and jurisdiction and considerable expense to a Breed Club can any alteration in a Breed Standard be accepted. All such Breed Standards, are, as I have said, lodged with the Kennel Club who have the final word as far as any dispute about its interpretation, should such a thing arise. I explain these facts at this stage so that anybody contemplating the purchase of a pedigree pup can be certain of how it should turn out. The Breed Standard is reproduced above. A careful study of this standard before going out to look for your puppy will pay you more dividends than any investment on the Stock Exchange.

While the above will read as gospel truth with ninety-nine breeds out of the hundred, I am going to have to admit that it does not honestly apply to the Yorkshire Terrier. Every breeder you approach in this breed will firmly and with deepest conviction, deny every item that the last breeder you spoke to swore to be true. This must either mean that the breed is being invaded by a lot of newcomers that have never bothered to study the Standard or have it explained to them in any way, or, that the breed has veered so far away from the standard that the description of the Yorkie laid down therein is not any more a true description. For instance: take the colours in the coat, which in the standard is quite clear and concise, namely — I quote:

ON THE BODY: The Colour a dark steel-blue (not silver-blue) extending from the occiput (or back of skull) to the root of tail, and on no account mingled with fawn, bronze or dark hairs. The hair on the chest a rich bright tan. All tan hair should be darker at the roots than in the middle, shading to a still lighter tan at the tips.

ON THE HEAD: The fall on the head to be long, of a rich golden tan, deeper in colour at the sides of the head about the ear-roots, and on the muzzle, where it should be very long. On no account must the tan on the head extend to the neck, nor must there be any sooty or dark hair intermingled with any of the tan.

ON THE EARS: Covered with short hair the colour to be a very deep, rich tan.

ON THE FORE QUARTERS: Front legs should be — 'well covered with hair of a rich golden tan, a few shades lighter at the ends than at the roots, not extending higher on the forelegs than the elbow'.

ON THE HIND QUARTERS: Legs should be — 'well covered with hair of rich, golden tan, a few shades lighter at the ends than at the roots, not extending higher on the hind legs than the stifle'.

ON THE TAIL: With plenty of hair, darker blue in colour than the rest of the body, especially at the end of the tail.

As a judge this wording seems to me to be most clear and explicit. The body that evolved this Standard have gone into the very tiniest detail to make every point clear to anyone who takes the trouble to study it well. It is so thorough in its definition (not leaving the tiniest detail to chance) that perhaps it has somewhat defeated its own ends and confused where it only set out to help. I have taken all the text referring to 'coat, colour and hair root colour' out of context and put it together so that the whole picture can be studied at a glance. This may enlighten somewhat and show how the colours should run.

This Standard was devised at the inception of the Yorkshire Terrier Club in 1898 and, with very little alteration, still stands today. So diverse are many breeders' opinions that I only hope they will learn far more about the breed than they know now, before daring to aspire to serve on any of the ruling bodies in the breed, lest their ignorance will lead them to attempt to change the essentials of this beautiful breed to suit their own ends and make the mediocre specimens that they own and that fall far short of the accepted standard, the new and easily achieved pattern for the breed. How can they think that a pale silver with cream markings can be accepted when they have it laid down in black and white that the colour must be *steel blue and deep, rich, mahogany tan* which in certain specified places can be allowed to shade out to a few shades lighter.

Not only in colour is the Yorkie a bone of contention. It is actually possible to find breeders of long-standing who still cannot tell a long back from a short one. The Standard is quite clear on this point. *VERY COMPACT* are the words it uses and 'very compact' means that the back should be shorter from the neck or withers to the root of the tail than the height from the withers to the ground when the dog is standing. Just 'compact' usually means 'square' which means the length from neck to tail should be the same as from withers to ground. It would appear that some people have been measuring from rather different places or they haven't known the standard. Legs should be straight, which means that the front legs do not stick out at the shoulders and the back legs do not stick out behind the dog's body. This helps the dog to look 'neat' as the standard requires. He must have a neck, although the wording does not mention it explicitly. It describes the carriage however as being very upright and conveying an 'important' air. The general outline should convey the impression of a vigorous and well-proportioned body. I cannot see him giving this impression if he is short of neck — looking as if his head came out of his shoulder-blades, which makes for a very 'stuffy' appearance.

The head too is qualified in very clear terms and here the many, many different types that confuse your eye when you are judging them means that somebody had better 'lay down the law' here. There are even two schools of thought, utterly opposed, and as unlike as any two heads can be — the 'terrier' head and the 'toy'. The standard calls for a rather small head, it should be flat on top, not too prominent or round in skull, nor too long in muzzle. It would appear, therefore, if the standard is to be considered that the head must be neither one nor the other but somewhere in between — a neat, fine head, with no coarseness in skull or cheek, little or no stop and no snipiness in muzzle. A head that has the eyesockets somewhere in the middle is fairly near. If the eyes are large and round it will follow that the skull is too round, so the eye will need to be oval to fit the socket that the skull formation denotes.

Ears should be small, V-shaped and carried erect, or semi-erect, and not too far apart. In the original standard the words 'or semi-erect', were not included. It was in 1950 that the Kennel Club approved the final wording and it is to be wondered whether this particular feature is improved by having the ears semi-erect. Might this be a case of the Standard being altered to suit someone's own particular failings to breed the correct ones. Whatever the reason, they are not looked on with favour by the majority of judges.

Ch. Deebees Penny Rose, owned and bred by Mrs S.D. Beech.

Before embarking on the venture of showing the Yorkie, the outcome will be better secured if a fair knowledge of the 'blue-print' is fixed in the mind. You will be less likely to be swayed by everybody's opinion for you will be told by one would-be seller that the Yorkie must have *three* different coloured stripes in his head. It doesn't matter what colours, as long as there is black, gold and tan. Above all there must be black in the head. The breeder who told me this in perfect faith had been showing Yorkies for years and honestly believed what he was telling me. When I quoted the Standard to him he was amazed and said the judges *always* put up dogs with black hair in their heads. Another breeder of many years' standing stated that people who looked for deep mahogany tan didn't know what they were looking for as that colour was decidedly unpopular in the breed and what was wanted was a pretty pale gold. Was he mistakenly thinking about the paling to gold of the deep tan required near the skin or was there some influence at work to change a feature, the importance of which in this particular breed carries no less than 50 points for coat alone. If so, then there is grave cause for concern. Those responsible are spoiling the breed and the time could come when it might even become a necessity to reintroduce the black and tan terrier into the breeding to bring the proper colour back. Although the history does not specifically mention Maltese blood in the foundation there is true evidence to think it had been introduced. The hanging ears so often found in the breed are almost sure to have come from this cross as the Clydesdale and Skye Terriers have mostly erect ears. I think the Maltese coats were the attraction and it seems that in order to get the desired coats there seems to be a certain amount of Maltese being introduced still to improve coats. Long backs are a common failing in

Maltese Terriers and woolly undercoats also. It may be these two faults from the Maltese that occur in the Yorkie.

If you have avoided the risk of buying without knowledge of the breed, with average luck you should now be able to think about showing your Yorkie. Check that he is not too large (under 5 lb is best for show), see that his back is level, legs are straight, that his coat is growing well and changing colour correctly, and is benefiting from regular grooming and bathing. As soon as he cuts his second teeth take him to your vet to have any stubborn milk teeth removed as so often a second row grows without the first teeth falling out, with dire consequences to the permanent ones. Study Fig. 12 and ascertain that the 'bite' is correct and that teeth are even, and the jaws level. A dog has 42 teeth in a full set, although many Yorkies are short of premolars which are not considered important in this country and America, but essential for all the European judges who make quite a fetish of what they call a 'complete' mouth.

The Kennel Club won't allow puppies to be shown before the age of six months. Check the K.C. registration papers and ascertain that you have had the pup's ownership transferred to your name. This must be done before entering for a show. If the puppy was unregistered when purchased you can obtain a signed breeder's form from the person who sold you the puppy and this must be sent to the Kennel Club fully completed and with the appropriate fee. If on the other hand the registration had been effected and you wish to add your own prefix or affix this can be done for a fee of £4.60.

Before showing your dog give him several weeks of intensive training in ring-craft — walking on a lead *on your left side*, standing on his show box in the correct pose for several minutes without relaxing; not being scared when placed on a high table and his mouth opened and other liberties taken, which he must undergo when he is actually in a show-ring.

Short, regular lessons are the best with the young show dog and he should never be taken to a show unless his schooling has been completed. It is unfair to your dog, to the judge and to the other exhibitors, to expect them to enjoy waiting about while you put your pup through his first lesson in showmanship right in the very ring where dogs are expecting to qualify for Crufts and so forth. This happens alas, all too often, and it isn't always the prerogative of the novice.

Most toy breeds work better for some tangible reward and the Yorkie is no exception to this. Little lumps of stale cheese rattled in a match-box will hold his attention when he knows he will get a piece in due course. When you feel he can be relied on to know his part in all this, he can be entered for his first show.

Since this book was first written ring training schools have opened up in most parts of the country. Would-be exhibitors, novices and even successful exhibitors who are very experienced find these training classes very successful as very young puppies are easily trained when they have some competition and everybody and all the dogs are absolute beginners.

Many schools allow babies as early as three to four months to join their schools just as long as their inoculations have been completed.

If you bought your Yorkie from a regular breeder or exhibitor you can look to them for help, which they will almost surely give you and will, no doubt offer to nominate you for membership of the Breed Club. When you join such a club you will automatically receive show schedules and all information with regard to matches, training classes and all other such activities. There is also a social side where you will meet and be able to discuss problems and seek advice from the experts.

It is wise policy to subscribe to one or both of the excellent weekly dog journals where you will find much information and news of forthcoming dog shows outside your own breed. Although a show confined to his own breed will be less alarming for his first outing, you will soon want to get him to an all-breed show to see how he measures up against other varieties. These shows are very interesting always and it is important that he gets used to meeting all sorts and sizes. These shows are the training ground for dogs and owners.

To get back to the first breed show, don't expect to win an award the first few times. Both of you will be novices and however good your exhibit you are bound to be awkward and make a wrong turn or two. Most first timers always get between the judge and the dog. Even if you don't make this major error it will be several shows before you even begin to feel at ease in a show-ring, so tell yourself that you are only there for the experience and not for the prize cards and your disappointment won't be so keen when you have to return home cardless. After all you have had a golden opportunity of comparing your dog with a lot of others and perhaps yours did not look so perfect against some of them. If there is any one point that does not look as good as his rivals see what can be done to improve it. Watch the judge too and if he shows any idiosyncracies about the dogs he likes or the way he prefers them shown, store this knowledge for this is valuable material to go into your memory file.

Leave championship shows alone at the start of your show career. Make a big effort to attend as many as possible as an onlooker, though, as this is where you will see the cream of the breed. Watch all you can, especially the Open Classes and the challenge for the certificates. After watching a good few you will gradually find yourself being able to differentiate between some and even find yourself disagreeing with the judge in some of his placings. If you are able to consistently pick out the best five, even if in different order from the judge, you can be said to be acquiring an eye for the breed. To be able to concentrate hard enough to do this you must leave your dog at home as you won't be able to give your undivided attention to the show ring if you have a distressed little fellow sitting on the show bench, feeling miserably neglected and ignored, for the Kennel Club rule is that no exhibit may be absent from his bench for more than 15 minutes unless in the show ring. Choose your seat carefully so that you have an uninterrupted view of the final placings in order that you can compare them properly. Also however, put yourself where you are directly behind the dogs as they are moving to and from the judge so that you have a chance to see how they all move, and, just how much a lot of them vary in movement. Some will turn their toes 'in' while others turn them 'out'. The long coat of the Yorkie makes it difficult to see this but watch the feet carefully and they will tell you a lot: 'feet turned in' — out at elbows, and, 'feet turned out' we say he will be 'cow-hocked' (another term for knock-kneed). You should be able to see the dogs that have a roach back, arch in the middle, droop down at the tail. This is very ugly and quite spoils the look of the Yorkshire Terrier, who can't do anything to hide it as with his coat parted in the middle, the spine sticks up for all to see. A bad roach should disqualify a Yorkie immediately but the judge will often give a bit of leeway to a thin puppy who has not enough flesh to cover the bones. Quite often too a very cold wind will cause the dog to tuck up his tummy and make him look roachy when he isn't really. The judge will be in a position to ascertain these facts but you won't, so although you will be able to get a very fair picture, the judge has the full view and can see a lot more than you. Don't forget to store away carefully all the tips you can for actually showing the dog. Watch the winners and see if they do anything to attract their dogs' attention when the judge is looking at them. See how much better an alert Yorkie looks than one whose attention is being allowed to wander. Ascertain which coats look the best and try to reason why. Is it because some are straighter and glossier than others? See how long they are and if they are of even thickness or are showing daylight underneath. Make a special note of the way the top-knots (or fall) are tied up and how they are allowed to fall. When you return home you will be able to practise walking your own pup the same way the exhibitors walked their's and you will be resolved to spend a part of every day working on the coat to get is as near as you can to the ones you have most admired. These are lessons that when learnt are better than struggling for years in the ring hoping to beat the winners but never quite knowing why you don't. You will be starting off with the equivalent of a degree in showing your Yorkie. If you are standing in the ring with the exhibitors you will never learn as much.

At last you feel ready for your first show and you should be able to look forward to it with pleasure instead of apprehension.

If your puppy is just over the six months, enter in the Special Puppy Class, which means for a puppy over six months and under nine months. This will make sure that the competition will only be for babies still in a very immature state. If there is only one Puppy Class this will include those up to twelve months and the competition from better coats and a longer ring experience will be keener. Don't enter in both if the two are scheduled. It will be a big ordeal for your baby and he might even get a little tummy upset. Let him return to the comfort of his pen as soon as the class is over, give him a treat and

Ch. Carmardy Marcus
owned and bred by Mr
and Mrs H. Parkin.

shower him with praise, however badly it went. He will look back on the experience as having been quite a lot of fun to meet so many other pups just like himself and won't be at all frightened in retrospect. If, however, you enter the higher Puppy Class as well, both you and he are bound to feel a bit of an inferiority complex, as you can't possibly look as good. This attitude will communicate itself to him and he may evince an inferior feeling next time he goes to a show. It is much better to write off completely the first four shows as just ground work. After years of showing I never worry how my puppies behave the first few times out. They may roll on their backs in front of the judge, jump all over me and anybody else that gets in the way, refuse to walk, lie down and go to sleep and even spend a penny in the ring. All this is completely ignored and the whole occasion made one of play and praise. Afterwards they get a specially good reward, not for all the naughty things they have done, which they, of course, have forgotten about as soon as they have done them, but for going into the ring at all and not being frightened by it. I am lucky in that none of my pups are ever frightened when they are with me. I think if they were I would leave them at home until they grew out of the condition. If they didn't I would get rid of them as I don't think such an attitude is correct in a Yorkie. I could not bring myself to force a tiny creature to face anything that would fill him with fear, just for the sake of showing him. When the initial ice is broken and the puppy walks round the ring with a complete air of unconcern, then is the time to push him up to a higher standard, if he reaches this stage before his age does it for him.

Puppy Class is up to 12 months and if and when the puppy wins a first prize he can still be entered in the Maiden Class, which is for dogs who have never won a first prize, as the Puppy Class wins do not have to count. Where they do count, however, is for a Junior Warrant Award. This is made up of 25 points which have to be obtained by the time a dog is eighteen months of age counting one point for every first prize won at an Open Show and three for a Championship Show. Once the puppy passes the age of twelve months, he can be shown in Maiden Class until he has won a first prize. The next class for him will then be the Novice. He can enter in Junior until he is eighteen months, but, it must be remembered that C.C. Winners and even Champions can be entered in this class as the only stipulation is one of age — he must be under eighteen months. The same thing applies for Special Yearling which takes him up to two years of age. After Novice let him try Graduate — a sort of intermediate class. If he wins in this then Junior and Special Yearling can be taken in his stride and he is ready for the Limit Classes and the Open. Keep him in Limit until he wins a C.C. or Res. C.C. It is a pity to force him out of his weight in a high class. He may easily need another year or so to come to his real maturity.

If you are unlucky enough to win a C.C. with him while he is still under two years it will be a big pity. I mean this in all sincerity. You are still a novice with perhaps only one dog and going to dog shows is going to be your hobby. You will, naturally, wish to enter for *all* the shows once you get going. There are only a limited number of championship shows held during the year and they are dotted all over the country. Once you have won a Challenge Certificate with your dog you are ineligible for entry in any Limited or Members Shows and so miss all the fun of winning on your own doorstep and showing at all the mid-week and week-end shows that make up the show-goers' calendar. Another snag is that you will never again be so thrilled with just an ordinary first prize. After winning a C.C. it can actually be a disappointment to only win a Res. C.C., whereas when you start out this very high award may be beyond your wildest expectations.

These early days of showing can be among the happiest. Until you win a high award you can call everybody a friend but, human nature being what it is, once you start to make your presence felt in the ring you will find a certain number of acquaintances start to give you the cold shoulder. It is only envy rearing its ugly head, but if you want to win you must expect the consequences. Don't be in too much of a hurry to leave these friendships behind however. This is a competitive world, this world of dog showing. Some people are born without this spirit of competition and are content to remain just one of the 'also presents' and they are no worse for this. They are quite content just to have a dog to show at all and seem to have no wish to win with it.

Such people are worth their weight in gold in any doggie fraternity as they help to keep one's head out of the clouds and are usually very level-headed and sensible. Friendship with such a steadying influence will be a great asset. Too

Ch. Daisybell Tinker.

many people take the dog showing part of their hobby far too seriously and as a result become tense and over-wrought at the first sign of defeat. Good sportsmanship is a must. Good manners essential. Even if you feel angry and disappointed never, never show it in the ring. Any display of temper there, while it might make you feel better for the moment will be held against you for ever-more by the ring-siders. If you take all that comes to you quietly and politely, you will earn the respect of the people watching. Onlookers see most of the game, so they will probably be ready with their sympathy if they think you have been treated unfairly and you will find that you will be surprised by the warmth of the unexpected applause that you will have when your dog is finally recognised as a good one.

I am the proud possessor of a very well-known champion in another breed. I bred him myself and always knew that he would be a 'flyer'. To my great surprise, however, I showed him fearlessly all over the country and although he was usually placed, he never made any sort of impression. In my eyes he kept on improving and started to win but never made the high spots. I might have given up showing him, for even though I could see how special he was, it didn't look as if the judges ever would. However I never carried him out of a ring anywhere without some of the onlookers coming to ask what was wrong with him as they thought he looked marvellous. After a while he had a big circle of fans who would sit round waiting for him to be eliminated. Their sympathy was of great help and he must have appreciated it. Whenever he heard their appreciative murmurs he would play up to them and not notice the judge. After a time he won his first C.C. and I don't think I have ever heard such rapturous applause. No one will ever know why he was ignored for so long. He never looked back again and is now acknowledged as one of the 'greats' of his breed. He always showed on top of his form — never put his tail down in his life, was ever a happy, endearing personality and is now proclaimed as a perfect example of the breed.

What I want to convey by this is that even when you think you have produced the perfect dog, you are still a long way from getting other people to appreciate him. My dog was shown for over a year before he made much impression in his breed classes although he was winning well in any variety ones. A good one will usually come to the top though without any blood-letting.

Besides the restrictions of age the Yorkshire Terrier is, of course, limited to classes where his coat and its varying stages are acceptable. It would be useless to enter a puppy whose coat had still not cleared in colour in the Limit or Open Classes. Limit Class is for dogs which have not won three C.C.s under three different judges or seven or more First Prizes, etc. Although Open Class is open to all the breeds or varieties for which a class is provided and eligible for entry at the Show it would seem to the uniniated to be the obvious choice. This, however, is not the case at all as the Open Class is the highest of them all and often filled right up with Champions and dogs who are almost champions. While it is the most thrilling and interesting class of all to watch, no newcomer should mistakenly enter it. Show entries nowadays are very expensive and no puppy can hope to stand a ghost of a chance of gaining the lowest award in a breed like this where points for coat are rated as half of the whole amount counted.

At one time it was policy for a judge to judge each entry on a standard of points system. They are not accepted now and it is a good thing, for completely diverse types of dogs could end up with the same number of points and the judge may even not have liked the dogs he had to give his awards to. The present Kennel Club practice of giving the judge his 'head' as it were and letting him place the dogs according to his own preference is much better. If every man that judges him acclaims one particular dog as a good one, that means that the dog must be an extra good one. If, however, twenty judges add up their points and twenty different dogs win certificates, it either means that the breed has sunk to mediocrity or that every dog is good and there is none better than another. It is extremely interesting to study these scales of points, however, because they were allotted by the Founders of the Breed and show just how much importance they placed on certain features. Coat is of paramount importance with the Yorkie and merits 50 points out of 100. We are not interested here in other breeds but any aspiring judge should make himself acquainted with the values in every breed.

It is wise practice to arrive at a show a good half hour before the official judging time. Consult your schedule under 'Show Regulations' and you will find all the times stated. Dog Puppy Classes are judged first, Bitch Puppies after all the dog classes, unless as sometimes happens the two are mixed together in a Mixed Puppy Class, when bitches will be first as well.

Let us suppose, by way of an example, that you have entered your Yorkie in the Special Dog Puppy Class at the Open Show run by one of the Yorkshire Terrier Breed Societies. You will have sent off your schedule and received back an admission ticket with your dog's name on it. This won't arrive many days before the show so don't worry about any delay. When you know you are going to show buy a travelling case large enough to take your dog, with plenty of room to line it all through. These used to be made of wicker, which was quite cheap, light to carry and easy to sew the padding to. However, they were neither proof against the cold or wet and were quite wicked against nylon stockings. Today we use fibre glass which is rather more expensive but very much more practical. It is light to carry, hygienic to clean, draught and weather proof, and not so attractive to little terrier teeth as wicker, neither does it damage delicate nylons or equally delicate coats. Linings, which should be smooth American cloth or similar plastic, can be stuck on with one of the excellent glues made specially for this purpose. Do the glueing a week or so before using the box to make sure there will be no unpleasant fumes. Stick plastic foam straight on to the fibre glass inside the box then stick the shiny plastic material on top of this. A piece of sheepskin cut to fit is a luxurious floor covering but a blanket folded up to fit is just as good and easier to wash. It is a good idea to have your name and address on the box. Some kennels get this done professionally and it is a good form of advertisement, besides proving who the box belongs to if there is any dispute about ownership.

Have this box ready the night before, with the blanket already waiting so that you only have to pop the pup in the next morning. The day before you must bath the puppy according to instructions in the chapter on getting ready for a show. Make sure that the oil has been washed well out and use an anti-static in the rinsing water. Do not oil coat before putting it in papers. There will not be time to attend to the coat before leaving for the show so take the dog in its papers and do all the necessary grooming when you arrive. Pack a spray of coat dressing and water so that you can almost drench the coat in order to get all the wrinkles out of it. You then comb it through and through for it to dry straight. Only the very tiniest smear of grease should be allowed on your brush for the final flick before entering the ring. Tie the fall in a rubber band and then tie the ribbon on top. This will hold in the puppy coat much better than the ribbon alone. Match the ribbon to the cover on your travel box and, if you haven't been able to find a nylon lead to match your colour scheme dye one to match. Tiny nylon leads adjusted with a tiny bead are all that is necessary for such a small dog. They are very cheap to buy — in fact several can be bought and dyed to match different ribbons. It will be quite enough for you to cover your travelling box with a matching towel or blanket. You will see the smartly draped boxes of the other exhibitors and can then decide if you wish to cover yours in the same way. They are made with a hole for the handle in the middle. A small pocket in one side holds extra rubber bands and a spare ribbon, brush and comb and some sort of special treat to encourage your exhibit to perk up at the crucial moment. Furnish yourself with a safety pin or a special clip which will hold your ring number card. You will obtain the latter from the ring-steward as you enter the ring. All you can do now is wait and see how the judge reacts to your puppy. Don't talk to the other exhibitors but concentrate on your baby who might easily have stage fright. Keep talking to him in a soft gentle tone, telling him what a clever boy he is and how nice he looks. If he wins an award show him the card and let him see how pleased you are, if he doesn't win, sound just as pleased with him and take him back to his show pen, putting him in with a special hug and something he particularly likes by way of a treat. Offer him a drink and leave him to rest until his lunch-time. This is the best moment for you to have the coffee you so wisely brought in a Thermos and you can now relax with a cigarette and know that all your efforts are over for the day. You will be so glad you only entered in one class.

If you were lucky enough to win this first class, however, you would have to keep your dog groomed and ready for, when the judge has finished judging all the dog classes, he will get all the unbeaten dogs in the ring together and chose the best, to award him the Best of Breed. If it was a Championship Show the Best Dog would be awarded the Challenge Certificate. Three of these under three different judges are required to make a champion. The next best dog will be awarded the Res. C.C. but this does not count towards becoming a champion. Provided that you have chosen a Yorkie that conforms to the Standard of the Breed and also has a good show type of temperament, and you do all the necessary preliminary groundwork, you should start to do a bit of winning after you have been to a few shows. It takes more than just the looks and behaviour to be a champion, though, as some sort of star quality is required to make one good looking dog stand out from the rest.

14 How to Judge a Yorkshire Terrier

The most vital aspect of judging dogs is a profound knowledge of the breed and application of its Standard. Not every judge starts at the top as I did. Most gain knowledge by breeding, selling, going to shows as an onlooker and exhibiting. At first all one's geese are swans and no fault will be found with any of one's dogs. After a time a few dogs will look better and it will be thought possible that some tiny detail might have been better – it might take quite a long time for a breeder to start to discriminate between various individuals but even the smallest sign of an attempt at selection is commendable and although most criticism is most likely to be of the other exhibits at first, when the time eventually comes when an owner can find fault with his own dog and make an effort to improve what he has got with a mixture of another owner's stock, then he can be said to be getting an 'eye' for a dog, and in this case for a Yorkshire Terrier in particular.

This 'eye' can take years to achieve. It sometimes evades a person for years and then suddenly a genuine critical power is acquired that is almost second nature. This can be so convincing that every group of dog is automatically put into order of preference.

Such a quality added to plenty of breeding experience at first hand, exhibiting, stewarding, and then judging at matches will be the best foundation for a judging career to be based on. Those would be judges that are only exposed to a single breed are called specialist judges but with the necessary experience in this country only available at all breed matches and exemption shows it behoves a novice judge to acquire as broad a spectrum as possible. Ring control is also a perquisite of any good judge. How often we find a new judge, when her steward has left her to herself or him to himself wander about the ring not knowing where to start, sending the dogs around the ring and stopping them somewhere in the middle instead at the last of the line, running the exhibits in different directions and with different orders, up and down straight or in a triangle; placing her winners in different parts of the ring in each class and starting at the end where her VHC was last time. This can be very confusing for the exhibitors and they also get very alarmed when a judge reverses a position. This of course while it can be annoying to the winners in the previous class and the cause of trouble for the steward, is quite admissible. I have done it myself in cases where I was unable to get a puppy to show properly in the first class for a number of possible reasons – say arriving late at the show and being made to go to the showring before having a chance to relieve an uncomfortable bladder, etc. Once nature has been attended to and the efforts of his first appearance forgotten, a puppy who is entered in the Junior Class as well will very often acquit himself quite creditably at a subsequent class and then worthy of being placed over the puppy that beat him that was of a poorer quality but showing well. When I started showing, Yorkshire Terriers were the only breed that was allowed to be shown without a lead until such time as a judge insisted that they be put on the lead in case the larger dogs made a meal of them.

Exhibitors did not like to disturb their exhibit's perfection of coat and so the tiny dogs were allowed to wander all over the place as they are not all that obedient. The days of the small entry, enclosed garden or tiny hall available for holding dog shows is over and the rings are enormous and very well-filled and a dog allowed to roam at will will soon be in trouble either by being bullied by the other exhibitors trodden on by them and exposed to all kinds of danger.

Only the Yorkshire Terrier is allowed to be shown posed on a draped-box because the coat is said to be too long and trails on the floor and so only looks its best in this way. The Yorkie puppy has to spend long hours on his box during his lifetime so it is imperative that he is taught to like it. With the present day large entries it should be promoters' policy to give the breed one of the larger rings but most often this point is ignored and the dogs have to be judged by splitting the classes into sections − taking the best two from each section, eliminating all the others and so enabling the judge to have enough room to gait and pose his reduced class.

left Mrs Mary Hayes with her champion Chantmarles Proper Madam winning Reserve Best in Show at Windsor Championship Show, 1980.

A consistent winner is Ch. Wyebank Tinkerbell who conforms very well to the Standard. Best of Breed, Crufts 1981, Best in Show 1980; owned by Mr and Mrs A. Blamire.

I like to stand in the middle of the ring and watch the entry move as I send them round. Often but not always my eventual winner will be one that attracted me in that instance but a lot of factors have to be taken into account before I do hand that one the red card. After the run round I stop them at the first person to lead off and invite that one to be placed on the table. I like to have the dog placed with the head at my left hand and the tail end in my right hand. The next exhibitor should move up to the table ready to place his dog there as soon as the first one has finished so there is no unnecessary waiting, and it is important that the handler keeps within sight of his charge and ready to open the mouth and to prevent the dog being frightened. Before the onset of parvo virus I always used to open the mouth myself and examine the teeth for formation, number and cleanliness. Since my last judging appointment in America, however, I now ask the handler to show me the mouth. This takes time because the whole picture is not seen at one glance and so needs to be repeated. Still it is quicker than washing and drying hands between each examination. I then take the head and examine it for shape, size, length of muzzle, shape and colour of eye and expression. Expression and a sweetly pretty face are essential in my book and I look for small erect ears. If out of puppyhood I make sure there are no sooty markings in the forehead, examine the fall for length and the correct colour of bright golden tan each hair darker at the roots than at the middle and paler on the tips. A check needs to be made that the tan on the head does not extend into the hair on the neck.

Because the Standard mentions carriage, and asks for an 'upright' carriage I am trying to envisage what sort of a neck this would require. Apart from the colour of the hair on it there is no mention of neck as such at all. Anyway one Yorkshire Terrier with its head coming out of its shoulder blades will not have nearly such an important carriage as one with a reasonable neck which in turn needs a lay-back of shoulder blades otherwise the head will stick out like a pig's. So I look for a good slope in the shoulder blades which with straight front legs gives a good sound appearance. After the sloping shoulder I like to get my hands around the rib-cage, good and well-sprung with plenty of 'heart room', behind the ribs the required good loin – I feel the breadth with my hands and then the tail set which leaves the tail at an angle just slightly above the back. Here I feel for a short coupling, (space between ribs and stern) and a very level top-line. I abhor a dipping, hollow back, and camel back and a roach back equally and would prefer not to have to give them a prize. Next I turn the dog with his back to me, run my fingers down his hind-legs ever so gently and without hardly touching I can tell if there is patella luxation or slipping stifles, because the stifle bone 'clicks'. This is a sign that all is not well and closer examination will show that the cord at the stifle joint is either loose and moveable or tight and off the joint altogether. This is a very serious hereditary disease and Yorkshire Terriers with this condition should not be bred from. Then a look at the feet for thick cat-like pads and good round feet. They should always be pointed forward and to check that the back legs are parallel just lift them up gently and let them drop and they should point forward. Toenails must be short or they hurt. Now is the time to take the handlers hairbrush and part the hair above the fore-leg and check that there are no tan hairs above the elbow then take the brush and make the same parting in the coat of the hind-leg and make sure there is no tan hair present above the stifle bone. With the brush check under the chin for beard and length and colour and under the tail for the required tan shading there, and part the hair along the side to look for the body hair.

Now is the time to watch the dog on the floor – and the sounder and gayer he is the better and when there is a challenge the one that keeps showing the best would always win under me. A gay happy mover who is quite at home on his box and shows with style and assurance always has a good chance under me. In all my years of Championship Judging of the highest standard in every part of the world I can honestly say that I have never given a high award to an exhibit with its tail between its legs. When all my class winners are assembled I watch them carefully for any of the faults in movement I have described and usually the one that moves soundest and makes the most of his good qualities with a free and positive action has the edge on the others and wins the C.C. The next best to him gets the Res. C.C. in males. When the bitches have all been judged the best in each class challenge each other and the best of all competes against the best dog for Best of Breed. At an All Breed Show the Best of Breed in every Breed goes into its applicable Group and competes against all the others in that Group and after all the Groups have been judged the Best of Each Group has to be sorted out. These Group Winners then go under the Best in Show judge who will pick the one that is most preferred and the winner of this challenge automatically becomes the Best in Show. Sometimes the Best Opposite Sex to the Best in Show is called for and sometimes the second best, whatever its sex or breed.

The Standard of the Yorkshire Terrier as adopted by the Committee of the Kennel Club in January 1950 and reproduced by permission

GENERAL APPEARANCE. Should be that of a long-coated toy terrier, the coat hanging quite straight and evenly down each side, parting extending from the nose to end of the tail.

The animal should be very compact and neat, the carriage being very upright and conveying an 'important' air. The general outline should convey the impression of a vigorous and well-proportioned body.

HEAD AND SKULL. Should be rather small and flat, not too prominent or round in skull, nor too long in muzzle, with a perfect black nose. The fall on the head to be long, of a rich golden tan, deeper in colour at the sides of the head about the ear-roots, and on the muzzle, where it should be very long. On no account must the tan on the head extend to the neck, nor must there be any sooty or dark hair intermingled with any of the tan.

EYES. Medium, dark and sparkling, having a sharp, intelligent expression and placed so as to look directly forward. They should not be prominent and the edge of the eyelids should be a dark colour.

EARS. Small V-shaped, and carried erect, or semi-erect, and not far apart, covered with short hair the colour to be a very deep rich tan.

MOUTH. Perfectly even, with teeth as sound as possible. An animal having lost teeth through accident not to be faulted providing the jaws are even.

FOREQUARTERS. Legs quite straight, well covered with hair of a rich golden tan, a few shades lighter at the ends than at the roots, not extending higher on the forelegs than the elbow.

BODY. Very compact, and a good loin, level on the top of the back.

HINDQUARTERS. Legs quite straight, well covered with hair of a rich golden tan, a few shades lighter at the ends than at the roots, not extending higher on the hind legs than the stifle.

FEET. As round as possible; the toenails black.

TAIL. Cut to medium length, with plenty of hair, darker blue in colour than the rest of the body, especially at the end of the tail, and carried a little higher than the level of the back.

COAT. The hair on the body moderately long and perfectly straight (not wavy) glossy like silk, and of a fine silky texture.

COLOUR. A dark steel blue (not silver-blue), extending from the occiput (or back of skull) to the root of tail, and on no account mingled with fawn, bronze, or dark hairs. The hair on the chest a rich bright tan. All tan hair should be darker at the roots than in the middle, shading to a still lighter tan at the tips.

WEIGHT AND SIZE. Weight up to 7 lbs.

All the earlier dog history books and the Yorkshire Terrier books specifically make a very big issue of the value of the points as set out in Mrs Annie Swan's *The Yorkshire Terrier Handbook* and as I am going to examine these values in detail I am setting them out herewith:

Value of Points in Judging

Formation and Terrier appearance	....	15	points
Colour of Hair on Body	....	15	,,
Richness of Tan on Head & Legs	....	15	,,
Quality & Texture of Coat	....	10	,,
Head	....	10	,,
Mouth	....	5	,,
Legs & Feet	....	5	,,

Ears	....	5	points
Eyes	....	5	,,
Tail (carriage of)	....	5	,,

Now it should be pointed out that these values have absolutely no use to any of the present day judges as the Kennel Club have completely done away with such points systems and we are compelled as Championship Show judges to study the Kennel Club's own Standard which is available to all judges and anybody else who is interested. If they examine it carefully and in detail as I have done they are going to be very disappointed with the quality of the Standard that all judges are empowered to judge by and dismayed, as I have been when they try to interpret this Standard as the blueprint of a breed as numerically strong and internationally popular and desirable as the present day Yorkshire Terrier. Everybody who exhibits Yorkshire Terriers at any of our Championship Shows knows that if the exhibit is out of Puppy Class and its coat does not reach the ground no judge will give it a prize and there is no hope of such an exhibit ever receiving a C.C. or any title that would go towards its championship.

Now I have examined the Standards of four different Kennel Clubs and nowhere can I see a reference to the Yorkshire Terrier's coat having to touch the ground. In fact the American Kennel Club in their Standard says that the dog's coat should hang evenly down each side of body. Coat on the body is moderately long and perfectly straight; it may be trimmed to give ease of movement.

The British Kennel Club says that general appearance should be that of a long-coated toy terrier, the coat hanging quite straight and evenly down each side. All it says of the coat is that the hair on the body should be moderately long, perfectly straight (not wavy), glossy like silk and of a fine silky texture. (No mention here either that the judge should look for a coat of any specific length). It certainly does not call for the coat to touch the ground.

The Swedish Kennel Club follow that of the British Kennel Club and the French and Belgian together with Holland, Denmark, Germany, Switzerland, Monaco, Italy and Spain and they all belong to the Federation Cynologique International and they judge on a Standard du Terrier de Yorkshire in which *Poil Moyennement Long* is used to describe the coat.

How then can so many British judges explain by what criterion they base their criticisms when judging Yorkshire Terriers by asserting that the coat was not down to the ground and that one could see 'daylight' under it.

There is no part of the Standard that calls for this declaration and yet I have seen exquisite little specimens of great soundness, type and style, of perfect colour and texture of coat, showing their hearts out be put at the end of a line by a judge who puts up a large, course, ugly untypical exhibit with a roach back, bowed front and very unsound rear, and with a dark woolly coat and with sooty marking in the top-knot with the award described in the report in the dog papers that it was 'beautifully coated, very well presented and well deserved its high placing'. This needs some redress as, however long the length of the coat with such colour and texture faults and with so many hereditary construction faults this prize-winner can do nothing but harm to the breed in general while a good coloured, blue-coated one with the correct bright tan and gold in the correct places, good bodily construction and typical size and outlook even if there is a lack of coat in the length will do no harm to the breed in any way.

A study of the Standard will confirm this. There is mention of colour, quality, texture and straightness are all qualities that a judge is instructed to pay special attention to but there is no mention of length except that it be moderate. I assert that as long as the coat conforms to all the requisite features there is absolutely no virtue in an over-long coat, especially when its length can interfere with movement, which could lose the exhibit its 'important air' and impression of vigour that the Standard calls for. It is necessary for the parting to be straight and the ends of the coat should be perfectly even and well-groomed, silky and straight without waves. If judges paid attention to the Standard and used it when judging puppies and juniors it would mean that the correctly coated and coloured exhibits would take their rightful place in the line and allowances would be made for the immaturity of their jackets and less credit would be given to those quite undesirable specimens whose only claim to fame is the extra long length of their hair. Too much hair often conveys a totally wrong texture and colour and many stars of their early life are still at two and three years of age waiting to 'clear'. The steel blue hasn't 'broken' and the sooty markings have not cleared because they were wrong all the time. When judging for coat colour in the younger Yorkshire Terrier it is necessary to lift the coat and examine the hair under the body for early evidence that the coat is going to 'break' correctly. Mrs Swan allows thirty points for colour of hair on body and richness of tan on head and legs but only ten altogether for quality and length of coat.

While I personally love the 'Coated' Breeds and get a great deal of satisfaction out of caring for them and seeing them put down to the minute, I have to admit that in all cases the beauty and presentation of the coat is only the icing sugar on the top and it is absolutely useless to spend a great part of one's life caring for the coat of an unsound dog. Fortunately for me I learned all about 'unsoundness' in a very hard school among several types of livestock, where a wrong judgement and a bad choice would affect our livelihood for many years. For instance it took nine years to prove the merits and failings of your stock bull so a bad choice in him and the whole herd was affected for a decade before any improvement could be expected. Steep shoulders, slab-sides, low set tail, cow hocks and being 'tied in the pin' were all construction faults that I could spot at a glance without ever getting my hands on an animal. As a member of the Guernsey Club I was often invited to prove my assertions so that when I was invited to judge my first ever Dog Show at

Crufts itself, I was fortunate enough to be asked to judge Chihuahuas which in 1956 were all smooth coated, so that I could watch their movement and have a pretty good idea of their construction faults before I ever got to handle them.

With coated breeds it is much more difficult unless the fault is a glaring one like 'running up behind' which always means incorrect low set shoulders and a straight hind leg without any bend of stifle. When judging poodles I know that if an exhibitor has grown the hair on the feet so long that they are obliterated then I can expect flat feet for if the feet are good everybody wants to trim the foot so as to reveal their excellence. Mention of feet reminds me that I should mention that I was taught by one of the country's top All-rounders, Jimmy Garrett, how he could assess how a dog is made by the way he wears his feet − just like a human shoe 'that wears down at the heel'. This applies to dogs that exercise a lot on hard ground but does not necessarily refer to Yorkies.

As far as a guide to assessing conformation and sound construction is concerned the Yorkshire Terrier Standard is just about useless. For instance read what it has to say about 'The Mouth':

> 'Perfectly even with teeth as sound as possible. An animal having lost any teeth through accident not to be faulted provided the jaws are even.'

Now how does one define such a statement? What is 'even'? Does it mean every tooth should be smoothly in place or does it refer to the 'bite'? Should the top teeth and the bottom teeth meet together? Mrs Edith Stirk gave me the diagrams opposite showing mouth formations. A and B are obviously incorrect and I do not care for C with its missing teeth and yet this much more typifies the correct mouth required by the Standard than D which Mrs Stirk says is considered perfect. While it can be admitted that it would be the only one accepted on the Continent for show and breeding purposes, they are extremely particular about mouths even to demanding forty-two present in the mouths of all the dogs they breed from and show. All the same our Standard's requirement of 'even' would not seem to describe a scissor-bite. In order to bring our ruling closer to our more demanding overseas adherents of our Breed some clarification could well be considered. The American Kennel Club allows for 'scissor' or 'level bite'. The head is to be rather small and flat − not round in the skull and the muzzle must not be too long. There is absolutely no mention of 'Terrier' head. In fact the Standard does not describe a 'Terrier' head at all, not a Working Terrier at any rate. So often one reads of the 'perfect Terrier head' that some judges enthuse over in their reports.

Body must be very compact with a good loin. Compact means square from the withers to the tail and from the withers to the ground. Very compact means that the measurement may be taken from the brisket which makes the

(a)

(b)

(c)

(d)

Fig 14 The mouth: (a) Overshot. The upper jaw protudes over the lower. (b) Undershot. The lower jaw protudes beyond the upper. (c) Level bite, with upper and lower teeth meeting. This is recognised as correct. (d) Scissor bite, considered perfect animal even shorter backed. So much for all those long-backed specimens that can be found at every show. Good balance is most important in the Yorkshire Terrier, as is a level back. The Standard calls for a good 'loin'. Now this is the region of the body on either side of the vetebrae (back bone) and is situated between the last rib and the hindquarters.

Feet as round as possible signifies that 'cat feet' are essential. Tail carried just a little higher than the level of the back and cut to medium length; while the tail continues to be docked the actual quality of the tail does not need to be worried about. All the same, if the protaganists who are lobbying the Kennel Club and media to do away with tail-docking completely have their way it will be necessary to be able to recognise all the faulty tails that could come into being, especially as no notice has ever been taken of imperfections in this direction. You could find gay tails or ring tails that spoil the appearance nearly as much as squirrel tail does. Nothing would look more horrible than a 'screw' tail though, so let's hope the reformers never get their way.

Forequarters − legs to be quite straight and well covered with hair. Now there is no mention of the shoulders and, if they are to be straight also, that would make the dog most unsound. In fact the American Kennel Club have altered it to make it more readily described and in order to give their judges what to look for they add 'elbows neither in nor out'. I would go further and call for the position of the shoulders to be indicated in much the same way as in the Interim Standard of the Australian Silky Terrier which I have judged in Sweden to Championship Status and where the description of the shoulder is so exact as to leave no doubt at all in a judge's mind:

> Forequarters − Shoulders fine and well laid back, fitting with well-angulated upper arms snugly to ribs, elbows turned neither in or out, forelegs refined, round bone, straight and set well under body with no weakness in pasterns.

It would be a poor judge indeed who could not follow this very detailed and knowledgeable guideline. Whoever evolved the Yorkshire Terrier Standard had no such understanding for when it comes to the all-important hind-quarters his description of what is required is the worst I have ever studied; I quote in detail for obvious reasons:

> Hindquarters − Legs quite straight.

The rest of the requirement covers hair and hair alone − well-covered with hair of a golden tan (rich) a few shades lighter at the ends than at the roots, not extending higher on the hind leg than the stifle.

Any animal with the kind of straight legs described above would be a complete cripple with absolutely no mobility at all. It is imperative that there is angulation in order for the leg to be propelled forward. How much of an angle depends on how the dog is constructed. As a level top line is asked for and the dog must be 'important' and give the impression of a vigorous and well-proportioned body it would appear that plenty of angulation is called for and a well-bent stifle.

The American Kennel Club has it that the hind legs are 'straight' when viewed from behind but stifles are moderately bent when viewed from the side. Obviously the American judges were as puzzled as I am and they have had to readjust our very inadequate description of one whose only concern was with coat and colour. My friend with the Silky Terrier puts it most beautifully:

Hindquarters —Thighs well developed. The stifles should be well turned and the hocks well bent. When viewed from behind the hocks should be well let down and parallel with each other.

This is exactly what is wanted for the Yorkshire Terrier. What a pity this expert on dog anatomy wasn't alive when the Yorkshire Terrier Club was formed in 1898.

Judging the Yorkshire Terrier abroad

America

The American Kennel Club have their own Standard and exhibitors have much more say in where and when their challengers have to compete. American judges like a large type which can move and keep up with the biggest of the big breeds and the gundogs and hounds. The handlers like a dark coat that can be glossed to shine and attract the judge's eye and if the tail is erect, it saves them holding it up. They always show their Yorkshire Terriers on a lead and do not use a box to stand them on. They have to collect points to become a champion and these are allotted on the number of entries so the exhibitors can boast of a five point major etc. The Best of Sex is the Winner. According to the number of entries per class there is a scale of points and an exhibit needs fifteen points to become a champion. This position is not considered very important except that the Americans have a class for champions and the winner of this class competes against the winner of the Champion Class for Best of Variety. It is the winners in each sex that add up to championship points and when a champion goes round the shows competing against other champions it is called 'specialing' and when the Best of Variety wins a group against all the other group winners of the Toy Section he can then compete against all the other groups and so become Best in Show. Nearly all the shows in America and Canada are championship shows so that they can all help qualify an exhibit for championship status. Judges are trained at puppy matches and they have a system of sweepstakes wherein the owner of a dog declares it as a puppy and enters it in its appropriate class for puppies only. A separate judge is appointed for the puppy sweepstakes and

The fabulous Ch. Cede Higgins going Best in Show at Westminster Show 1980 with his proud owner Mrs Barbara Switzer and the famous judge Mrs James E. Clark (nee Anne Hone Rogers).

they are a way of getting extra funds.

In this country we have a red ribbon for a first prize and a blue for the second but in America they have a blue ribbon for first prize and a red one for the second prize. This always confuses me to start with when I am judging over there but the ring steward takes charge of the ribbons and I only have to hand them out.

One very good arrangement at all the American shows is that places are marked clearly 1st, 2nd, 3rd and Reserve (which fourth place is known as in this country). Five dogs are called out in case one is eliminated. In this country if there is a big class five places are filled and the fifth is known as Very Highly Commended or VHC. At Crufts there are cards for sixth place HC (Highly Commended) and C (Commended). At such an important show even a seventh place is appreciated and prized.

We have Crufts, and America has Westminster which is held at the Madison Square Garden which sees the top boxing and sporting events over there much as our Albert Hall does here. I have visited it on very many occasions and as I have very important friends who have private boxes right up in the roof, I have had the opportunity of watching events through binoculars. The groups are judged at night and it is a full evening dress affair.

The Yorkshire Terriers favoured in America are rather sturdier than ours and with a strong hind action which propels the dogs around the ring. Showmanship more than soundness is often thought to be vital but the Yorkshire Terrier Club of America is a very lively one and is active up and down the States with every area having its breed club and then a big get-together at the New York Statler Hilton each year the day before Westminster Show and all the Yorkshire Terrier followers from each individual Club bring their exhibits to show at both events. I stay at the Statler because it has a tunnel across to the Garden which saves a lot of hassle and the show is in a beautiful ballroom with chandeliers. Annie Swan refers to the first and only breeder of the thirties as 'Mr Goldie Stone' but Goldie is very much a lady and a very important one in American Yorkshire Terrier history. Back in the early thirties and forties Goldie made everybody want to own a Yorkshire Terrier. Mrs Myrtle Durgin was just such a one and obtained Mickey in 1940. He was Best of Breed in Yorkies at Westminster in 1945 and he was winning Best in Show awards for at least ten years without ever being beaten in the breed. When I was in the States in 1971 Myrtle had just attended her thirty-second Chicago International and she had then, in her eighty-sixth year, celebrated over forty years in the breed. She won her first award under my old friend Alva Rosenberg, one of America's all time greats in the judging world, who has given my own dogs very high awards. His death some years ago was deeply mourned by all the dog showing fraternity.

Another very important Yorkshire Terrier prefix is Wildweir belonging to the two sporting sisters Miss Janet Bennett and Mrs L.S. Gordon Jr of Glenview, Illinois. Their foundation was 'Ch. Star Twilight of Clu-Mor' bred by the Misses M. and F. Loton of Eire. 'Ch. Wildweir Pomp and Circumstance' was probably the greatest stud force in the breed in America. The Mayfair Yorkie House of Ann Seranne and Barbara Wolferman is one of the top kennels having the famous Wendell J. Sammet for their handler, and you can't get much better than that. On the other hand Margaret L. Spilling handled her own bred 'Ch. Shareen Mr Tee See' to Best in Show, which in the U.S.A. is an incredible accomplishment. When I was over in '69 'Ch. Topsy of Lodestar' was doing all the winning and she was bred by Ethel Tole in England and she won forty-three Best of Breed awards including Westminster in 1962 and she also won the Veteran Class at Beverley Hills and New York City. She was owned by Ann Seranne and Barbara Wolferman and was the dam of two very famous children in 'Champion Dandy Diamond of Mayfair' and 'Ch. Dandy Duke of Mayfair' both sired by 'Kelpie's Belsiehill Dondi'. He was born on the 14 July 1958. One adorable tiny Yorkie from Mayfair had an quite awkward name − 'Barban Yam 'N Yelly'.

Am. Ch. Wildweir Pomp N' Circumstance owned by Mrs Leslie Gordon and Miss Janet Bennett; top producer of all time. Featured in the pedigree of Emmrill Jigsaw who was imported by the author in 1970 to improve her breeding programme.

right English and American Ch. Star Twilight of Clu-Mor, foundation sire of the Wildweir Yorkshire Terriers.

Wolpert's owned by Alberta Walsh and handled by Fred Wolpert were my favourites when I saw them in New York. I especially liked 'Ch. Mayfairs Anchovy', who was a better colour than his kennel mates.

'Ch. Deebee's Beebee' bred by Mrs C.M. Pitchey and sold to America by Mrs S.D. Beech of the famous Deebee's Yorkshire Terriers. 'Beebee's' sire was 'Deebee's Bumble Boy' and her dam 'Wee Polly Fisher of Whipton' and she was born on 11 September 1969. After winning well over here she was sold for a very high figure to Mrs Gloria Lipman of Shelter Bay Drive, Great Neck, New York. The Lipman's home was on what is known as Long Island, and I was friendly with them for a long time before they moved out to the West Coast, which has never been a port of call of mine. Once when my daughter and I were staying at the Statler Hilton in New York the Lipmans sent a limousine to drive us down to their home in Long Island. It was February and the roads were snowbound and when we came to the River Hudson that too had huge boulders of ice in it. We had a warm welcome from humans and dogs and if any home of any Yorkies could be likened to a palace the Lipman's place certainly could, it was near the river with lawns on two levels, the boys and girls separated. The boys had the ground floor with a huge lawn bounded by the river and the girls were on an upper floor with an enormous balcony leading from the living quarters and also another huge lawn. All the floors were covered with the best velvet finish towels everywhere the little dogs ran, and they ran everywhere, even up their own special little staircase and on to their owner's glamorous bed. As the towels were soiled they were whipped up by one of the servants and taken to a shute and sent down to the basement where a huge washing machine was housed. In the machine and out and into an equally huge tumbler drier which dried them completely and back onto the floors again on a sort of conveyor belt system. They were all as happy as Larry and had the best food and a staff to care for their grooming, which was also continual like the towel laundry. We spent a most interesting time as the beautiful house was chock-a-block with treasures, and we saw the dogs' food being cooked in a microwave oven, which was the first time we ever saw one of those in action — straight out of the freezer, a couple of minutes and ready cooked completely.

I had taken Gloria a signed copy of my book and a few months later I had a most excited 'phone call from them at four o'clock in the morning telling me that they had actually 'borned' a litter themselves with the aid of my book. Gloria had read out my instructions and Stan had actually been the midwife and doing all the usual things that we others do without thinking, but which for a high-powered business man like Stan was certainly something, as all the other whelpings had been performed by their veterinarian. Gloria sat in bed in the bedroom and watched Stan operating in the bathroom the other side of a wall, on a closed circuit television. Four puppies were produced and everything went perfectly and it was a very pleased Stan who telephoned me quite proudly.

15 The Yorkie Abroad

OUT of the 8,842 Yorkshire Terriers that were registered at the English Kennel Club in 1968 no less a figure than 1,743 were exported, the majority of them going to the United States of America. This works out at a fifth of the number registered. Yorkies were the top export breed, a fact which places a great onus on the people who send these little ambassadors around the world to make sure that only the best of their breeding ever leaves Britain. If breeders of Yorkshire Terriers made quite sure that only the pick of all their breeding was ever exported there would not be any need to write this chapter. The reverse, however, seems to be happening and anything that can vaguely answer to the name of Yorkshire Terrier can find a place on a plane these days bound for some place or other.

Perhaps some breeders have no care for what might befall their stock after it has left their hands but, for those people who are in complete ignorance of the requirements of buyers from other countries, here are just a few details that may have escaped their attention.

Only send the best and make sure that the price asked is commensurate with the quality you are sending. It is expensive rearing and exporting and the people receiving the dog would much rather pay a sensible, fair price and get a good quality Yorkie and a fair deal than pay a lower price and get rubbish. Only dealers who buy a good many puppies at a time have a right to expect a price reduction. Put a fair price on your pup and stick to it. Some people are sending Yorkie puppies abroad for much less than the fare. This, of course, is ridiculous and they deserve to lose their market altogether. Who would value or treasure a diamond ring that cost no more than the box it was packed in.

Make sure that all the documentation required for the country of the dog's reception have been obtained and all the requirements attended to. Some expect a stamped consular certificate something like a visa, which would cost about £3–£4 to accompany the dog, and every exported pup *must* be accompanied by a veterinary certificate of good health to say he is fit for the journey — this is required by all air and shipping lines. Also vital is an Export Certificate issued by the Ministry of Agriculture, Fisheries and Food to say there has been no RABIES in this country during a stated period. For some of the African Countries you may have to swear before a Commissioner of Oaths, on the Holy Bible, that the dog you propose sending to their country has been bred in this country and has never left it. This may sound silly but it is in order to make sure that the dog came only from Great Britain and was not just stopping here on its way from some other country where it may have picked up rabies infection. Because of our strict quarantine laws other countries are willing to give dogs from our country a more lenient time on arrival than from some others. Even Mauritius demands six months' quarantine, Australia about 10 weeks for dogs from England, up to 120 days for dogs from elsewhere. Australia is very strict about dogs arriving in their country and used not to receive any dog arriving by air under any circumstances. New Zealand allows the entry of dogs from Great Britain if accompanied by a statutory declaration as well as the normal health certificate. The new owner must keep the dog away from all other dogs for eight weeks. Exhibitors seem to manage to keep dogs in country districts in New Zealand but the life of a dog in the urban areas is very restricted and no dog is allowed on public transport, in public parks, in shops, taxis or on beaches.

For some countries it is necessary to obtain an import licence or a special permit from the government of that country before a dog can be sent. It is wise to ascertain that there are no such requirements before sending a dog to any country. Don't listen to the people that say their dogs always travel without such trifles. Their dogs may be smuggled in but, that is not the way to ensure the best and safest journey for your own dog. Many tiny dogs have suffered greatly, some have even died, when being squashed in a bag or suitcase, dosed with sleeping drugs and given no air or water for hours on end. I heard of one such buyer who had 15 tiny puppies in a large carpet bag and they travelled by sea and train from Dover to Paris as one dog only with one permit. Of the fifteen several were quite dead on arrival and several very near it. The dead ones were chucked in the Seine from the taxi and as soon as that lot were sold the seller was back looking for more. The taxi-driver reported the matter but nothing could be proved.

Dogs exported to Sweden must undergo a blood test for leptospirosis within seven days of shipment. They are confined for up to a month when they will be subjected to another blood test for the same purpose and, if found positive the dog is destroyed or returned to the sender. I had the misfortune nearly to lose a tiny puppy once when the vet collapsed the vein trying to obtain a blood sample. Prompt attention just saved his life but, I was reluctant to put him through the same procedure again so cancelled the sale. At a later date another tiny dog, but this time much older than the four months old pup just mentioned, was in the same predicament. I went to the Swedish Embassy and saw the Agricultural Attaché, requesting him to let my tiny through without the test. He, apparently, had no say in such a matter and suggested that I take the dog to Sweden myself and explain to the inspector there just as I had done to him. I did so and the inspector was most sympathetic but still maintained that the pup would have to be tested. He took him away and was supposed to keep him a month but the very next morning he was sent round to my hotel, none the worse for his adventure, and although I looked most

Ch. Wildweir Bumper Sticker winning at the International at Chicago, 1980. Owned by Mrs Leslie Gordon and Miss Janet Bennett.

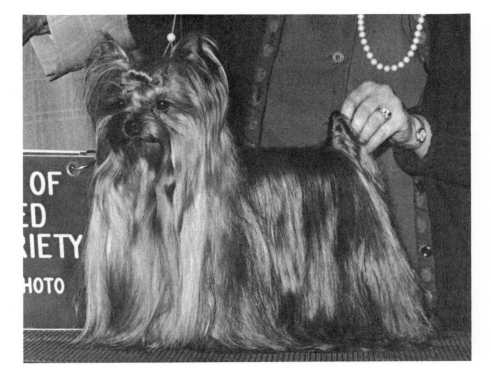

carefully I did not find any mark of a blood sample having been taken. I did not question the matter, however, as I was so thankful to have the baby safe and sound for delivery to his new owner. I think they probably took some blood but not from a vein. Anyway the rules are most strict and I now make sure that any puppy I send to Sweden is on the extra robust side and will not turn a hair at losing the required amount of blood.

People bent on exporting their stock should have the sense to study their markets too. What suits one country's requirements would be all wrong for another's:

AMERICA: All the North American countries are most interested in very small Yorkies and coat quality is of utmost importance. Exhibitors complain that they are being sent Yorkshire Terriers with broken coats, woolly coats that won't lie flat and Yorkies that turn pale silver at six months. They are not fussy about the total number of teeth as are most of the European countries but they do appreciate what they call 'a good bite' — meaning level and properly set teeth. Above all they insist on a gay ring temperament and an upright tail carriage even if we don't like it over here. They are shown on the ground, not on a box, so a little training in this respect will not be wasted. Many professional handlers are in charge of the Yorkies in the ring and they insist on the ability to grow coat above everything else, as competition is very keen. Yorkies have been in America since 1880 and are very popular.

AUSTRALIA: They are very much liked in that country and some of the older breeders have a long line of their own strains to show. New owners are very keen to learn and should be given instructions on guarding the coat from the heat and on suitable diets. There is not much of a pet market yet, except perhaps in the main towns.

BELGIUM: The exhibitors here attend the French and German shows, so have a good chance to study the types favoured by these two countries, which are really very wide apart. There is a great partiality in Brussels and the major towns for very tiny pets and so the smaller type of show stock is probably the safest to send. As all the continentals do, Belgium puts great importance on evenness and number of teeth. Full 42 teeth is preferred.

BRAZIL: Like U.S.A. — the more glamorous looking the better and will pay for the trouble taken to send out with a good coat.

CANADA: Often exhibitors travel to shows in the United States so much the same requirements exist.

DENMARK: Dogs in Denmark are shown in Germany and associated countries but not in Scandinavia because Germany has rabies. Very particular about soundness in limbs and body and, as a contingent of breeders is present at Crufts most years and very often at other shows, they are very knowledgeable about the state of the breed over here. Ch. Blairsville Royal Seal's litter sister is over there so the standard is very high.

EIRE: It is normally possible to travel between Eire and U.K. without any quarantine regulations. Shows in Eire give Green Stars instead of C.C.s and three green stars enables a dog to be called an Irish Champion. If he is already an English Champion he can then be known as an International Champion. Many famous little Yorkies have won this double honour. Northern Ireland comes under the English Kennel Club rules and C.C.s are available there.

FRANCE: During many visits to France and a fairly regular attendance at the Paris Exhibition which is the most important show in the French calendar, I have seen much disappointment expressed because the Yorkshire Terriers many of the exhibitors had received from England had grown far too big. Actually, many of these ladies only bought their Yorkie for a pet, in the first instance, but it is the fashionable thing for Parisian ladies to exhibit at the Paris Exhibition even if they never go to another show. The standard may not be as high as over here, or many of the coats put down with the finesse we are accustomed to see, nevertheless, they adore their little Yorkies and treasure them highly. It is a pity that some of them look so out of place among the mink

CAC winner Sophie
from France.

and diamonds, and nothing worth the large sum of money that would have
been paid for them. They would all have cost their owners at least £200 or
more and some looked expensive at £5. Size was, often as not, of the widest
variance, and while the most favoured size is between 3 lb. to 4 lb. some of
them would turn the scale at 14 lb. at least.

English breeders are obviously unaware that only very few licences to
import dogs are issued by the French government and the people who possess
them are quite able to pay good prices for the dogs they import as they are in a
very good way of business indeed. If buyers come and say that they can only
sell their pups for £30–£40 they are not genuine dog dealers and would
possibly be selling the pups in the street markets. I know for a fact that stud
fees are about £75 a time and no French breeder would sell or need to sell the
pups at a loss to himself. Don't forget that Paris is one of the world's biggest
centres for overseas visitors and people from all over the world go there and
the South of France, and so buy expensive puppies to take home. English
breeders who sell cheap pups to France are losing not only the price of a good
puppy but the possible market as well. The Yorkshire Terrier has only been
so desirable to many people abroad because he was difficult to find. Make him
two a penny and his popularity will vanish overnight.

When my middle daughter was studying in Paris she met a doctor's wife
socially and this lady asked what the Yorkshire Terriers were like in England.
When she heard that we bred them she was more than interested and to cut a
long story short when I visited my daughter I took a little Yorkie bitch with
me in the plane, to show her, and if it was good enough to enter at the Paris
Exhibition. My daughter's friend was delighted with the bitch and asked if I

would sell her. As I couldn't take her home I was glad she liked her and so began my long association with the President of the Yorkshire Terrier Club of France, which she founded. When this book was translated into French Mme Duchatel wrote the introduction and was instrumental in supervising the translation, all the pictures, which were taken by a French photographer of very high standing and she arranged the veterinary article which was done by one of the leading French Veterinary Surgeons. The book contains a picture of us both in the Yorkshire Terrier ring when we were judging at the Paris Exhibition.

Since the arrival of such sires as Hampark Dandy there has been a big improvement in the colours of the coats but they divide their classes into weight which is the only country I have visited that does so. It has changed again and there is only one class under 3,500 kg. For a time exhibitors from Belgium and Germany brought boxes covered with drapes as we have them here. Mme Duchatel thought they had an unfair advantage so she banned them.

GERMANY: The German Kennel Club (Verband für das Deutsche Hundewesen (VDH), Schwanenstrasse 30, Dortmund) is the only club in Germany recognised by our Kennel Club and they have full control over all breeding. Stud dogs and brood bitches cannot be mated together until inspected by the VDH and satisfy them as to the suitability of the proposed mating. When the litter is born it also is inspected and any discards are taken away and destroyed. No dogs can be registered with the VDH unless they pass inspection and the standard is very high as to number of teeth, colour of coat, conformation and lack of inherited maladjustments. The German exhibitors are very anxious to buy the best and keep their breeding to a high standard. It is up to British breeders to see they are not disappointed.

HOLLAND: As this country does much business with Germany and shows are attended in both countries it is safest to comply with the highest standard if repeat orders are required. It may not be generally known that hind dew claws are a sign of degeneracy and no dog who was born with hind dew claws can be bred from in Holland. Don't send such stock even if the dew claws have been removed as the scar will disqualify it just the same.

SWEDEN: In 1958 I went to Sweden to watch one of my Poodles being shown at Gothenburg show by Mrs Connie Runefels, who I had met at Blackpool Show some years before and who had admired the dogs I was showing and asked to buy one. I visited her home after the show − she lived in Dalby a lovely country place near the old university city of Lund and we had many good times together. She had a tiny little Yorkie as a house pet named Cotton and she really wanted to breed from her but did not have a dog. I had been entertained so lavishly that I promised to help and when I returned to England set about finding what she wanted. Her son was a well known terrier

International Ch. Carmardy Benjamin bred by Mr and Mrs H. Parkin and owned by Bernice Undên of the famous Debonaire kennels in Sweden. Best of Breed at Gothenberg International Show.

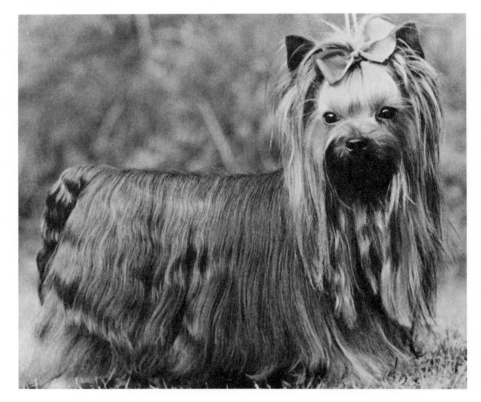

man and he said get a 'sound' dog. Cotton was tiny so I knew I wanted a tiny one. I had been brought up with Yorkies so I went to my contacts who all told me to go to Edith Stirk. Edith had only short-legged dogs at that time and I did not like them, however she put me in touch with Mrs Chorlton Haw, who lived near me and incidently supplied me with dog meat and biscuit. In the end I had to fall back on Edith who came up with something a bit longer in the leg and so I bought it and sent it off to Connie. Apparently it did the trick and was the foundation of Connie becoming the top Yorkshire Terrier Breeder in Sweden. I visited her in 1979 and she still has some of her Yorkies although she has stopped breeding in a big way and only does so as a hobby. A bitch she had bred was Best of Breed at Malmo International Show under the Japanese judge Honda. I had bought Carmardy dogs from Mr and Mrs Parkin and Connie liked them so she used a Carmardy bred dog and produced her present winning strain.

ITALY, SPAIN, SWITZERLAND AND PORTUGAL: All these countries' shows are attended by the others as travel between them is easier. The South of

France and Monaco are also included in this group. Entry is easy and many good dogs are shown at some of the shows but many of the venues are better than the entries. Yorkshire Terriers have yet to gain a foothold in these countries and when they do they will put on special classes for them.

KENYA: Much interest in Yorkshire Terriers for many years and they have topped the shows several times. ZIMBABWE AND S. AFRICA are also enthusiatic and hold regular shows where classes are put on for Yorkies and many exports have become champions.

JAPAN: There is a great demand for Yorkshire Terriers in Japan and anyone wishing to export to this country should ascertain if the dog will live in the house and what arrangements will ultimately be made for euthanasia if and when this is necessary. Many Japanese are only too willing to give their dogs the same benefits that we do ourselves but it is always best to be sure about this before sending to this country, as they have different laws and customs to ours. Dog breeding and exhibiting has been a hobby with many Japanese over a great many years and it was not until a company appeared on the scene, buying large numbers of dogs to breed from on a sort of battery system or to put bitches out on terms with families, that it was decided to boycott the practice as no provision is made in the 'Loan of Bitch' agreement for what happens to the bitches when their breeding days are over. Many articles have been written and most frightening pictures drawn of the misery that they can expect and breeders are, naturally loth to risk the same thing happening to the dogs exported. An agreement with the buyer that a painless death will end the dog's life can be suggested but it could only be a gentleman's agreement, and most people will prefer not to send dogs at all.

As there is so much interest there is really no difficulty in finding foreign buyers and an advertisement in the dog papers will produce any amount of enquiries from overseas. Any dogs winning at shows will have an audience of foreigners soon grouped round it and Crufts is the best shop-window we have in this country. Any Yorkshire Terrier who has won a 1st, selected prize at a championship show during the year previous can be entered at Crufts. Other championship shows make no such stipulation. The Kennel Club will print your kennel prefix under each breed heading for a quite modest sum of per year and many overseas buyers contact the Kennel Club for information, in the first instance.

When enquiries arrive for your stock, reply as soon as possible and give as exact a description of the dogs you have to offer as you can. Explain about the breeding quite briefly and there is no need to send off pedigrees as they cost a great deal to post and the Kennel Club's official one will be the only one acceptable to other countries anyway. Some people abroad are interested in obtaining as many British pedigrees as they can get, and they do not realise that it costs the sender a great deal of money to post back airmail as they always request. Stamps of foreign countries, although nice to receive are not usable when sending from this country. Always give a fairly accurate assessment of the cost of the dog plus all the expenses that will be met and get a payment for the complete amount. Never send a dog abroad that has not been paid for. If your client does not want to trust his money to you get him to pay it into a London bank and, when he lets them know that the dog has arrived safely and meets with his satisfaction, then he must advise the bank to pay the money either to you direct or into your bank. This is quite a businesslike method of doing business with strangers and the banks are quite used to such matters.

Get a quotation from the airline you propose using, sending them the measurements and cubic capacity as well as the weight of the travelling box with the puppy inside. Charge the fee for transport to the airport, if you have to employ an agent to do this, and add the cost of the Health Certificate and the Monorchid Certificate which will have to be signed by your vet, if you are shipping a male. The Kennel Club will not issue an Export Pedigree to a dog that is a Monorchid or Cryptorchid and the vet will charge a fee for his examination and for signing the K.C. Certificate which you will receive from the Kennel Club when you apply for the transfer form to a person in a foreign country. The Kennel Club issues three generation pedigrees for £15 plus £2.25 VAT plus the £4.60 transfer cost.

The Ministry of Agriculture form of Export Certificate referring to Rabies must be applied for beforehand. There is no charge.

The Airline will give all details of the requirements that the country importing the dog will lay down and you would be wise to contact them as soon as your client decides on one or more of your dogs. Never export any dog under 12 weeks and make sure there is time to give it a full inoculation.

Make a tentative booking with the airline and inform your client of the flight number and day and time of arrival. If any alteration occurs you will have to cable the change of plans. Arrange for a radio message to be sent ahead to enable your client to meet the plane, if possible. Obtain a travelling kennel of wood or fibre glass (the latter will cost more but weigh less and so your freight cost will be lower). Make sure that the dog has room to stand upright and the box is long enough for him to stretch his tail without hitting the end of the box. It should be narrow in width so that he won't fall over if the plane lurches. Label the box with the name and address and possible telephone number of the buyer and add any feeding instructions that may be necessary for the airline staff on the journey. A water container can be built into the box. Put the dog's pet name on the label so that he can be talked to as he is bound to feel apprehensive, on the way over. When you value the dog for customs don't forget to subtract the cost of his journey from the sum you received for the dog. Only the net amount is chargeable. You will have to make out an Air Way Bill and on this you must put the instructions about the journey and how the dog is to be collected at the other end. Insurance charges are also allowed for. You will receive a copy of this bill for your own files and one will go to the consignee. If kept together in a file these Air Way Bills will contain much useful information for future export business. Don't forget to tie some food on for the journey.

Dogs to Australia used to go by sea and this takes about five weeks. The booking will have to be made well in advance and it may be better if you put the whole matter into the hands of a shipping agent who will collect the dog from your house and get him delivered the other end and see to all the paper work and bookings, etc., which are quite considerable as food must be taken for the whole journey. I have always found the ship's officers very kind and interested in the small dogs I have sent to Australia and they have often travelled in style with regular visits to the bridge at the captain's request. It is obvious that Yorkies will stand a journey of this sort much better than bigger dogs. The work entailed in exporting dogs is quite considerable and if the time taken is added to the cost of shipping, etc., it is doubtful that much profit will be made on the deal unless the price asked was three figures at least.

Mass exports of young puppies are a bad thing as the pups sometimes stay in warehouses until sold to shops and dealers.

16 Ailments and First Aid

WHILE being the first to summon professional help for any serious condition, an owner of a number of dogs will acquire a working knowledge of dozens of conditions and emergencies that, with the right remedy and a little common-sense and 'know-how', can save a considerable sum in vets' bills and, in a real crisis, can often mean the difference of life and death, by being able to act in time.

No kennel would be complete without its medicine chest and a little guidance as to its contents and their use is included for the novice breeder. Most readers have their own favourite specifics and, if you are ever successful with a certain remedy, you will find that you will always resort to that until something even better is found.

I should like to state at the beginning that all drugs should be used under veterinary supervision only. If, for instance, your vet suggests that you should use a certain specific for the relief of diarrhoea, it would be wise to always have a fresh supply of this drug handy as this is one of the commonest ailments found in any kennel. Any sudden change in temperature, food or routine can trigger off an attack and besides being a very messy business to deal with, it is so weakening that unless toy breeds are dosed very early on, they get very weak and can die sometimes before veterinary aid has been summoned.

For very tiny pups, and older toys also, I find 'Vansup', manufactured by Stevenson, Turner and Boyce of Reading, Berks., a safe and very effective specific. My vet supplies it and it not only contains the safe amount of Neomycin, Streptomycin, etc., but is fortified with Vitamin A, Vitamin D, Vitamin E and Vitamin K. The dose is half an inch of the paste per pound of bodyweight daily. It is supplied with a spatula and tube for ease in dosing and we have had very swift results.

All the items in your medicine chest need checking over regularly as many of them may have deteriorated in storage.

The medical chest

Bandages — various sizes
Cottonwool and roll of cellular padding or baby's Paddi-pads
Thermometer

Surgical scissors and tiny nail scissors
Borax
Bicarbonate of Soda
Kaolin Powder
Permanganate of Potash
Epsom Salts
Flowers of Sulphur
Zinc Oxide
Boracic Powder
Fuller's Earth
Canker Powder
Tooth Powder
Insect Powder (containing Gammaxene)
Savlon Ointment
Cetavlon
T.C.P.
Hydrogen Peroxide (best thing for deep wounds and bleeding)
Cough Mixture (Liquefruta is good as it contains garlic)
Dinneford's Magnesia (for very tiny puppies)
Milk of Magnesia
Castor Oil (especially good for immediate first-aid for eye injury)
Liquid Paraffin
Friar's Balsam (for inhaling)
Glucose
Travel Sickness Pills
Baby Aspirin
Penbritin (Penicillin)
Rhubarb Tablets (the best and safest cure for constipation)
Raspberry Leaf Tablets for Whelping difficulties
Garlic Tablets
Honey
Nestlés Milk
Worm Tablets or Medicine
Cod Liver Oil
Halibut Oil
Olive Oil
Mange Dressing (Tetmosol)
Sweet Oil
Soft Soap
Benbow's Conditioner or similar
Linseed Oil
Eye drops and dropper
Tubes of Eye Ointment
Gentian Violet

Tannic Acid Jelly (for burns)
Parrish's Food (for anaemia and poor appetite)
Arrowroot
Slippery Elm Food (both these are good to feed in cases of sickness)
Burroughs & Wellcome's Hydralised Protein (kept in the fridge)
Bottle of Calcium Gluconate
Hypodermic syringe
Crooke's Collo Cal D or Adexolin
Tin of SA 37 (complete Vitamins Supplement), Interpet Ltd.,
    Milton Road, Cambridge CB4 4BH
Small jar Virol
Tweezers and Safety Pins

Ailments

ABSCESSES: Poultice with Kaolin on a piece of lint covered with a bandage or bathe in a hot solution of salt water — one dessert-spoonful to one teacupful of hot water.

ACCIDENTS: Call the vet immediately if a limb is broken. If a front leg, place it in a long cigar case to prevent movement until it can be set. Keep warm, give sugar water for shock and move as little as possible.

ANAL GLANDS: A very painful condition caused by a secretion accumulating in these glands. On no account should any attempt be made by an inexperienced person to squeeze the mess out. Irreparable harm can be done to a tiny Yorkie and lasting injury. A vet will soon empty the gland and then the trouble can be avoided by a sensible diet containing roughage — All Bran or Bemax. This condition is usually found among 'meat only' subjects.

ANAEMIA: Red corpuscles in the blood in short supply due to the result of severe illness, any haemorrhage or a shortage of red meat or liver from the diet. Iron and B12 injections or regular doses of a tonic such as Parrish's Food or Benbows will be beneficial.

BALANITIS: Inflammation of the sheath often found in old dogs. It appears as a creamy discharge at the end of the penis. Cure is an antibiotic injection and a mild antiseptic douche for which a jam jar can be utilised.

BALDNESS: If caused through alopecia, it is not contagious and may be helped with injections and added vitamins. Seaweed meal sprinkled over food is very beneficial. Massaging the head with an astringent such as eau-de-Cologne and bay rum. In old dogs regular grooming and conditioning baths are as effective as hormone treatments. B Complex and Folic Acid and Seaweed Meal are useful.

BAD BREATH: Decayed or dirty teeth, worms, indigestion and mouth infections cause bad breath. Ascertain the cause and treat accordingly. Chlorophyll tablets cover up the smell but do not cure the condition and charcoal biscuits will help disguise stomach odours.

BURNS: Treat bad burns with a compress of bicarbonate of soda and cold water and cover with lint to keep the air out. Treat for shock and get veterinary help.

BRONCHITIS and TRACHEO-BRONCHITIS: This condition should respond to antibiotics and will often clear up on its own without ever making the dog very ill. If despite treatment the cough persists it may be due to a worm in the larynx.

CAR SICKNESS: Don't feed for eight hours before a journey. Travel pills can be a help but a drink of milk and glucose before starting off sees most dogs all right. A travelling crate and a comfortable rug with a nice juicy bone or toy to chew and never let the dog look out of the window.

CORTISONE (BAD REACTION TO): This can make the dog bald, have fits. The vet can give a drug to counter-balance and a long course of Vit. C and Vit. E and all the B complex is indicated. It can be a long process.

COUGHS and COLDS: Being rather low to ground Yorkies can easily get chilled from draughts and cold floors. Beds should be raised eighteen inches off the ground. Half-hooded ones are cosy in winter.

CONCUSSION: Yorkies often concuss themselves by jumping up against a table or such. Very tiny ones often have a molero (like a baby's fontenal) which never completely closes up. Summon veterinary help, put a hot water bottle in a blanket and place near the patient, in case the shock will prove fatal. Give nothing — in fact put nothing in the mouth or it will choke him. It is a good idea to pull the tongue forward as it can cut off the supply of air through the passages. The sooner he is in the vet's care the better chance he has of recovering, for any form of unconsciousness means some damage to the brain.

COLIC: Violent stomach pains which can be caused by chill, worms or eating poison can cause death by shock in such a tiny dog as the Yorkie. Dr. Collis Browne's Chlorodyne given in minute doses in water is an effective first-aid remedy. This famous old remedy saved many thousands of lives in the Boer War and since but, as it contains Choloroform, Cocaine, Morphia, Opium, etc., to name but a few, it is hoped the small patient won't get hooked. An alternative treatment — Brandy in warm water with sugar can be equally habit forming! The vet will use Chlorotone or similar, but early treatment is essential.

CHOKING: If anything ever sticks in the throat hold the dog upside down and get someone with a small finger to try to hook it out. If unsuccessful get veterinary help quickly or he could choke to death very quickly.

CONJUNCTIVITIS: Inflammation of the eyes is very common in this breed as the hair of the head will often rub against the eyeball and cause much discomfort. Washing the affected eyes with an eye lotion (boracic) is good but must not be allowed near the mouth as it is very poisonous. Let the lotion run from the inner to outer corner so as to keep the tear duct clear. Ointment containing Neomycin sulphate is excellent. Corto-caps are good but must be obtained from your vet.

CONSTIPATION: These lively active little dogs should not suffer in this respect as long as they get plenty of exercise and their diet contains enough roughage. An over-fat dog will often suffer though, and a weekly fast day started off with one or two rhubarb tablets is an excellent corrective. A safe mild laxative for young puppies and invalids is Milk of Magnesia. Three-quarters to half-teaspoonful daily until trouble disappears.

DANDRUFF: Very common in Yorkies and sometimes attributed to too much cow's milk. Change to Lactol or Nan or some such bitch equivalent milk and give an increased dose of cod liver oil and halibut oil or sunflower oil. To treat the skin wash in a shampoo made from two parts of Stergene to one part T.C.P. or Dettol. This is a very safe remedy for even the tiniest puppy. Selenium Sulphide is a modern and effective remedy as is Hexetidine. A cold tar shampoo is often all that is needed. Head and Shoulders is my vet's choice.

DIABETES: Recognised by the presence of sugar in the urine and the dog's breath having a sweet sickly smell coupled with an unusual craving for water. Kits are obtainable from Boots to test for sugar or your vet will soon do so if you let him have a sample of urine. Regular doses of Insulin have proved to be as effective with dogs as with humans.

DIARRHOEA: More often a symptom rather than an illness in itself. Nevertheless, it can cause an early death in tiny dogs as if prolonged it causes extreme weakness. Kaolin mixed with morphine is a quick and efficient first-aid treatment as it acts like blotting paper. This, of course, does not cure the cause, and it is often better to put the Yorkie on to a mixture of antibiotics which will then attack the particular bacteria which is the cause of the trouble. Infection or chills are the main cause and also eating infected or poisonous substances. Deep frozen meat must be thoroughly defrosted before feeding and all feeding vessels scrupulously cleansed. Stale sour biscuits can be the cause and also over-eating and worms. Neo-Sulphentrin is a fairly comprehensive mixture of antibiotics and covers a wide range of disorders. First-aid treatment — give a few drops of brandy in a teaspoonful of warm water and glucose. Never re-freeze defrosted meat.

DISTEMPER: Once the scourge of dogdom when whole kennels of dogs would die in a matter of days and none escaped crippling consequences. Anyone who has gone through the mental agony and soul-destroying numbness of nursing a kennel full of dogs through this very terrible illness is the best of all advocates in favour of immunisation of all puppies — pure and cross-bred — from the earliest possible moment. Anyone who buys an expensive Yorkie and then fails to protect it with a complete immunisation as soon as possible is a bigger fool than a man who buys a car and puts no oil in it. In fact, well deserves to go through all the horrors of nursing this dreadful disease through its many phases and then to end up with a little nervous cripple at the end of it. Effective immunisation is available from as early as three weeks of age with Measles Vaccine and complete protection is given with the present-day vaccines against Hardpad and Distemper (similar diseases), Hepatitis (Rubarth's Disease), which is transferable from the mother to her unborn pups, and Leptospiral Jaundice, etc., which is rat-borne. I could write a book about the symptoms and phases of this disease which was an inevitable hazard when I started to breed dogs. Protection is better than cure and we can be thankful we have the answer today in every vet's surgery. Parvo virus vaccine can now be included with the above.

ENTROPIAN: This is the medical term for ingrowing eyelashes, a very painful condition causing conjunctivitis and often 'blue eye'. Corto-caps are a very useful aid for soothing the condition but the only real cure is an operation. This condition is hereditary so care is needed in breeding.

EAR CANKER: More often the bane of long-eared dogs such as poodles and spaniels. If a Yorkie shows evidence of it suspect the family cat of breeding the mites which are the cause of this condition, boring about in the inside of the ear and driving the dog mad. The black discharge is from the inflammation this mite sets up and much damage can be done by the dog's own toenails when scratching. Ears must be cleansed out with Cetavlon solution or T.C.P. and a powdered mixture containing iodoform shaken well down inside to kill the mite, clear up the messy discharge and soothe the affected skin.

ECLAMPSIA: Only affects bitches during lactation. They go into fits and become unconscious and will die quickly if help is not sought without delay. An injection of Calcium Borogluconate will work wonders as the strain of making milk has put too much stress on the little mother and drained all the calcium from her blood stream. When this is replaced the mother will recover miraculously but the puppies should be taken away and hand fed.

EUTHANASIA: The lifespan of the dog being a lot less than our own there comes the time when our much-loved pets must be parted from us. If there is danger of a long, painful or distressing illness to be borne it is so much kinder to the dog, though not to ourselves, to have him or her put quietly to sleep. There is no benefit to a very old dog to keep him alive to just 'tick over' when he has known the delights of a vigorous life. Veterinary surgeons, R.S.P.C.A. inspectors and the P.D.S.A. are all equipped to put animals to sleep painlessly. You can do your part to this end by giving him a final feed of his favourite dish and including a large dose of a sleeping drug. He can then be played with or nursed and, as soon as the drug has taken effect, the vet. can give the injection which will put him even deeper to sleep so that he will not wake up again. This is by far the least distressing for owner and dog than see him struggling for breath with a bad heart or undergoing the intense pain of arthritis or malignant growths and such.

EYE ULCER: Fill the eye with cod-liver oil – the refined type given to babies and keep the dog in pitch darkness for six to eight weeks if you don't wish the eye to be permanently scarred. Exercise after dark if necessary but the worst looking eye can become sound again.

FITS and EPILEPSY: The animal will thrash about with his legs, his eyes look glassy, he may foam at the mouth. Wrap a large towel round the Yorkie and be careful he doesn't bite you as he is not aware of his actions. Hold him near the cold water tap and soak his neck and back of head until the limbs subside, then apply an ice-bag and wait for the vet to inject a sedative. Give nothing by mouth for fear of choking — a wooden spoon handle held between jaws will save the tongue being bitten. Keep very quiet for several weeks and give extra Vitamin B complex to help restore the nervous system.

FRACTURES: If you suspect that your dog has internal fractures or, in fact, any broken bones, slide a flat tray or similar object (I once used the children's blackboard), fill a hot water bottle and wrap the whole in a blanket and get the vet or, better still, get to the vet's surgery as quickly as possible as the bones will need X-rays.

GASTRITIS: Often caused by a Yorkie eating a too fatty diet. Give nothing but glucose and warm water until vomiting ceases. If very bad just wet tongue with white of egg. Do not let him have unlimited water as he will drink too much. Return to normal diet very slowly and omit fats, milk, cod liver oil until dog is quite normal. Fish and white meat such as chicken and rabbit are better than red meat for a few days.

HARDPAD: See under Distemper.

HEART ATTACK: Giddiness, shortness of breath and congestion of the lungs are all symptoms of heart trouble and veterinary help is essential as the machinery of the heart must be kept working for the dog to live. Much help is available and dogs have lived to a ripe old age on a daily quota of Digitalis and such-like drugs. Recognising the condition and getting help quickly are all-important. If the tongue is turning blue gently pull it forward and drop an eye dropper of brandy on the back of it. Vitamin E appears to have a restorative effect on the heart.

HEAT STROKE: Most likely to affect dogs shut up in cars or left on a show bench in the full sun. Always see the dogs have some shade in hot weather, that drinking water is always available and that if left in a car enough windows are left open for there to be a through draught. No dog should be left in a closed box, however much ventilation there appears to be. If a dog is found to be suffering from heat stroke his body temperature must be reduced at once. His life depends on how quickly this is done. Ice-packs on the head and a block of ice under his body, icy cold water poured all over him or his body immersed in icy water (his head free, of course). If all these fail to reduce the heat, tie him safely in a strong bag, attach it to the door of the car, let the bag hang outside the window and by holding it in your arms get someone else to drive the car at great speed for several miles. This will probably give him pneumonia but will save him from dying of heat stroke. This method was described to me by a doctor who had used it successfully to save men in the desert dying of heat stroke during the last war.

HEPATITIS: Like distemper this is better prevented than cured as it is one of the commonest causes of sudden death in young puppies and can be transmitted through the mother who is apparently in the best of health. The dog looks miserable and arches up its back, has sickness and diarrhoea which can suffer death very quickly. As this disease is really inflammation of the liver the dog is always likely to suffer the effects of an attack in after-life and many vets have a theory that the disease commonly known as 'Fading-out of Puppies' is closely allied, if not actually caused by, Canine Virus Hepatitis.

HYSTERIA: This was very often caused by the whitening agent in the flour from which dog biscuits were made and for years I used to cut up brown bread baked in the oven to feed my dogs. Now I have so many I make sure that I only buy wholemeal biscuits. I also use a finely kibbled meal as partly soaked biscuits with a very hard centre can cause very bad indigestion and the pain from this can make dogs scream with hysteria. Teething, worms and being of a highly strung and nervous disposition will often make a dog scream on that certain high-pitched note that points to hysteria and he may run madly round whining and barking with a glassy stare in his eyes. If you cannot get the dog into a darkened room throw a dark blanket all over him and hold him still until the attack subsides. The dog will need quiet, light diet, a good laxative and a course of Vitamin B Complex. Skull-cap is an old-fashioned remedy but still a very effective one for strengthening the nerves.

INTERDIGITAL CYSTS: Painful swellings between the toes which some terriers seem to have in a chronic form. They are probably caused by cuts with brambles or coarse grass or maybe through getting thorns or grass seeds embedded in the sensitive skin between the toes. Kaolin poultice, Basilican ointment or Epsom Salts and glycerine mixed to a paste are all good applications. Bathing with T.C.P., Dettol or Cetavlon after the cyst has burst will help clean up the trouble and reduce the chance of infection. It may be necessary to ask the vet. to give a Penicillin injection or a course of Penicillin tablets.

KENNEL COUGH: After many years of frustration over this nasty dry and very contagious cough there is now a new vaccine called INTRAC-1 from Mycofarm which is given by a special applicator into the nostrils and immunity is complete in five days and lasts ten months.

LEPTOSPIRAL JAUNDICE: This can be prevented with two injections at monthly intervals and can give protection against Leptospira Canicola (a disease of the kidneys which is transmitted from the urine of infected dogs and passed on to another dog when he sniffs it), and Icterrohaemorrhagia, which is a rat-borne disease and can be transmitted to humans. By the time the dog's eyeballs show the yellow that denotes this disease he is probably too ill to be helped. Temperatures are sub-normal, urine turns to deep orange in colour and vomiting of frothy white or yellow bile all are indications of this disease. Yearly booster injections are usually recommended to produce complete immunity.

LEAD POISONING: Usually caused through chewing paintwork with a lead base. Make sure that all paint that the dog comes in contact with is said to be safe for pets and children — in fact 'lead free'. Dogs with this trouble act just as though they were going mad and the brain gets very quickly affected before death mercifully intervenes.

MANGE: Sarcoptic or red mange is caused by a mite that burrows under the skin, lays eggs and then reappears on the skin again ready to burrow somewhere else. The skin is red and terribly itchy, the dog scratches and bites distractedly and the surface of the skin that isn't covered with the blotches of mange is made raw and inflamed with the scratching and biting. The cure can only be effected if the life cycle of the mite is observed and treatment is carried out accordingly. The first sign of the trouble and the dog should be bathed in Tetmosol (I.C.I.) or any other mange dressing. Kur Mange is also effective. Two days later, bathe again to kill the female as she emerges and three days later repeat the bathing to kill the hatched eggs that will emerge from the burrows. Leave for about a week and give three further baths and the dog should be cured. Burn all bedding, treat all woodwork with paraffin rubbed over it and burn sulphur candles in any kennels used after plugging up all air-inlets. Benzyl Benzoate solution will cure this trouble but is rather dangerous in use and could burn the eyes very badly. As it removes nail varnish as easily as varnish remover sold for this purpose its strength can be judged. Only a third of the dog at a time should be covered with Benzyl Benzoate, so its efficiency is not as sure.

Follicular or Dermodectic Mange is not as contagious as Sarcoptic (which is easily transmutable to humans) and appears to be a congenital disease passed on from the mother to the unborn puppies as the mite that causes

Follicular Mange lives right at the roots of the hair. The whole hair is destroyed and the skin gets to look hard and dry — just like elephant skin. There is no hope of treatment being effective with home remedies as in the previous case and your veterinary surgeon will have several different treatments to try perhaps and it may not necessarily be possible to cure it at all.

OBESITY: There were no fat people in Belsen and if your dog is too fat you are feeding him too much and of a too-starchy nature. Change to raw meat and feed at ½ oz. to each lb. and reduce this even further after a few weeks and you will add years to your dog's life.

PARVO VIRUS: This most frightening new disease has caused dog shows to be cancelled, kennels to be closed and long queues at vet's surgeries waiting for the feline vaccine previously used only for cats but which has proved effective for dogs as a preventive measure. Felocell by the Smith Kline Animal Health of Welwyn Garden City is recommended by my vet. The disease shows itself in some cases by violent vomitting followed by diarrhoea that lasted a week. Because of the lack of fluid that results saline drips are administered at the earliest possible moment and Kaoline and Morphine can be given by mouth to cope with the enteritis. Some of the litter affected will have no systems at all and they will quite likely have taken the type that affects the heart only and they could drop dead without warning even a year later. Autopsy will show dangerously enlarged hearts as the cause of death and there is absolutely no chance of saving them. A lot of literature is available and I have attended a symposium at Keele University. Given by the Small Animal Veterinary Association combined with Beechams and Irene McCandlish of Glasgow University showed us X-ray pictures to prove the points of her very informative lecture on this terrible disease. It is carried in the air and humans can bring it back from anywhere, the disease has been transmitted in the excreta of the dogs affected. Regular boosters are essential.

PERTHES DISEASE: Although tiny dogs like Yorkies don't suffer from Hip Displasia this is mostly confined to large breeds and can and do suffer an almost identical condition in their hips where the joint is widened and the femoral head displaced. It can affect puppies from two months to fourteen months and the peak age is about seven months and intense lameness is the result. It will get progressively worse over a matter of weeks, much pain will be caused and the hip will waste away and the limb will become shorter which in some cases can be caused by muscular spasm. After many months this condition appears to right itself and dogs get the use of their legs again. It is not thought to be hereditary but a similarity of upbringing and the same inbalance of hormones can trigger off this condition so the mother and her children could both suffer from it.

POISONS: In most cases of poisoning the sooner you can get the dog to vomit the better chance he has of recovery. Soda lumps pushed down his throat have an almost instant effect. So also do salt and water, mustard and water, bicarbonate of soda. Always have a list of poisons and their antidotes in your medicine chest as it is difficult to commit them to memory. Once when a dog of mine ate Slug Death and was writhing about in convulsions the vet diagnosed hardpad. I knew he had been perfectly all right the night before and so I poured warm treacle down his throat. His recovery was remarkable as he had been in the fits for several hours without coming round at all. He ate a good feed that night, but the outcome was the he was completely sterile for the rest of his thirteen years although he had been quite sound before.

PYMETRIA: A very dangerous condition of the womb which usually results in a complete hysterectomy or very urgent veterinary attention. Temperature will be 105° or even higher and pus will be discharging from the womb.

RABIES: The reason that all dogs and cats entering Great Britain from abroad have to spend six months in a special quarantine kennel authorised by the Ministry of Agriculture. The dog turns mad, froths at the mouth and his bite can pass the disease on to other animals or people. Injections in other parts of the world with rabies vaccine seem to have a very high degree of efficiency but are not compulsory here.

RICKETS: A disease of puppyhood due in most part to a calcium and Vitamin D deficiency. Adequate supplies of these plus phosphates in the daily diet will avoid this disease. Care should be taken with such a small dog as the Yorkie, however, to avoid giving too big a dose of Vitamin D as this can have the opposite result and so it is better to feed natural sources rather than synthetic ones.

RINGWORM: Fungus disease of the skin communicable to man. Can be speedily dealt with if noticed before the dog becomes hairless. Signs are round, bald spots ringed with a thin red line. Dress with Stockholm Tar or Linseed Oil and Creosote applied with a longhandled paint brush. Cut the coat short and after the sore places have healed several baths will be needed to clear the coat of the agents. Burn all bedding and spray woodwork, floors, walls and beds, etc., with a fungus killer.

STINGS and BITES: Remove bee stings from skin and cover with blue bag, bicarbonate of soda mixed to a paste with water or any special anti-histamine cream or spray. If eyes, mouth, tongue or lips are stung use bicarbonate solution or T.C.P. in a mild form.

Wasp stings do not get left behind but keep on stinging. Dab with vinegar, lemon juice or onion.

Snake bites are only met with in certain parts of Great Britain where the tiny adder is the only poisonous one we have. Their bites can be lethal so rush the dog to a hospital or vet's surgery for serum. Our local doctors will always help in this respect. In the warm south where much of the undergrowth and bracken are undisturbed for long periods the snakes have a natural habitat and it is a wise precaution to take a box of permanganate crystals on country walks. These can be applied to the bite until serum can be obtained. Shock treatment will be necessary as the pain is very severe.

SUNSTROKE: Apply ice-bags to head, plunge body in icy cold water and keep in a dark room under sedation.

TARTAR: The nasty accumulation that affects the teeth of so many toy dogs who do not get enough hard chewing on biscuits or bones to keep them clean in the proper way. Clean the teeth daily with a mixture of half milk and half peroxide of hydrogen, using a cottonwool pad. Neglected tartar will need removing with dental scrapers done professionally under a complete anaesthetic. A tartar pencil from the chemist used according to instructions is a slow but much cheaper and safer method.

WORMS: See chapter ten.

Appendix 1:

YORKSHIRE TERRIER REGISTRATIONS IN THE U.K. FROM 1932–1949

Year	Registrations
1932	300
1933	275
1934	285
1935	283
1936	208
1937	208
1938	265
1939	147
1940	47
1941	56
1942	132
1943	236
1944	366
1945	479
1946	727
1947	953
1948	931
1949	1041

REGISTRATIONS AT THE KENNEL CLUB FROM 1950 IN FIRST COLUMN

EXPORT FIGURES FOR YORKSHIRE TERRIERS IN SECOND COLUMN

Year	Registrations	Year	Export Figures
1950	1217	1950	
1951	1331	1951	
1952	1241	1952	
1953	1248	1953	
1954	1462	1954	
1955	1708	1955	
1956	2148	1956	
1957	2313	1957	
1958	2824	1958	
1959	3244	1959	
1960	3863	1960	338
1961	4385	1961	
1962	4908	1962	
1963	5130	1963	
1964	5531	1964	
1965	6129	1965	
1966	6306	1966	1047
1967	7389	1967	1213

1968	8842	1968	1743
1969	10,212	1969	2,361
1970	11,016	1970	2,265
1971	10,577	1971	2,106
1972	12,832	1972	1,936
1973	13,780	1973	2,395
1974	15,147	1974	2,805
1975	14,640	1975	2,521
1976	7817	1976	2050
1977	5428	1977	1654
1978/79	19187	1978/79	1596

Yorkshire Terriers have topped the export figures from 1966 to 1979, and in 1974 they replaced Alsatians as first in registration order, a position Alsatians had held since 1965. Yorkshire Terriers retained this lead in registrations in 1979 also.

Appendix 2:

YORKSHIRE TERRIER CLUBS

(Taken from the Kennel Club's Year Book 1980–81)

	NORTHERN COUNTIES YORKSHIRE TERRIER CLUB
Hon. Sec.	Mr A. Blamires
	482, Bradford Rd, Brighouse, W. Yorkshire HD6 4ED
	CHESHIRE & NORTH WALES YORKSHIRE TERRIER CLUB
Hon. Sec.	Mrs P. M. Grunnill, 16 Brook Lane, Chester, CH2 2AP
	EASTERN COUNTIES YORKSHIRE TERRIER CLUB
Hon. Sec	Mrs L. Hilton, 18, Ridgewell Road, Gt. Yeldham, Essex
	MIDLAND YORKSHIRE TERRIER CLUB
Hon. Sec.	W. A. Jackson, Esq., Foxhill Close, Langwith Road, Scarliffe, Chesterfield.
	SOUTH WESTERN YORKSHIRE TERRIER CLUB
Hon. Sec.	Miss I. M. Millard, 6, St. Andrews Road, Blackwell, Bristol BS 19 3DL
	ULSTER YORKSHIRE TERRIER CLUB
Hon. Sec.	Miss M. Callen, 19, Woodvale Road, Belfast BT13 BN
	THE YORKSHIRE TERRIER CLUB
Hon. Sec.	Mrs B. F. Whitbread, 13, Weltmore Road, Luton, Beds.
	YORKSHIRE TERRIER CLUB OF SCOTLAND
Hon. Sec.	Mrs M. Hay, 43, West Saville Terrace, Edinburgh EH9 3DP

Appendix 3:

YORKSHIRE TERRIER CHAMPIONS SINCE WORLD WAR II

Champion's Name	Sex	Sire	Dam	Breeder	Owner	Birth Date
1947						
Bens Blue Pride	D	Blue Flash	Jill	Mr Roper	Mr Williamson	8.7.44
Lady Nada	B	Wee Willie Winkle	Little Flower	Mrs R. Allen	Mrs Hebson	9.9.42
1948						
Hebsonian Jealousy	B	Gay Prince	Hebsonian Harana	Mrs Hebson	Mrs Hebson	10.3.49
Weeplustoo of Achmonie	B	Sweet Memory of Achmonie	Isolda of Achmonie	Miss Macdonald	Miss Macdonald	9.5.45
Starlight	D	Marten Teddy	Adora	Mr Orford	Mrs Hargreaves	15.10.45
1949						
Wee Don of Atherleigh	D	Don Progress	Beauty of Atherleigh	Mr Hayes	Mr Hayes	13.9.45
McCay of Achmonie	D	Nigella of Pagham	Sophie of Achmonie	Miss Macdonald	Miss Macdonald	21.4.46
Splendour of Invincia	D	Invincia Masher	Olie of Invincia	Mrs Swan	Mrs A. Swan	16.7.47
Venair Parkview Preview	D	Parkview Prince	Parkview Dinky	Mr Bain	Mrs Mair	12.5.46
Tufty of Johnstounburn	B	Midge's Pal	Hazy of Johnstounburn	Mrs Crookshank	Mrs Crookshank	3.5.45
1950						
Blue Dolly	B	*Ch. Bens Blue Pride*	Little Marionette	Mr Coates	Mr Coates	2.4.46
Mr Pim of Johnstounburn	D	Parkview Prince	Flea of Johnstounburn	Mr Sturrock	Mrs Crookshank	29.2.47
Dinah Beau	B	Bridle Copper King	Beauty of Atherleigh	Mr Hayes	Miss Hartley	24.6.48
Winpal Arine	B	Soham Carlyle	Anita of Soham	Lady E. Windham Dawson	Miss Palmer	13.2.47

Name		Sire	Dam			Date
1951						
Wee Gertrude	B	Monican Punch	Queenie's Pride	Mr Thurlow	Mrs Chard and Miss Fairchild	16.1.48
Feona of Phylreyne	B	Christoferobin of Phylreyne	Phylreyne Irrepressible	Mrs Raine	Mrs Raine	12.2.48
Vemair Principal Boy	D	Parkview Prince	Frosty of Johnstounburn	Mr Bain	Mrs Mair	28.6.49
Sorreldene Honey Son of the Vale	D	Harringay Little Dandy	Pretty Paulette	Mrs Sharpe	Mrs Bradley	25.11.48
Hopwood Camelia	B	Invincia Masher	Invincia Margretta	Mrs A. Swan	Miss Martin	9.3.48
Wee Blue Atom	D	Little Blue Boy	Our Sue	Mr Latliff	Mrs Overett	20.7.48
Martinwyns Golden Girl	B	Marten Teddy	Marian Martinette	Mr Coates	Mrs Montgomery	24.4.48
Martinwyns Surprise of Atherleigh	D	Invincia Masher	Pat of Atherleigh	Mr Hayes	Mr Coates	24.11.47
1952						
Adora of Invincia	B	Invincia Masher	Ollie of Invincia	Mrs Swan	Mrs Swan	5.6.48
Titania of Invincia	B	Pride of Invincia	Nancy of Invincia	Mrs Swan	Mrs Stirk	25.9.48
Sunstar of Invincia	D	Invincia Masher	Margie of Invincia	Mrs Swan	Mrs Swan	5.6.50
Blue Belle	B	Wee Blue Atom	Blue Bonnet	Miss Noakes	Miss Noakes	21.8.50
Someone of Achmonie	D	*Ch. McCay of Achmonie*	Fiona of Achmonie	Miss Macdonald	Miss Macdonald	11.6.49
Wee Eve of Yadnum	B	*Ch. Mr Pim of Johnstounburn*	Scotford Queen	Mr Scott	Mrs Munday	10.8.51
Kelsbro Quality Boy	D	Gayways Little Trotters	Dinkie Blue	Mrs Cross	Mrs Cross	28.6.49
Firhill Fairy	B	Midge's Pal	Miss Monty	Mr Anderson	Mrs Pannett	30.9.48
Winpal Henriella	B	Henry of Soham	Prunella of Achmonie	Miss Macdonald	Miss Palmer	30.3.49
Jacaranda Beauty	B	Little Blue Boy	Bridle Sweetbriar	Mrs Montgomery	Mrs Montgomery	25.1.51
1953						
Vemair Spider	D	Midge's Pal	Coogee Dinah	Mr Johnstone	Mrs Mair	30.9.48
Martinwyns Debonaire	D	Little Blue Boy	Our Sue	Mr Latliff	Mr Coates	4.10.49
Medium of Johnstounburn	B	Midge's Pal	Misty of Johnstounburn	Mrs Crookshank	Mrs Crookshank	23.10.50
Aerial of Winpal	B	Prince Cosmo of Winpal	*Ch. Winpal Arme*	Miss Palmer	Miss Palmer	4.7.52

YORKSHIRE TERRIER CHAMPIONS SINCE WORLD WAR II

Champion's Name	Sex	Sire	Dam	Breeder	Owner	Birth Date
Eoforwic Envoy of Yadnum	D	Blue Guinea of Yadnum	Florentina of Yadnum	Mrs Prosser	Mrs Munday	1.7.50
Jessica of Westridge	B	Martinwyns Surprise of Atherleigh	Pauline of Westridge	Mr Grist	Mr Grist	19.7.51
Stirkean's Chota Sahib	D	Splendour of Invincia	Empress of Invincia	Mrs Swan	Mrs Stirk	22.8.51
Butibel Perseus	D	Bowdigan Prince Charming	Lovely Blue Princess	Mrs Russell	Mrs Russell	20.11.49
1954						
Midnight Gold of Yadnum	D	Pip the Piper	Lady Prudence of Yadnum	Mrs Donaldson	Mrs Munday	29.4.53
Myrtle of Johnstounburn	B	*Ch. Mr Pim of Johnstounburn*	Misty of Johnstounburn	Mrs Crookshank	Mrs Crookshank	8.7.49
Faye of Phylreyne	B	Sorreldene Honey-son of the Vale	Fiona of Phylreyne	Mrs Raine	Mrs Raine	10.4.52
1955						
Burghwallis Little Nip	D	Burghwallis Waggie	Stanhope Queen	Mr Howard	Mrs Betton	29.6.52
Sehow Independent	B	Pagham Sehow Special	Pennywort of Pagham	Miss Marter	Miss Howes	18.5.53
Wadeholme Little Mitzi	B	Peddler Boy	Sehow Hopeful	Mrs Drake	Mrs Wade	19.12.52
Stirkean's Kandy Boy	D	*Ch. Stirkean's Chota Sahib*	Trix of Invincia	Mrs Stirk	Mrs Stirk	23.12.53
Martinwyns Adora	B	Martinwyns Teddy	Wee Suzetta	Mrs Latliff	Mrs Seymour	25.1.53
Epperstones Bon Ton	D	Epperstone Surprise	Mam's Little Pal	Mrs Read	Mrs Hill	5.6.53
Vemair Uncle Sam	D	*Ch. Vemair Principal Boy*	Nemorosa Jill	Mr Wall	Mrs Mair	4.7.52
Eastgrove Gay Boy	D	Gayways Little Trotters	Susan's Wee Lady	Mr Ford	Mrs Hargreaves	14.1.52
1956						
Delia of Erlcour	B	Victory Boy	Miretta Marianne	Mrs Batsford	Mrs Batsford	10.6.53
Blue Symon	D	Golden Fame	Dinah is Good	Miss Armstrong	Mrs John	29.9.51
Pipit of Johnstounburn	B	*Ch. Mr Pim of Johnstounburn*	Pixy of Johnstounburn	Mrs Crookshank	Mrs Crookshank	6.9.54

Name	Sex	Sire	Dam			Date
Buranthea's Angel Bright	B	*Ch. Mr Pim of Johnstounburn*	Buranthea's Paris Jewel	Mrs Burfield	Mrs Burfield	29.4.54
Hilaire of Pookshill	D	*Starlight of Pookshill*	Rosalinda of Erlcour	Mrs Wood	Mrs Batsford	23.1.54
Moon Glow of Yadnum	D	*Sir Gay of Yadnum*	Pretty Paulette	Mrs Munday	Mrs Sharpe	13.6.55
Aureola of Winpal	B	*Butibel Mercury*	Aimee of Winpal	Miss Palmer	Miss Palmer	24.10.52
1957						
Cressida of Erlcour	B	*Dandini of Erlcour*	Miretta Marianne	Mrs Batsford	Mrs Batsford	22.4.56
Martini	B	*Ch. Splendour of Invincia*	Cherie of Invincia	Mrs Beech	Mrs Swan	1.8.53
Blue Orchid of Hilfore	B	*Totis Treasure*	Midget of Hilfore	Mrs Seymour	Mrs Seymour	8.8.55
Prim of Johnstounburn	B	*Ch. Mr Pim of Johnstounburn*	Lady of the Lake	Mrs Rossiter	Mr Brown	25.7.55
Pimbron of Johnstounburn	D	*Ch. Mr Pim of Johnstounburn*	Lady of the Lake	Mrs Crookshank	Mr Brown	4.7.54
Symons Querida of Tolestar	B	*Blue Symon*	Honey Queen	Mrs Tole	Mrs John	16.9.54
1958						
Bystander's Replica	D	*The Young Aristocrat*	Jill	Miss Logan	Miss Logan	22.8.54
Coulgorm Chloe	B	*Coulgorm Remus*	Versatile Veronica	Mrs Hutchin	Mr Hughes	10.5.56
Deebees Stirkean's Faustina	B	*Ch. Stirkean's Chota Sahib*	Stirkean's Astolat Enchantress	Mrs Beech	Mrs Stirk	15.2.57
June's Boy	D	*Little Blue Boy*	Dainty Princess Suzanne	Mr J. Latliff	Mrs Latliff	19.10.53
Ravelin Gaiety Boy	D	*Ravelin Golden Boy*	Chingford Sweet Sue	Miss Noakes	Mrs Latliff	13.10.55
Sir Lancelot of Astolat	D	*Pagham Sehow Special*	Astolat Nicolette	Mrs Charlton Haw	Mrs Charlton Haw	6.2.56
Societyrow Dog Friday	D	*Fawn of Friskerton*	Lassie of Societyrow	Mr & Mrs Barrs	Mrs Barrs	27.4.56
Stirkean's Rhapsody	D	*Ch. Stirkean's Chota Sahib*	Stirkean's Anne Marie of Winpal	Mrs Stirk	Mrs Stirk	21.2.57
1959						
Buranthea's Doutelle	D	*Ch. & Irish Ch. Mr Pim of Johnstounburn*	Buranthea's York Sensation	Mrs Burfield	Mrs M. Burfield	8.5.57

YORKSHIRE TERRIER CHAMPIONS SINCE WORLD WAR II

Champion's Name	Sex	Sire	Dam	Breeder	Owner	Birth Date
Don Carlos of Progresso	D	Ch. Martynwyns Wee Teddy	Shirlorn Sally	Mrs C. Hutchin	Mrs C. Hutchin	20.12.57
Elaine of Astolat	B	Pagham Schow Special	Astolat Nicolette	Mrs P. Charlton Haw	Mrs P. Charlton Haw	6.2.56
Pagnell Prima Donna of Wiske	B	Ch. Burghwallis Little Nip	Prism of Johnstounburn	Mrs S. Groom	Mrs Renton	1.5.57
Pedimins Piper	D	Bonclad of Invincia	Pedimins Parade	Mr Porter	Mr Porter	22.10.57
Stirkean's Astonoff Horatio	D	Stirkean's Teekhai	Astonoff's Victory Victorios	Mrs M. Etherington	Mrs Stirk	31.3.58
1960						
Deebees Campari	D	Ch. Stirkean's Chota Sahib	Deebees Lillet	Mrs Beech	Mrs Beech	1.5.59
Burghwallis Vikki	D	Ch. Burghwallis Little Nip	Prism of Johnstounburn	Mrs Groom	Mrs Betton	1.5.57
Hampark Dandy	D	Ear-Wi-Go of Tzumaio	Chota Memsahib	R. Wilkinson	W. Wilkinson	26.6.58
My Sweet Suzanne	B	Totis Treasure	Gloria's Girl	Mrs D. Baynes	Mrs D. Baynes	24.6.58
Sungold of Supreme	B	Happy Warrior of Saughey	Tauntsom Polly Anna	Mr D. A. Smith	Mr D. A. Smith	22.5.58
Wadeholme Happy Quest	D	Wadeholme Staraza of Clu-Mor	Wadeholme Merry Maid	Mrs L.J. Wade	Mrs Wade	12.7.57
1961						
Adora Junior of Hilfore	D	Ravelin Golden Boy	Ch. Martinwyns Adora	Mrs V. Seymour	Mr H.T. Seymour	30.7.58
Burghwallis Brideen	B	Ch. Burghwallis Little Nip	Little Sheba	Mrs A. Brown	Mrs M. Betton	15.2.58
Deebees Isa La Bella	B	Ch. Stirkean's Chota Sahib	Deebees Lillet	Mrs S.D. Beech	Mrs S.D. Beech	1.5.59
Doone of Wiske	B	Burghwallis Sukyboy	Madcap Molly	Mr W. Quinn	Mrs Renton	12.3.59
Fuchia of Fiskerton	B	Fiskerton Limelight of Lilactime	Stirkean's Frisky Dot	Mrs V. Moyes	Mrs. V. Moyes	26.3.58
Glamour Boy of Glengonner	D	Little Tot of Glengonner	Queen of Birkburn	Mr A. Bennie	Mr D.A. Peck	11.6.59
Leyam Mascot	D	Ch. June's Boy	Kim's Starlight	Mrs D. Mayell	Mrs D. Mayell	31.12.58
Mamma's Little Topper	D	Beechrise Dandy	Hallowe'en of Grenbar	Mr J. Walker	Mrs K.H. Cherryholme	20.7.58

Progress of Progreso	D Don Carlos of Progreso	Ch. Coulgorm Chloe	Mrs C. Hutchin	Mrs C. Hutchin	2.4.59
Stirkean's Puff Puffin	B Ch. Stirkean's Chota Sahib	Stirkean's Astolat Enchantress	Mrs E.A. Stirk	Mrs E.A. Stirk	18.5.58
1962					
Deebees Hot Toddy	D Ch. Deebees Campari	Deebees Phoebe	Mrs S.D. Beech	Mrs S.D. Beech	9.6.60
Elmslade Galahad of Yadnum	D Elmslade Chuffty	Elmslade Moon Maiden	Mrs M. Slade	Mrs E. Munday	11.8.60
Guyton's Spring Blossom	B Bonnie's Apple Blossom	Our Pepita	Mr G. Kniveton	Mr G. Kniveton	17.5.60
Jacaranda Blue Mischief	B Jacaranda Jolly Boy	Jacaranda Petite	Mrs J. Montgomery	Mrs J. Montgomery	1.2.61
Kelsbro Blue Pete	D Kelsbro Brigadier	Kelsbro Pretty Peggy	Mr H. Cross	Mr H. Cross	6.11.59
Melody Maker of Embyll	B Ch. Don Carlos of Progreso	Little Blue Wonder	Mr W. Everitt	Mrs C. Hutchin	11.12.59
Pontana Prodigy Dainty	B Pedimins Prodigy	Tulip Design	Mr G. Howells	Mr G. Howells	9.12.60
Stirkean's Mr Tims	D Stirkean's Titmouse	Stirkean's Krakawin	Mrs E. Stirk	Mrs E. Stirk	13.5.60
Sundance of Wiske	B Burghwallis Vikki	Vanessa of Wiske	Mrs Renton	Mrs Renton	18.8.59
1963					
Charm of Wadeholme	B Wadholme Staraza of Clu Mor	Wadholme Wee Rebel	Mrs L. Wade	Mrs L. J. Wade	7.10.59
Deebees Caronia	B Ch. Deebees Hot Toddy	Deebees Invincia Rosemary	Mrs S. D. Beech	Mrs S. D. Beech	7.11.61
Hopwood Desirable	D Hopwood Torville Majestic	Hopwood Fantasia	Miss E. Martin	Mr J. W. Hutchinson	8.3.59
Pagnell Peter Pan	D Ch. Burghwallis Little Nip	Prism of Johnstounburn	Mrs S. I. Groom	Mrs S. I. Groom	17.10.61
Tzumaio's Cheetah of Martinez	B Ear-Wi-Go of Tzumaio	Victoria's Pride	Mr & Mrs J. Martin	Mrs E. Gilbert	25.5.60
Wenscoe's Wendolene	B Ear-Wi-Go of Tzumaio	Pedimins Proposal	Miss W. A. Schofield	Miss W. A. Schofield	26.5.61
Yorkfold Wrupertbear	D Yorkfold Chocolate Boy	Yorkfold Koala	Mrs D. Rossiter	Mrs D. Rossiter	6.9.61
1964					
Buranthea's Saint Malachy	D Piccolo Patrico	Buranthea's Doutelle Replica	Mrs H. D. Burfield	Mrs H. D. Burfield	25.11.60

YORKSHIRE TERRIER CHAMPIONS SINCE WORLD WAR II

Champion's Name	Sex	Sire	Dam	Breeder	Owner	Birth Date
Deebees Little Dodo	B	Deebees Stirkean's Drummer Boy	Deebees Prunella of Invincia	Mrs S. D. Beech	Mrs S. D. Beech	11.2.62
Goodliff Blue Dragon	D	Ch. Hampark Dandy	Trixie of Winpal	Mr M. G. Taylor	Mrs G. Crowther	6.10.61
Millfield Mandy	B	Pagnell Brigadier	Solandra Blue Binky	Mrs C. Bailey	Mrs M. Hepworth	9.3.62
Minerva of Johnstounburn	B	Ch. Pimbron of Johnstounburn	Muffit of Johnstounburn	Mrs M. U. Crookshank	Mrs M. D. Lowrie	9.10.61
Phirno Magic Moment	B	Ch. Ravelin Gaiety Boy	Phirno Miss Mandy	Miss P. Noakes	Miss P. Noakes	12.9.62
Progreso Lover Boy	D	Ch. Progress of Progreso	Pink Gin of Progreso	Mrs C. Hutchin	Mrs C. Hutchin	14.1.62
Romance of Wiske	B	Templevale Pertinacious	Miss Bessie Boo	Mrs J. R. Milnes	Mrs Renton	2.10.62
Skyrona Blue Prince	D	Baby Peachy of Rosehara	Woldsdene Blue Rose	Mrs G. Sykes	Mrs G. Sykes	15.7.62
Yorkfold McPickle	D	Buranthea's Saint Malachy	Gold Dinky of Arcady	Mrs D. Rossiter	Mrs D. Rossiter	17.5.62
Golden Button of Yadnum	B	Emperor of Yadnum	Bonny Blue of Yadnum	Mrs E. Munday	Mrs E. Munday	7.5.61
1965						
Anston Cindy Loo	B	Anston Blue Emperor	Alfeebas Joy	Mrs A. L. Buxton	Mrs Moore	29.2.60
My Precious Joss	D	Ch. Pimbron of Johnstounburn	Bonny Jean	Mrs C. Flockhart	Mrs C. Flockhart	21.2.63
Ruswel Chorus Girl of Brendali	B	Ch. Glamour Boy of Glengonner	Mandy of Glengonner	Mr D. A. Peck	Mrs R. Marshall	20.8.62
Templevale Niaissmo of Wiske	B	Templevale Benissimo	Templevale Lady Monia	Mrs L. H. Briggs	Mrs K. M. Renton	11.7.63
Viada Rosina	B	Wylhylda Tiny Tim	Sadie of Invincia	Mrs V. A. Monger	Mrs V. A. Monger	15.8.63
Wedgewood's Starmist	D	Fair Victor of Clu Mor	Wedgewood's Vickey	Mrs C. I. Morris	Mrs M. Logue	4.5.62
Whisperdales Phirno Carmen	B	Ch. Ravelin Gaiety Boy	Blue Biddy	Miss P. I. Noakes	Mr R. Wardill	26.2.63

1966

Name	Sex	Sire	Dam			Date
Carlwyns Wee Teddy Toff	D	Ch. Stirkean's Astonoff's Horatio	Stirkean's Cherry Ripe	Mrs W. E. Nichols	Mrs W. E. Nichols	7.10.63
Phirno St. George	D	Ravelin Little Jimmy	Phirno Dawn Delight	Miss P. Noakes	Miss P. Noakes	23.4.64
Skyrona Blue Girl	B	Ch. Skyrona Blue Prince	Woldsdene Blue Rose	Mrs Sykes	Mrs Skyes	22.6.64
Templevale Jessica of Wiske	B	Templevale Simonson	Templevale Giselle	Mrs Briggs	Mrs Renton	17.10.64
Beechrise Superb	D	Ch. Pagnell Peter Pan	Beechrise Pixie	Mrs Griffiths	Mrs H. Griffiths	5.8.63
Leyam Scampie	D	Leyam Tuppence	Leyam Starbright	Mrs D. Mayell	Mrs D. Baynes	19.11.62
Progreso Pearl	B	Progreso Melody Son	Fairmead Jane	Mr Brown	Mrs C. Hutchin	2.7.64
Lillyhill Pimbronette	B	Ch. Pimbron of Johnstounburn	Fair Blossom	Mr W. Dores	Mrs W. Wilson	12.3.62
Stirkean's Reenie	B	Ch. Stirkean's Astonoff's Horatio	Stirkean's Romance	Mrs E. Stirk	Mrs E. Stirk	2.4.65
Progreso Prospect	D	Ch. Progreso Lover Boy	Topsy Jane	Mr Langley	Mrs Hutchin	4.1.64

1967

Name	Sex	Sire	Dam			Date
Buranthea's Luscious Lady	B	Buranthea's Ben Braggie	Buranthea's Prime Mover	Mrs Burfield	Mrs Burfield	1.8.63
Blairsville Tinkerbelle	B	Leodian Smart Boy	Blairsville Lady	Mr & Mrs B. Lister	Mr & Mrs B. Lister	7.9.65
Dorrit's Suzanne's Treasure	B	Ch. Buranthea's Saint Malachy	Ch. My Sweet Suzanne	Mrs D. Baynes	Mrs D. Baynes	10.10.65
Heavenly Blue of Wiske	D	Ch. Pagnell Peter Pan	Ch. Doone of Wiske	Mrs Renton	Mr & Mrs L. F. Palframan	28.2.63
Skyrona Blue Bobby of Streamglen	D	Ch. Skyrona Blue Prince	Enchanted Lady of Rosehara	Mrs G. Sykes	Mrs M. Waldram	3.6.65
Macstroud's Sir Gay	D	Ch. Carlwyn's Wee Teddy Toff	Macstroud's Little Nell	Mr D. Stroud	Mr D. Stroud	15.1.66
Blue Flash of Streamglen	D	Wee Tich of Streamglen	Fifi Petite	Mrs Marsden	Mrs Waldram	3.6.65
Pagnell Blue Peter	D	Ch. Pagnell Peter Pan	Issabel Lady	Mrs D. Smith	Mrs Groom	4.4.64
Anston Lucy Locket	B	Anston Scampy Gem	Anston Sally Ann	Mrs Moore	Mrs Moore	28.9.64

YORKSHIRE TERRIER CHAMPIONS SINCE WORLD WAR II

Champion's Name	Sex	Sire	Dam	Breeder	Owner	Birth Date
Stirkean's Gerrard's Little Guy	D	*Ch. Stirkean's*	Stirkean's	Miss E. Thomas	Mrs E. Stirk	5.11.65
1968						
Murose Storm	D	*Astonoff's Horatio* / *Ch. Beechrise Superb*	Polyanthus Murose My Sheree	Mrs E. Burton	Mrs E. Burton	21.8.66
Deebees Blue Mist	B	Hopwood Super Star	Deebees Hopwood Golden Orchid	Mrs Beech	Mrs Beech	21.5.64
Dandini Jim	D	*Ch. Beechrise Superb*	Little Enchantress	A. Blamires	A. Blamires	1.11.65
Luna Star of Yadnum	D	Bright Star of Yadnum	Bonny Blue of Yadnum	Mrs E. Munday	Mrs E. Munday	7.7.65
Tolcarne Brandy Soda	D	Lambsgrove Pinnochio	Tolcarne Grenbar Kanzette	Mrs O. Wood	Mrs O. Wood	28.6.65
Chantmarles Mycariad Wild Silk	B	Macstroud's Whitecross Dandini	Mycariad Astonoff Lady Virginia	Mrs M. Childs	Mrs Hayes	16.7.66
Deebees Don Cella	B	Deebees Tommy Tucker	Deebees Sweet Celeste	Mrs D. Beech	Mrs D. Beech	14.9.66
1969						
Ch. Whisperdales Temujim	D	Ravelin Little Jimmy	*Ch. Whisperdales Phirno Carmen*	R. Wardill	R. Wardill	8.11.66
Bobby of Beachdale	D	Little Gay Boy of Beachdale	Jannette of Beachdale	Mrs A. M. Beach	Mrs A. M. Beach	9.8.67
1970						
Deanchel Beau Caprice	D	Ozmilion Noble Boy	Deanchel's Suki Blue Caprice	Mrs E. M. Taylor	Mrs E. M. Taylor	10.2.68
Nelmila Berryfield Beauty	B	Chunky of Archombeau	Whitecross Twinkletoes	Mrs I. M. Millard	Mrs I. M. Millard	10.9.67
Newholme Marcopolo	D	Wee Boy Blue	Beechrise Pixie	Mrs K. Cherryholme	Mrs K. Cherryholme	14.9.66
Deebees Gold Penny	B	Deebees Golden Prince	*Ch. Deebees Little Dodo*	Mrs S. D. Beech	Mrs S. D. Beech	13.2.67
Anston Lucy Locket	B	Anston Scampy Gem	Anston Sally Ann	Mrs Y. Moore	Mrs Y. Moore	28.9.64
Elspeth Serenade	B	Elspeth Wonder Boy	Kelsbro Moonbeam	Mesdames Lomas & Pass	Mesdames Lomas & Pass	18.3.66

Name	Sex	Sire	Dam	Breeder	Owner	Date
Macstroud's High Society	B	*Ch. Macstroud's Sir Gay*	Macstroud's Jack's Memory	D. Stroud	D. Stroud	3.1.68
Pretty Debbie of Yadnum	B	Bright Star of Yadnum	Fair Phillipa	Mrs B. Bulgin	Miss V. E. Mundey	10.2.66
Star of Keeth	B	Sketrick Shi-Shi-Bu	Stetrick Sharon Rose	J. Gardner	Mrs I. Copley	18.9.66
1971						
Blairsville Aristocrat	D	*Ch. Beechrise Superb*	*Ch. Blairsville Tinkerbelle*	Mr & Mrs B. Lister	Mr & Mrs B. Lister	11.9.68
Blairsville Boy Wonder	D	Leodian Smart Boy	Blairsville Lady Adora	Mrs R. Lister	Mr & Mrs B. Lister	13.7.66
Lyndoney Timothy Tuppence	D	Little Master of Hilfore	Junior of Hilfore	Mrs D. A. Johnson	Mrs D. A. Johnson	27.6.67
Macstroud's Noble Lad	D	*Ch. Macstroud's Sir Gay*	Plantationhall Susan of Wiske	D. Stroud	D. Stroud	1.2.69
Murose Wee Pippa	D	*Ch. Murose Storm*	Murose Blue Dawn	Mrs E. Burton	Mrs E. Burton	13.6.68
Superfine of Yadnum	D	Star Superb of Yadnum	Gay Rosalinda of Yadnum	Mrs V. E. Mundey	Miss V. E. Mundey	3.7.68
Blairsville Shirene	B	*Ch. Blairsville Boy Wonder*	Blairsville Belinda	Mr & Mrs B. Lister	Mr & Mrs B. Lister	29.9.67
Chantmarles Snuff Box	B	Macstroud's White-cross Dandina	Mycariad Stargazer	Mrs M. C. Hayes	Mrs M. C. Hayes	31.10.68
Elspeth Nina of Ravaldene	B	Kelsbro Top Choice of Sweetloves	Elspeth Sweet Susy	Mesdames Lomas & Pass	V. Ravald	1.6.67
Skyrona Blue Victoria	B	*Ch. Beechrise Superb*	*Ch. Skyrona Blue Girl*	Mrs G. Sykes	Mrs G. Sykes	15.11.68
1972						
Brave Warrior of Naylenor	D	*Ch. Heavenly Blue of Wiske*	Sombrero Daisy May	P. Naylor	P. Naylor	18.5.69
Gaykeys Gold	D	Gaykeys Firecracker	Gaykeys Sorreldene Lucy Locket	Mr & Mrs J. Heskett	Mrs M. Heskett	19.7.68
Blairsville Samantha	B	*Ch. Blairsville Boy Wonder*	Blairsville Belinda	Mr & Mrs B. Lister	Mr & Mrs B. Lister	5.6.70
Deebees Bee Bee	B	Deebees Bumble Boy	Wee Polly Fisher of Whipton	Mrs C. M. Pitchey	Mrs S. D. Beech	11.9.69
Raveldene Graybet Rhapsody in Blue	B	Graybet Master Mike	Graybets Blue Rose	Mr & Mrs F. Mitchell	V. Ravald	8.9.69
Wyebank Amethyst	B	*Ch. Murose Storm*	Wyebank Emma Peel	A. Blamires	A. Blamires	28.8.68

YORKSHIRE TERRIER CHAMPIONS SINCE WORLD WAR II

Champion's Name	Sex	Sire	Dam	Breeder	Owner	Birth Date
1973						
Beechrise Surprise	D	*Ch. Beechrise Superb*	Jane Cuttler	Mrs A. Dean	Mrs H. Griffiths	2.8.70
Deanchel's Prince Pericles	D	*Ch. Whisperdales Temujin*	Deanchel's Suki Blue Caprice	Mrs E. M. Taylor	Mrs E. M. Taylor	25.4.70
Foxclose Little John	D	Quornhill Fuss Pot	Foxclose Blue Jean	Mrs D. M. Jackson	Mrs D. M. Jackson	22.6.70
Mycariad Ragged Robin of Yadnum	D	Mycariad Tam-o-Shanter	Mycariad Merry Go Round	Miss M. V. Childe	Miss V. E. Mundey	20.1.70
Ozmilion My Imagination	D	*Ch. Blairsville Aristocrat*	Ozmilion Tender Moment	O. A. Sameja	O. A. Sameja	14.7.70
Tolcarne Drambuie	D	*Ch. Tolcarne Brandy Soda*	Tolcarne Blue Rain	Miss O. Wood	Miss O. Wood	2.12.68
Wyebank Super Solitaire	B	Pagnell Pandarus	Wyebank Debutante	A. Blamires	A. Blamires	10.5.68
Brashcaysh Bezzer of Murose	D	*Ch. Murose Wee Pippa*	Macstroud's Starshine	Mrs M. Pritchard	Mrs E. Burton	23.6.71
Candytops Blue Peter	D	Candytops Deebees Peter Piper	Candytops Pandora	Mr & Mrs E. H. Oakley	Mr & Mrs E. H. Oakley	3.7.71
Chantmarles Sauce-Box	D	*Ch. Macstrouds Sir Gay*	*Ch. Chantmarles Snuff Box*	Mrs M. C. Hayes	Mrs M. C. Hayes	3.5.71
Kellaylis Miss Sophie	B	Chunky of Archombeau	Kalleylis' Ramleaze Mighty Atom	Mrs G. Kellar	J. Thrupp	18.4.70
Murose Exquisite	B	*Ch. Murose Wee Pippa*	Murose Delight	Mrs E. Burton	Mrs E. Burton	9.9.70
Whisperdales Deebees Halfpenny	B	*Ch. Whisperdales Temujin*	*Ch. Deebees Gold Penny*	Mrs D. Beech	R. Wardill	12.5.70
Dorrits Macstroud's Hot Toddy	D	Macstroud's White-cross Dandini	Macstroud's Mitzi	D. Stroud	Mrs D. Baynes	9.1.67
Broharrons Leisa	B	Crumbell's Alley Shuffle	Broharrons Lucy	Mr & Mrs Harron	Mrs H. Harron	1.2.69
Ozmilion Jubilation	D	*Ch. Ozmilion My Imagination*	Ozmilion Justine	O. A. Sameja	O. A. Sameja	4.10.71
Blairsville Most Royal	B	*Ch. Whisperdale Temujin*	*Ch. Blairsville Shirene*	Mr & Mrs B. Lister	Mr & Mrs B. Lister	12.5.71
Finstal Sugar Baby	B	Skyrona Blue Boy	Streamglen Beatrice of Finstal	Mrs S. Pritchard	Mrs S. Pritchard	24.2.72

Name		Sire	Dam	Breeder	Owner	Date
Lloydslee Lass	B	Simon Stroller	Ox Car Dinkie	E. Lloyd	E. Lloyd	20.4.71
Wykebank Impeccable	B	Beechrise Splendid	Wykebank Debutante	A. Blamires	A. Blamires	14.7.71
1974						
Chantmarles Miss Boniface	B	Macstroud's Whitecross Dandini	Mycariad Stargazer	Mrs M. C. Hayes	Mrs M. C. Hayes	17.2.68
Robina Gay of Yadnum	B	Ch. Mycariad Ragged Robin of Yadnum	Gay Rosalinda of Yadnum	Miss V. E. Munday	Miss V. E. Munday	14.4.71
1975						
Blairsville Royal Seal	D	Ch. Beechrise Surprise	Ch. Blairsville Most Royal	Mr & Mrs B. Lister	Mr & Mrs B. Lister	2.5.74
Carmardy Little Henry	D	Captain Kydd of Carmardy	Cinderella of Parkabbey	Mr & Mrs H. Parkin	Mr & Mrs H. Parkin	18.4.73
Clarebeck's Moonraker	D	Ch. Chantmarles Saucebox	Clarebeck Candymint	Mrs J. Hughes	Mrs J. Hughes	9.11.72
Eburacum Paladin	D	Eburacum Priam	Eburacum Gem	Mr J. R. Haynes	J. R. Haynes	15.4.73
Foxclose Mr. Smarty	D	Foxclose Little John	Foxclose Peggy. O'Neill	Mrs D. M. Jackson	Mrs D. M. Jackson	26.1.72
Gerjoy Royal Flea	D	Ch. Beechrise Superb	Lambgrove Messalina	Mrs G. A. Wattam	Mr G. A. Wattam	9.4.72
Harleta Uno-o-Go-Go	D	Ch. Whisperdales Temujin	Harleta Prescious Joscelyne	Mr & Mrs L. Hilton	Mr & Mrs L. Hilton	9.5.73
Kellaylys Master Tino	D	Chunky of Archombeau	Kellaylys Ram-Leaze Mighty Atom	Mrs G. M. Kellar	Mrs G. M. Kellar	4.7.72
1976						
Macstroud's Soldier Blue	D	Int. C. Macstroud's Noble Lad	Macstroud's Society Girl	Mr D. Stroud	Mr D. Stroud	26.7.73
Ozmilion Modesty	B	Int. Ch. Ozmilion Jubilation	Ozmilion Blairsville Bidene	Mr O. A. Samejo	Mr O. A. Samejo	3.3.75
Katie Fare of Candytops	B	Candytops Cornelius	Wanesfield Lass	Mr & Mrs E. H. Oakley	Mr F. Morris	9.2.74
Phirno Gay Lord	D	Deebees Sunbeam	Phirno Rosie	Miss P. I. Noakes	Miss P. I. Noakes	11.4.71
Lyndoney Krishna	D	Ch. Dorritt's Macstroud's Hot Toddy	Lyndoney Suzette	Mrs D. A. Johnson	Mrs D. A. Johnson	11.11.72
Naylenor Blue Monarch	D	Ch. Brave Warrior of Naylenor	Wykebank Gaiety Girl	P. Naylor	P. Naylor	30.4.72
Swank of Beechrise	D	Beechrise Splendour	Thatcroft Superb Kate	Mrs H. Griffiths	Mr R. Marshall	14.1.72

YORKSHIRE TERRIER CHAMPIONS SINCE WORLD WAR II

Champion's Name	Sex	Sire	Dam	Breeder	Owner	Birth Date
Ch. Deebees Penny Rose	B	Ch. Deebees Cornish Echo	Ch. Deebees Gold Penny	Mrs S. D. Beech	Mrs S. D. Beech	1.7.73
Garsims Moonshine	B	Candytops Cornelius	Babette of Index	Mrs P. Rose	Mrs P. Rose	14.5.73
Deebees Cornish Echo	D	Deebees Cock Robin	Deebees Caromia's Carissima	Mrs S. D. Beech	Mrs S. D. Beech	2.10.71
Robina Gay Of Yadnum	B	Ch. Mycariad Ragged Robin of Yadnum	Gay Rosalinda of Yadnum	Miss V. E. Munday	Miss V. E. Munday	14.4.71
Myork Muffin	D	Carlwyns Wee John	Modern Morita	Mrs K. Kemp	Mrs K. Kemp	22.10.71
Chantmarles Sash-Box	B	Ch. Chantmarles Sauce-Box	Ch. Chantmarles Miss Boniface	Mrs M. C. Hayes	Mrs M. C. Hayes	16.6.72
Ozmilion Dream Maker 1977	B	Ch. Ozmilion Jubilation	Ozmilion Tickle	Mr O. A. Sameja	Mrs V. M. Williams	15.11.74
Wykebank Startime	B	Ch. Blairsville Royal Seal	Wykebank Twinkle Star	A. Blamires	A. Blamires	12.2.76
Blairsville Royal Warrant	D	Ch. Beechrise Surprise	Ch. Blairsville Most Royal	Mr & Mrs B. Lister	Mr & Mrs B. Lister	13.11.76
Jackreed Apple-Blossom	D	Jackreed Jiminy Cricket	Mistress Emma of Jackreed	Mrs J. Reader	Mrs J. Reader	25.3.76
Peglea Con Tutto	D	Ch. Chantmarles Sauce Box	Highmead Kumara of Peglea	Mrs P. Foster	Mrs P. Foster	14.11.73
Tayfirs Fire Gift	D	Mr Teddy of Phylreyne	Rosa of Recnad	Mrs J. Fairbrother	Mrs J. Fairbrother	18.8.65
Jackread Whisky-a-go-go	D	Ravelin Little Jimmy	Jackread Cara Tina	Mrs J. Reader	Mrs J. Reader	19.8.71
Leadmore Lady Angela	B	Leadmore Tiny Sparkle	Leadmore Blue Sapphire	W. Cusack	W. Cusack	12.8.75
Ir. Ch. Bellebanes Krakatoa	D	Macstroud's Joy Boy of Bellebanes	Carlwyns Charlotte	Mrs I. Salisbury	Mrs I. Salisbury	17.8.75
Deebees Speculation	D	Deebees Dancing Dan	Deebees Penny's Sunshine	Mrs S. D. Beech	Mrs S. D. Beech	21.8.75
Ozmilion Premonition	D	Ozmilion Distinction	Ozmilion Just-Imagine	O. A. Sameja	O. A. Sameja	1.8.76
Candytops Strawberry Fayre	B	Ch. Candytops Blue Peter	Sophie of Candytops	Mr & Mrs E. H. Oakley	Mr & Mrs E. H. Oakley	29.6.75
Candytops Chantilly Lace	B	Ch. Candytops Blue Peter	Candytops Clarissa	Mr & Mrs E. H. Oakley	Mr & Mrs E. H. Oakley	3.11.73
Chantmarles Elegance	B	Ch. Chantmarles Sauce Box	Chantmarles Nelmila Briar Rose	Mrs M. C. Hayes	Mrs M. C. Hayes	3.2.75

Craigbank Blue Cinders	B	Southwardedge Blue Spark of Craigsbank	Southwardedge Josephine	Mrs Mann	Mrs Mann	31.1.76
Macstroud's Noble Boy	D	Ch. Macstroud's Sir Gay	Chantmarles Miss Silk	D. Stroud	D. Stroud	14.10.71
Chantmarles Sauce Box	D	Ch. Macstroud's Sir Gay	Ch. Chantmarles Snuff Box	Mrs M. C. Hayes	Mrs M. C. Hayes	3.5.71
Empress of Murose	B	Ch. Murose Wee Pippa	Thornhow Lady Gipsy	Mrs M. Holmes	Mrs E. Burton	2.9.74
Peglea Salamander	B	Ch. Beechrise Surprise	Peglea Mon Cherie	Mrs P. Foster	Mrs P. Foster	12.9.72
Chevawn Sweet Shonah	B	Mogid Watacharmer from Chevawn	Astolats Jasmine	Mrs Campion	Mrs E. Layton & Mrs. Chiswell	28.3.76
Typros The Devil of Spice Box	D	Chantmarles Spice Box	Snowdrop of Typros	Mrs G. Da Silva	Mrs G. Da Silva	14.7.75
Ozmilion Tradition	D	Ch. Ozmilion Premonition	Ozmilion Exageration	O. A. Sameja	O. A. Sameja	1.1.78
Fascination of Daisydell	D	Daisydell Mid-Summer Lad	Miss Tina of Haymor	A. Taylor & Miss S. Morelli	Mrs J. Turner	23.3.77
Harleta's Fernando	D	Evenwood Ambassador	Chantmarles Miss Rosebud	Mr & Mrs H. Hilton	Mr & Mrs H. Hilton	12.3.76
Verolian Justajule with Ozmilion	D	Ch. Ozmilion Jubilation	Ozmilion Wild Temptress	Miss V. M. Sameja-Williams	Miss V. M. Sameja-Williams	28.2.76
Eburacum Plutocrat	D	Eburacum Paladin	Murose Jasmine of Eburacum	Mr R. Haynes	Mr R. Haynes	1.7.76
Carmardy Marcus	D	Captain Kidd of Carmardy	Cinderella of Park Abbey	Mr & Mrs H. Parker	Mr & Mrs H. Parker	1.3.77
Chantmarles Stowaway	D	Chantmarles Tartar Sauce	Chantmarles Caress	Mrs S. M. Hayes	Mrs S. M. Hayes	18.4.76
Candytops Candy-Man	D	Ch. Candytops Blue Peter	Candytops Florence	Mr & Mrs E. H. Oakley	Mr & Mrs E. H. Oakley	3.12.77
Barntoys Cherry-brandy of Gillmins	B	Barntoys Brandy Punch	Moonlight Madonna of Barntoys	Mrs E. Barnaby	Mrs E. Gillot	1.5.77

1978

Candytops Raffles	D	Ch. Candytops Blue Peter	Melody Fare of Candytops	Mr & Mrs E. A. Oakley	Mr & Mrs E. A. Oakley	12.11.76
Deebees My Fascination	D	Deebees Dancing Dan	Wellshim Madam of Deebees	Mrs S. D. Beech	Mrs S. D. Beech & Mrs A. C. Shimwell	17.5.77
Shaun of Beechrise	D	Speculation of Beechrise	Two Pennorth of Copper	Mrs H. Griffiths	Mrs P. Gay	29.6.75
Ozmilion Exageration	B	Ch. Ozmilion My Imagination	Ozmilion Modesty	O. A. Samejo	O. A. Sameja	13.9.76
Wykebank Wild Rose	B	Ch. Blairsville Royal Seal	Wykebank Twinkle Star	A. Blamires	Mrs K. I. Henderson	12.2.76
Wellshim Madam of Deebees	B	Deebees Oberon	Dainty Dinah of Wellshim	Mrs A. C. Shimwell	Mrs S. D. Beech & Mrs A. C. Shimwell	25.12.75

YORKSHIRE TERRIER CHAMPIONS SINCE WORLD WAR II

Champion's Name	Sex	Sire	Dam	Breeder	Owner	Birth Date
Chantmarles Debutante	B	Chantmarles Tartar Sauce	Chantmarles Inis Cara	Mrs M. C. Hayes	P. Boot	8.8.76
1979						
Chantmarles Dolly Dimple	B	Chantmarles Stowaway	Chantmarles Maggie May	Mrs M.C. Hayes	Mrs M.C. Hayes	3.6.77
Mogad Million-iaress	B	Ch. Ozmilion Premonition	Mogad Just Dolly	Miss M. Giddings	Miss M. Giddings	1.9.77
Beechrise Sweet Solitaire	B	Ch. Swank of Beechrise	Sundae of Beechrise	Mrs H. Griffiths	Mr & Mrs D. Sargison	13.10.76
Naylenor Magic Moment	B	Naylenor Battle Cry	Naylenor Honey Bunny	P. Naylor	P. Naylor	3.12.76
Ozmilion Justimagine	B	Ch. Ozmilion My Imagination	Ozmilion Blairsville Bidene	O.A. Sameja	O. A. Sameja	3.3.75
1980						
Ozmilion Destiny	B	Ch. Ozmilion Jubilation	Ozmilion Winter Goddess	O.A. Sameja	Mrs J. Montgomery	26.7.74
Daisydell Tinker	D	Daisydell Midsummer Lad	Daisydell Spring Juill	Mr & Mrs W. Kneen	Mrs J. Turner	24.8.77
Chantmarles Proper Madam	B	Ch. Chantmarles Stowaway	Chantmarles Inis Cara	Mrs M.C. Hayes	Mrs M.C. Hayes	7.5.78
Ozmilion Distinction	D	Ch. Ozmilion Jubilation	Ozmilion Summer Illusion	O.A. Sameja	O.A. Sameja	5.5.75
Sladesmark Small Sample of Rienert	D	Macstroud's Noble Lad	Sladesmark Vested Interest	Mrs J. Dunning	Mr & Mrs J.M. Peel	27.2.78
Ozmilion Heart's Desire	B	Ch. Ozmilion Premonition	Ozmilion Justa-romance	O.A. Sameja	O.A. Sameja	3.1.78
Ozmilion Juliana	B	Ch. Ozmilion Jubilation	Ozmilion Dazzling Romance	O.A. Sameja	Mr & Mrs F.L. Voysey	10.4.77
Toy Top Tango	B	Ch. Beechrise Superb	Toytop Topsy	Mrs A.D. Kitchen	Mrs A.D. Kitchen	3.3.73
Juliette Bradstara	D	Ch. Foxclose Mr Smartie	Mistywinkle Belle	Mrs E.A. Kitching	Mrs G. Bradshaw	26.3.75
Ir.Ch. Elsworth Amber Gambler	D	Ch. Deebees Cornish Echo	Ir. Ch. Elsworth Amber Pearl	A. Lyons	A. Lyons	10.2.77
Craigsbank Miss Dior	B	Southwardedge Blue Spark of Craigsbank	Craigsbank Sweet Nanette	Mrs J.W. Mann	Mrs J.W. Mann	10.9.77
Ozmilion Brandy Soda	D					
Blairsville Gaiety Boy	D	Blairsville Royal Monarch	Blairsville Dream Girl	Mr & Mrs B. Lister	Mr & Mrs B. Lister	5.10.78

Appendix 4:

YORKSHIRE TERRIERS THAT HAVE BEEN BEST IN SHOW IN AN
ALL-BREED CHAMPIONSHIP SHOW

1. Ch. Pagnell Prima Donna of Wiske — owned by Mrs K. Renton
2. Ch. Pagnell Peter Pan (full brother to above) — owned by Mr & Mrs V. Groom
3. Ch. Chantmarles Snuff Box — owned by Mrs Mary Hayes
4. Am. and Eng. Ch. Deebee's Bee Bee — Best in Show Birmingham 1972 bred by Mrs C.M. Pitchey owned by Mrs D. Beech and exported to Mr and Mrs Stanley Lipman of U.S.A.
5. Ch. Blairsville Most Royale (also Res.Best in Show Crufts) — bred and owned by Mr & Mrs BrianLister and mother of the following
6. Ch. Blairsville Royal Seal won the Dog of the Show and leading Champion for a very long time — bred and owned by Mr & Mrs Brian Lister
7. Ch. Wykebank Tinkerbell Best in Show Darlington Ch. By Blairsville Royal Monarch exWykebank Vanity Fare. — bred and owned by Mr & Mrs A. Blamires.

Index